D0797047

This Hallowed Ground: Guides to Civil War Battlefields

SERIES EDITORS

Brooks D. Simpson
Arizona State University

Mark Grimsley
The Ohio State University

Steven E. Woodworth
Texas Christian University

ANTIETAM, SOUTH MOUNTAIN, AND HARPERS FERRY

A BATTLEFIELD GUIDE

ETHAN S. RAFUSE

Cartography by Christopher L. Brest

•

University of Nebraska Press

Lincoln and London

Library of Congress Cataloging-in-Publication Data
Rafuse, Ethan Sepp, 1968–
Antietam, South Mountain, and Harpers Ferry: a battlefield guide /
Ethan S. Rafuse; cartography by Christopher L. Brest.
  p. cm. –(This hallowed ground)
Includes bibliographical references.
ISBN 978-0-8032-3970-8 (pbk.: alk. paper)
1. Antietam, Battle of, Md., 1862. 2. South Mountain, Battle of,
Md., 1862. 3. Harpers Ferry, Battle of, Harpers Ferry, W. Va., 1862.
4. Antietam National Battlefield (Md.)–Guidebooks. 5. Battlefields
–Maryland–Burkittsville Region–Guidebooks. 6. Harpers Ferry
National Historical Park–Guidebooks. 7. Sharpsburg Region (Md.)
–Guidebooks. 8. Burkittsville Region (Md.)–Guidebooks. 9. Harpers
Ferry Region (W. Va.)–Guidebooks. 10. United States–History–Civil
War, 1861–1865–Battlefields–Guidebooks. I. Brest, Christopher
Lawrence, 1950– II. Title.
E474.65.R34 2008
973.7'3–dc22
2008018263

Contents

Acknowledgments

It is with great pleasure that I express appreciation to the many people who helped me put together this guide, starting with series editors Mark Grimsley, Brooks Simpson, and Steven Woodworth, who invited me to contribute this volume to their series and provided welcome guidance throughout the process of putting it together. Mark in particular provided extensive and thorough feedback based on his own extensive knowledge of the subject matter and visits to the field with earlier drafts of the guide in hand.

I owe an enormous debt to Thomas G. Clemens on many counts, the first among these being his willingness to provide me with a place to stay during visits to western Maryland, as well as guidance and feedback that not only enhanced my knowledge of the campaign but also forced me to rethink and correct many of the ideas I previously had. Tom also did me the great favor of putting me in contact with South Mountain authority Steve Stotelmyer, whose expertise greatly enhanced my understanding of the fighting at Fox's Gap. I also thank Mark Snell, director of the George Tyler Moore Center for the Study of the Civil War at Shepherd University, and Ted Alexander, chief historian at Antietam National Battlefield, for inviting me to participate in a number of programs that gave me opportunities to explore and think about the Maryland campaign. I also appreciate Ted's making available to me the resources of the battlefield library and the tremendous assistance that staff members at Antietam, especially Brian Baracz, Keith Snyder, and Keven Walker, provided me during my trips to the battlefield. I also thank Dennis Frye for taking the time to give me his expert feedback on the sections of the guide addressing the operations at Harpers Ferry. I have been fortunate to have had several opportunities, as a member of the faculty at the U.S. Military Academy and U.S. Army Command and General Staff College, to lead cadets and officers around the battlefields of West Virginia and western Maryland, and thank the officers and civilian instructors who have collaborated with me on those programs, especially Charles Bowery Jr., Dana Mangham, Sam Watson, Curt King, and Bob Kennedy.

As always, my warmest appreciation is to my wife Rachel for her love and support while I worked on this project. Finally, for being a source of joy beyond measure and making stops for ice cream mandatory parts of our travels together--and hoping she someday understands and finds some value in what her dad does--I thank and dedicate this book to my favorite little battlefield tramper, Corinne Lee Rafuse.

All illustrations reproduced in this book first appeared in the four volumes of *Battles and Leaders of the Civil War*, edited by Robert Underwood Johnson and Clarence Clough Buel (New York: Century, 1887–88). The volume and page number from which each illustration was taken are indicated at the end of each caption.

To Corinne

Up-hill work. BLCW 4:152

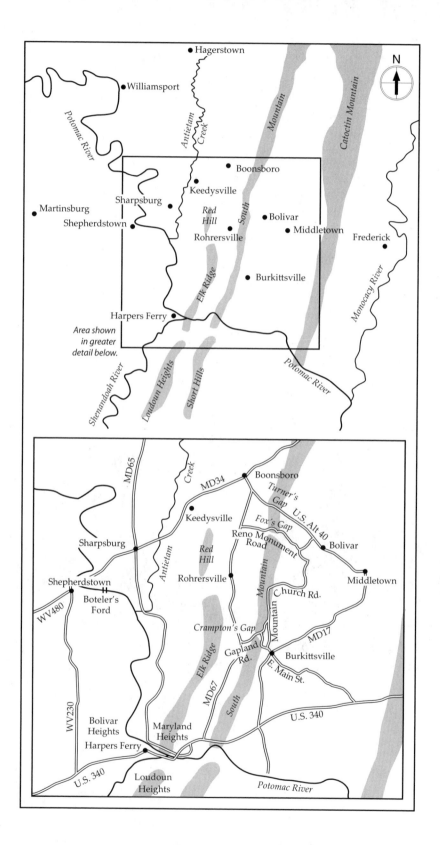

Introduction

In September 1862 the Confederate Army of Northern Virginia and the Union Army of the Potomac conducted one of the truly great campaigns of the Civil War. Gen. Robert E. *Lee* and his Army of Northern Virginia crossed the Potomac River during the first week of September looking to sustain and further extend a tide of Confederate victory that he hoped would persuade the Northern public that the costs of preserving the Union were too high and lead them to recognize Southern independence. *Lee* was confident and understandably so. Rarely, if ever, would a Confederate army operate with the boldness and brilliance the Army of Northern Virginia had demonstrated in the weeks prior to the Maryland campaign. In contrast, the Army of the Potomac began the campaign badly shaken after a stunning series of battlefield setbacks. Moreover, the Federals would conduct the campaign under the leadership of a man whose standing with his political superiors could hardly have been lower. Nonetheless, Maj. Gen. George B. McClellan was a commander in whom the men in the ranks had the utmost confidence, and under whose leadership they were eager to make the rebels pay for having the temerity to cross the Potomac.

At South Mountain, Harpers Ferry, and Antietam, Billy Yank and Johnny Reb would clash in engagements whose magnitude and importance would earn the 1862 Maryland campaign a notable place in American military history. The siege of Harpers Ferry produced the largest surrender of U.S. troops in the nation's history until World War II, while the day-long battle at Antietam on September 17 still holds the distinction of being the single bloodiest day of combat in American military history. When it was all over, the Yankees could claim victory. *Lee's* hopes for a decisive victory north of the Potomac that would induce the North to give up the war were destroyed, and only by great good fortune and the slimmest of margins did the Confederacy avoid the complete destruction of its greatest army. The Union victory also led Abraham Lincoln to issue a proclamation declaring war on slavery in the disloyal states, a signal event in the evolution of the Civil War from a limited war to preserve the Union "as it was" to a hard war that would transform the nation.

This guide is designed to provide visitors to the sites associated with the Maryland campaign with a better understanding of what happened in 1862 and why events followed the course they did. It is written for those who have a day to devote to their visit to Antietam and provides sections on South Mountain and Harpers Ferry, as well as more detailed excursions, for those who have more time to devote to their study of this campaign. Visitors need not do any previsit preparation, but can simply pick up this book and immediately head out to the field for the main tour, which can be completed in about eight hours. The tours of South Mountain and Harpers Ferry will take approximately four and three hours, respectively. For those with even more time, a number of excursions can add several more hours to your visit.

Major-General George B. McClellan. From a war-time photograph. BLCW 1:92

How to Use This Guide

The main tour is divided into fourteen main stops, proceeding from one part of the Antietam battlefield to another in chronological order. That is, the tour follows the battle as it progressed on September 17. Most stops require about twenty to twenty-five minutes to complete. A few, such as Battlefield Vista and West Woods, take a bit longer. Few stops require users to walk more than fifty yards from their cars or the Visitor Center.

The tours of South Mountain and Harpers Ferry are divided into five stops and two stops, respectively. Including driving time, the South Mountain tour should take about four hours to complete. Although a bit more walking is involved for the Harpers Ferry tour than for the Antietam and South Mountain tours, it should still require no more than three hours, even including time riding a shuttle bus into town. There is so much else to see in Harpers Ferry, however, that budgeting more time is strongly suggested.

All of the stops on these tours are divided into two or more substops. Substops seldom ask you to do any additional walking or driving around. They are simply designed to develop the action at each point in a clear, organized fashion, and there are as many substops as required to do the job. In the guidebook, each stop, and many substops, has a section of text "married" to a map. This enables you to visualize the troop positions and movements at each stop without having to flip around the guide looking for maps.

The stops and substops follow a standard format: **Directions, Orientation, What Happened, Analysis**, and/or **Vignette**.

The **Directions** tell you how to get from one stop to the next. They not only give you driving instructions, but they also ask you, once you have reached a given stop, to walk to a precise spot on the battlefield. When driving, keep an eye on your odometer as distances are given to the nearest tenth of a mile. The directions often suggest points of interest en route from one stop to another. We have found that it works best to give the directions to a given stop first and then to mention the points of interest. These are always introduced by the italicized words *en route*.

Once you've reached a stop, the **Orientation** section describes the terrain around you so that you can quickly pick out the key landmarks and get your bearings.

What Happened is the heart of each stop. It narrates the action succinctly but without becoming simplistic, and whenever possible it highlights how the terrain affected the fighting.

Some stops have a section called **Analysis**, which explains why a particular decision was made, why a given attack met with success or failure, and so on. The purpose is to give you additional insight into the battle.

Some stops have a section called **Vignette**, designed to give you an additional emotional understanding of the battle by offering a short eyewitness account or by telling a particularly vivid anecdote.

Although the basic tour can be completed in about eight hours, you can also take **Excursions** to places of special interest. These excursion tours follow the same format as the basic tour.

A few conventions are used in the guidebook to help keep confusion to a minimum. We have tried not to burden the text with a proliferation of names and unit designations. Names of Confederate leaders and units are in italics. The full name and rank of each individual is usually given only the first time he is mentioned at a particular stop.

Directions are particularly important in a guidebook, but they can often be confusing. We have therefore tried to make them as foolproof as possible. At each stop, you are asked to face a specific direction. From that point, you may be asked to look to your left or right. To make this as precise as possible, we may ask you to look to your left front, left, left rear, and so on, according to the system shown below:

straight ahead

left front	*right front*
left	*right*
left rear	*right rear*

behind/directly to the rear

Often, after the relative directions (left, right, etc.), we add the ordinal directions (north, south, etc.) in parentheses. The maps can also help you get your bearings.

The many monuments and troop-placement plaques at Antietam are excellent tools for understanding the battlefield. Every significant Union and Confederate command has a marker indicating a key point where it participated in the battle, and many Union and Confederate units have monuments at various parts on the field. The guidebook uses some monuments and markers to help you orient yourself.

Although this guidebook is intended primarily for use on the battlefield, it also contains helpful information for further study of the battle. Introductory sections at the beginning of each section of the book describe the events that preceded and shaped the battle, and help to establish context. The stops for each phase of the main tour are preceded by overviews that outline the main developments of that phase of the battle. Appendices at the end of the book give the organization of each army (Orders of Battle), a glossary of terms, and a discussion of tactics and weaponry. Suggestions for further reading are provided as well. Finally, although users might benefit from perusing the guide before visiting the battlefield, such preparation is not essential. They can simply pick up the guide, drive out to the battlefield, and begin their tour immediately.

We hope you will enjoy your battlefield tour of Antietam.

Ethan S. Rafuse   *Mark Grimsley,*
                                     Brooks D. Simpson,
                                     & Steven E. Woodworth
                                     SERIES EDITORS

North of the Dunker Church—A Union charge
through the corn-field. BLCW 2:630

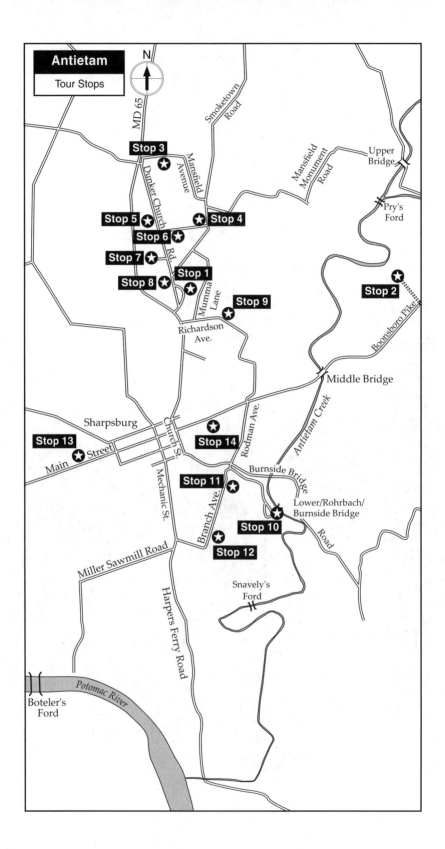

The Road to Antietam

In June 1862 a massive Union army commanded by Maj. Gen. George B. McClellan advanced seemingly inexorably up the peninsula formed by the York and James rivers toward Richmond, and the Confederacy appeared to be on the verge of total defeat. Then, Gen. Robert E. *Lee's* Army of Northern Virginia attacked McClellan's army in late June and drove it from the gates of Richmond to the banks of the James River in the Seven Days Battles. Shortly thereafter, Union president Abraham Lincoln ordered McClellan's Army of the Potomac to evacuate the peninsula and join up with Maj. Gen. John Pope's Army of Virginia in northern Virginia. *Lee* immediately rushed his army north and, in a spectacular campaign, smashed Pope's army at the August 28–30 battle of Second Manassas.

Nonetheless, as he stood on Ox Hill a few miles west of Fairfax Court House on September 2, 1862, *Lee* was not fully satisfied. Recognizing that the South could never destroy the North's ability to make war, he pinned his hopes for securing Confederate independence on winning battlefield victories of sufficient decisiveness to break the North's will to continue committing its overwhelming manpower and material resources to the effort to restore the Union. The Seven Days Battles and Second Manassas had driven the Federals from the gates of Richmond to the defenses of Washington, but *Lee* believed he needed to do more to reach the point where the North would break.

As *Lee* considered the courses of action available to him, only one made sense: to cross the Potomac and enter Maryland. A direct attack on Washington was out of the question. The Federals had a ring of forts around their capital that was too strong for *Lee* to take by assault or siege. Moreover, Union and Confederate armies had stripped northern Virginia of provisions, and in the course of the Second Manassas campaign, the railroad supply route from Richmond to Manassas Junction had been thoroughly wrecked. In addition, many Confederates believed that Marylanders eagerly awaited relief from Federal pressure so they could rise up and act on their desire to join the Confederacy. The preeminent factor shaping *Lee's* thinking, however, was his desire to force the Union to fight at a disadvantage. By crossing into Maryland, *Lee* believed he would compel the Federals to take the field before they could recuperate from their defeat at Manassas, sort out the organizational mess caused by the evacuation from the peninsula, and train the thousands of new troops reaching Washington from the North in the aftermath of Lincoln's July call for 300,000 troops.

Lee decided to cross the Potomac at White's Ford and move into the Monocacy River valley between Parr's Ridge and Catoctin Mountain. By doing this, he would enter Maryland close enough to Washington to provoke the Union government to pursue him. He could then lure the Federals west beyond Catoctin Mountain and South Mountain into the Cumberland Valley. There, Lee hoped to strike and annihilate the Union columns. Such victories would, he hoped, be so decisive that the Union will to continue the contest would be destroyed—just in time for the November elections, where disgruntled Northerners would have the opportunity to replace the current U.S. Congress with one willing to grant Southern independence.

The Maryland campaign began on September 3, when Lee ordered his infantry to march to Dranesville and Leesburg. The following day, he directed Maj. Gen. Daniel H. Hill to move his division into Maryland. On September 5 Maj. Gen. Thomas J. "Stonewall" Jackson led his wing of the army across the Potomac, followed by Maj. Gen. James E. B. Stuart's cavalry. Maj. Gen. James Longstreet's wing, accompanied by Lee himself, crossed the following day. By September 7 Lee's infantry was concentrated around Frederick with Stuart screening their movements and feinting toward Baltimore and Washington. Believing the Federals would not be able to respond to his move for at least a week, Lee decided to halt at Frederick for a few days to rest his men and issue a proclamation inviting the residents of Maryland to cast off the "foreign yoke" of the U.S. government. Few took him up on the offer.

More problematic for Lee was the fact that on September 2 Lincoln placed McClellan in command of the Union forces in and around Washington. Lincoln did this even though many of his advisors believed the general could not be trusted with a major command. Lincoln understood, though, that the army needed someone who could get it physically and morally ready for the field quickly, and McClellan's organizational skills and standing within the army were unmatched.

McClellan almost immediately vindicated Lincoln's decision. He abolished Pope's Army of Virginia, consolidated its units into the Army of the Potomac, and was ready for action within a few days. When reports from a signal station confirmed McClellan's suspicions that Lee would cross the Potomac, he began pushing two corps (Maj. Gen. Joseph Hooker's I and Maj. Gen. Jesse Reno's IX) under Maj. Gen. Ambrose Burnside north to the National Pike that connected Frederick and Baltimore. He also directed Maj. Gen. Edwin Sumner to advance two corps (Sumner's own II and the XII, then under the temporary command of Brig. Gen. Alpheus Williams) north and west on the direct road from Washington to Frederick. The southern wing of the army, commanded by Maj. Gen. William Franklin, consisted of Franklin's VI Corps and a division from the IV Corps commanded by Maj. Gen. Darius Couch. Franklin would advance west from Washington along the River Road, while Brig. Gen. Alfred Pleasonton's cavalry division screened the army's advance.

By September 9 the Union westward advance had begun in earnest. Unlike *Lee*, McClellan did not begin the campaign with a bold vision of decisive battlefield success. Only "sheer necessity," McClellan would later proclaim, could justify undertaking a campaign with an army that was still recuperating from Second Manassas and saddled with thousands of new troops. Consequently, McClellan established conservative operational goals. He would advance westward in a methodical, deliberate fashion in search of a position that would preclude a rebel push into Pennsylvania and compel *Lee's* army to return to Virginia, while avoiding any actions that might put his own army at risk.

Even though *Stuart* had already fought spirited skirmishes with Union cavalry at Hyattstown and Poolesville, when night fell on September 8 *Lee* was unaware of just how quickly McClellan was getting his army ready for the field. Consequently, he made a fateful decision. With a supply line via Manassas Junction no longer tenable, *Lee* decided to rely mainly on a line of supply through the Shenandoah Valley. However, Federal garrisons at Martinsburg and Harpers Ferry made the security of this supply line uncertain. Consequently, on September 9 Lee issued Special Orders No. 191 directing *Jackson's* three divisions, plus divisions commanded by Maj. Gen. Lafayette *McLaws*, Maj. Gen. Richard H. *Anderson*, and Brig. Gen. John G. *Walker*, to undertake an operation against Martinsburg and Harpers Ferry. The rest of the army, *Longstreet's* command of two divisions and D. H. *Hill's* independent division, would move west through South Mountain into the Cumberland Valley. There, when the operation against Martinsburg and Harpers Ferry was complete, the Army of Northern Virginia would be reconcentrated in the vicinity of Hagerstown or Boonsboro and readied for battle. Assuming the garrisons at Martinsburg and Harpers Ferry would flee rather than risk capture, *Lee* anticipated the forces operating against them would achieve their objectives by the morning of September 12—well before he thought any serious threat could materialize from the direction of Washington.

On September 10 the Army of Northern Virginia left Frederick. Not until September 13, however, would all of the Confederate forces operating against Harpers Ferry reach their respective destinations. To make matters worse, the Federal commander at Harpers Ferry, Col. Dixon Miles, decided to obey his orders from Washington not to abandon his post, which compelled *Jackson* to undertake siege operations. By September 13 *Lee's* army was in serious trouble.

After beginning his advance, McClellan steadily pushed westward into the Monocacy Valley despite complaints from Union general in chief Henry W. Halleck that he was doing so too fast. On September 12 Brig. Gen. Jacob Cox's division of Burnside's command drove Confederate cavalry from Frederick and took possession of the town. After learning of the capture of Frederick and receiving seemingly conflicting reports placing the rebels at Hagerstown and at Harpers Ferry, McClellan ordered Pleasonton to follow the National Pike over Catoctin Mountain and enter the Middletown valley on September 13. Cox's division would follow and, hopefully, join Pleasonton at the base of South Mountain by the end of the day. As Pleasonton and Cox pushed westward on September 13, Williams's XII Corps went into bivouac just outside Frederick. There, two soldiers discovered three cigars wrapped in a copy of Special Orders No. 191. In an incredible stroke of luck, before the war an officer on the XII Corps staff, Capt. Samuel Pittman, had worked in a bank that served the post at which Lt. Col. Robert *Chilton*, who drafted the orders for *Lee*, was stationed. Pittman recognized *Chilton's* handwriting and assured Williams the document was authentic. Williams then forwarded it to McClellan, who spent a few hours endeavoring to confirm the information contained in the document and developing a plan for acting on it.

The "Lost Order" explained why reports indicated there were considerable Confederate forces both at Harpers Ferry and in the Cumberland Valley and why *Lee* had divided his army. At the same time, it provided no clue as to Confederate numbers, and the rebel operation against Martinsburg and Harpers Ferry had clearly fallen behind schedule. Yet the fact that *Lee's* army was still divided had to be explained. One possibility was that *Lee* was unaware of just how fast McClellan's army had moved out of Washington and how close it was to his position. Although this in fact was the case, it would have been foolish for McClellan to assume this. He knew Pleasonton's and *Stuart's* cavalries had been skirmishing for nearly a week. Surely in that time, *Stuart* had figured out that Pleasonton's cavalry was the vanguard of a major Union advance and had reported this to *Lee*—unless he was completely incompetent, a conclusion that no observer of the war in Virginia to that point could possibly reach. But if in fact *Lee* knew how close the Federals were, why was his army still divided? One possibility was that *Lee* knew the contest for Harpers Ferry was nearly over. In that case, it was possible he might use the Harpers Ferry forces as the southern wing of a double envelopment of Union forces pushing through South Mountain, or have them swing east and attack the Federal rear. Another possibility was that *Lee* had enough force to feel confident that, even without *Jackson's*, *McLaws's*, and *Walker's* commands on hand, he could still crush any Federal attempt to push through South Mountain. Either way, there was plenty to suggest that a hasty thrust against the South Mountain passes carried some risk and a fair degree of caution was in order. Nonetheless, McClellan decided the rest of Burnside's wing would follow Pleasonton's and Cox's route to South Mountain on September 14. They would then attack Turner's Gap, where the National Pike crossed the mountain, and engage what Special Orders No. 191 indicated was *Lee's* "main body." To the south, Franklin would march to Burkittsville at the base of Crampton's Gap, seize the gap, and then move into Pleasant Valley to drive a wedge between Harpers Ferry and Boonsboro.

On September 10 *Lee* had received reports of Federal troops at Chambersburg, Pennsylvania, and of supplies of flour at Hagerstown. Consequently, on September 11 he ordered *Longstreet's* command to Hagerstown and moved his own headquarters to Funkstown the next day. There, he learned *Stuart* had been driven from Frederick, but was given the impression that there was nothing to be overly concerned with. During the evening of September 13, however, *Lee's* mood shifted from restless concern to grave alarm when he learned McClellan himself was in Frederick. This indicated that assurances by *Stuart* that the Federals merely had a reconnaissance in force in the Monocacy Valley had been horribly wrong. As if this were not enough, *Lee* also learned McClellan had somehow found out the Army of Northern Virginia was divided and was moving aggressively to take advantage of the situation.

Lee responded by directing *Longstreet* to place his forces north and west of Boonsboro behind Beaver Creek, ordering *Hill* to prepare to defend Turner's Gap, and sending a message to *Jackson* urging him to finish up his work at Harpers Ferry without delay. *Jackson* fully appreciated the need for urgency at Harpers Ferry. After receiving *Lee's* report of McClellan's faster-than-expected advance, *Jackson* finished placing his artillery around Harpers Ferry. Then, shortly after noon on September 14, Confederate artillery began bombarding the town. Although a horrible ordeal, Miles's men were able to endure it. *Jackson* then moved a division around the southern flank of the main Union line on Bolivar Heights to a position that rendered the Federal position untenable.

Meanwhile, the fight for South Mountain began early on September 14 with the arrival of Cox's division, the vanguard of McClellan's army, on the scene. Presuming the Confederates would be strongest at Turner's Gap, Pleasonton advised Cox to instead attack Fox's Gap to the south in order to turn the Confederate position. Cox immediately marched his division to Fox's Gap, where he encountered a single Confederate brigade and routed it. Then, however, he halted his offensive to await reinforcements, while to the south Franklin's command reached Burkittsville and prepared to attack Crampton's Gap. All the Confederates could scrape together to defend Crampton's Gap on September 14 was about 1,000 cavalry and infantry and Franklin was able to easily overrun their position and seize possession of the gap by nightfall.

At about the time Franklin made his attack, Burnside's wing was assaulting the Confederate positions around Turner's Gap. With McClellan approving every move, Burnside sent all of Reno's corps to Fox's Gap and directed Hooker's command to turn the rebel position at Turner's Gap from the north. By dark, the IX Corps had routed the rebels at Fox's Gap, although Reno was mortally wounded near the end of the battle, and Hooker's command had crushed the rebel left. As the fighting wound down, *Lee* concluded he had no choice but to return to Virginia and sent orders to *Jackson* and *McLaws* to abort the Harpers Ferry operation. Unfortunately for the Federals at Harpers Ferry, this message did not reach *Jackson* or *McLaws* until after the garrison's fate had been sealed. At first light on September 15, *Jackson* once again opened an artillery bombardment and by 8:00 A.M. was able to send a message to *Lee* announcing the imminent surrender of Harpers Ferry.

McClellan spent the evening of September 14 contemplating the victory at Turner's Gap, and shortly after midnight he learned Franklin had carried Crampton's Gap. A great victory, McClellan notified Washington, had been won at South Mountain; now it was time to exploit it. If *Lee* could be caught north of the Potomac and struck another such blow, a truly decisive victory might be achieved. The pursuit would begin the next morning. As McClellan pushed through the South Mountain passes on September 15, a message from Lincoln responding to news of the previous day's victories made its way to the front. "God bless you and every one with you," Lincoln wrote McClellan. "Destroy the rebel army if possible."

Antietam National Battlefield Visitor Center

The Antietam Visitor Center is an excellent resource for students of the battlefield. It contains a gallery of exhibits and artwork related to the battle, an upper-level observation deck, a theater in which audiovisual programs are offered, and a bookstore. Among the more interesting items in the Visitor Center is a collection of paintings by James Hope, who participated in the battle of Antietam as a captain in the 2nd Vermont, that dramatically depict various scenes from the battle.

After you have become acquainted with the Visitor Center, you are ready to begin your exploration of the Antietam battlefield. You need not return to your car at this point, for the first stop is right behind the Visitor Center.

Optional Excursions If you have more than a day to devote to your study of this campaign, before visiting the scenes of the fighting of September 17, you may want to first visit South Mountain and Harpers Ferry, where the Union and Confederate armies fought prior to Antietam. If so, directions to both South Mountain and Harpers Ferry from Antietam National Battlefield Visitor Center are provided in the sections of the guide devoted to those engagements.

An orderly at headquarters.
BLCW 2:406

STOP 1   Battlefield Vista

Directions   *Exit* the Visitor Center through the door at the top of the stairwell leading to the observation deck on the second floor. After passing through the door, *turn left* and *walk forward* until you are 25 yards from the door, leaving the pavement and walking out into the field. *Stop* and face forward (east) toward South Mountain, which should be visible in the distance, with the Visitor Center behind you.

Orientation   On a clear day, you will be able to clearly see a high peak of South Mountain to your right front with some modern towers on it. That peak is Lamb's Knoll, which slopes northward (to your left) to Fox's Gap, one of the gaps that played a significant role in the September 14, 1862, battle of South Mountain. Turner's Gap, which also figured prominently in the September 14 battle, is about a mile north of Fox's Gap. Crampton's Gap, which also saw significant fighting, is approximately five miles south of Lamb's Knoll but is not visible from this point.

From here on the Dunker Church plateau, you can see nearly all the important landmarks from the fighting north of Sharpsburg on September 17. The fighting south of the town occurred out of sight from this point. The first terrain feature you should take note of is the ground upon which you are standing. The view of the surrounding terrain that this high ground provides should help you understand why both sides fought so hard for control of it.

Next, look to your left rear and note Dunker Church, the small whitewashed structure on the other side of modern DUNKER CHURCH ROAD, which at the time of the battle was known as the Hagerstown Pike. Behind the church is a large woodlot known as the West Woods. As you scan to your right from the church, you will notice a large cupola. That is the monument to soldiers from Maryland on both sides who fought at Antietam. Just beyond it is the intersection of the old Hagerstown Pike and Smoketown Road. Next, raise your line of sight, scan to the right, and notice the line of markers in the distance. It is along modern CORNFIELD AVENUE, which is near the southern edge of a thirty-acre cornfield whose historic borders are marked by a split-rail fence. A line of monuments further in the distance is along modern MANSFIELD AVENUE, which in 1862 would have been on the other side of a woodlot known as the North Woods. If you follow to the right, you will note yet another woodlot. That is the East Woods.

As you continue to pan to your right, note the farm house

and barn just below the plateau upon which you are standing, the Mumma farm. The road that runs past it from left
to right is Mumma Lane. It terminates at the Sunken Road,
known after the battle of Antietam as Bloody Lane. Especially conspicuous in your line of sight now is the Bloody Lane
Observation Tower. The high ground in the distance beyond
the observation tower is Red Hill; pan to the right and you
will see Elk Ridge running behind it. On a clear day, you can
follow Elk Ridge south to its terminus at the Potomac River
overlooking the Harpers Ferry water gap. Closer to you, if
you scan to the right of the Bloody Lane Observation Tower, is an orchard located on Piper farm. On the other side of
the Piper house and barn from you is high ground about a
mile away. That is Cemetery Hill. Finally, you should note
the road that runs north from Sharpsburg and passes behind the Visitor Center. In 1862 it was known as the Hagerstown Pike. To bypass the northern part of the battlefield,
the modern SHARPSBURG PIKE (MD 65) was constructed west
of the original road in the 1960s.

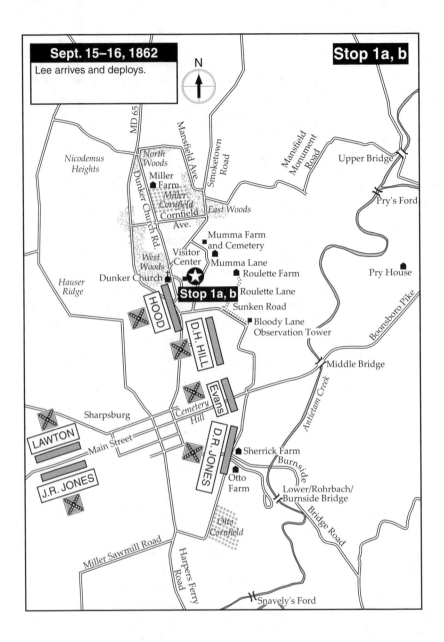

Sept. 15–16, 1862
Lee arrives and deploys.

Stop 1a, b

N

Nicodemus Heights

MD 65

Mansfield Ave.

North Woods

Miller Farm

Smoketown Road

Mansfield Monument Road

Upper Bridge

Pry's Ford

Miller Cornfield

Cornfield Ave.

East Woods

Dunker Church Rd.

West Woods

Visitor Center

Mumma Farm and Cemetery

Mumma Lane

Roulette Farm

Pry House

Hauser Ridge

Dunker Church

Stop 1a, b

Roulette Lane

Sunken Road

Bloody Lane Observation Tower

Boonsboro Pike

HOOD

D.H. HILL

Evans

Middle Bridge

Antietam Creek

Sharpsburg

Cemetery Hill

LAWTON

Main Street

D.R. JONES

Sherrick Farm

Burnside

J.R. JONES

Otto Farm

Lower/Rohrbach/ Burnside Bridge

Bridge Road

Otto Cornfield

Miller Sawmill Road

Harpers Ferry Road

Snavely's Ford

STOP 1A   *Lee* Arrives, September 15, 1862

Orientation   Turn right and face south toward Cemetery Hill, the center of *Lee's* line and his principal command post at Sharpsburg. As in 1862, after it crosses Antietam Creek at the Middle Bridge, the road connecting Boonsboro with Shepherdstown passes over Cemetery Hill just before it enters Sharpsburg. Boonsboro is approximately 6 miles to the north and east of Cemetery Hill, while the Middle Bridge crosses Antietam

Creek about 0.8 mile from the top of the hill; the Potomac River crossing at Shepherdstown is approximately 5 miles west of it. Hagerstown is about 13 miles north of where you are standing. Pleasant Valley is on the other side of Elk Ridge and separates Elk Ridge from South Mountain.

What Happened

Unable to ride a horse due to an incident on August 31 that badly injured both of his hands, Gen. Robert E. *Lee* arrived on Cemetery Hill in an ambulance at approximately 8:00 A.M. on September 15, 1862, as the 15,000-man main body of the Army of Northern Virginia finished a grueling night march away from the site of its defeat at South Mountain. When his forces began their retreat from Turner's Gap and Fox's Gap the previous evening, *Lee* intended to fall back across the Potomac at Boteler's (also known as Shepherdstown or Pack Horse) Ford and rejoin the forces under his immediate command with those that had been operating against Harpers Ferry in Virginia. *Lee* initially planned to rally his command about three miles east of Cemetery Hill at Keedysville before marching to the Potomac. Upon his arrival at Keedysville, however, *Lee* learned the terrain would not permit an effective defense east of Antietam Creek. After leaving Keedysville, *Lee* reached a clearing north of the Boonsboro Pike that provided a clear view of Sharpsburg Heights on the other side of Antietam Creek. *Lee's* keen engineering eye immediately told him the heights would make a fine position for defense that might make it unnecessary to retreat across the Potomac. A few minutes later, *Lee's* confidence was further bolstered by the arrival of a message from Jackson predicting "complete success" that day at Harpers Ferry.

Lee reached Cemetery Hill shortly thereafter and began looking over the terrain around Sharpsburg. He was joined there around 9:30 A.M. by Maj. Gen. James *Longstreet*, who, after a brief discussion with *Lee*, began posting artillery to support Maj. Gen. Daniel H. *Hill's* division, which was deploying north of the Boonsboro Pike halfway between Cemetery Hill and Antietam Creek, and to deter the Federals from making a determined push that day. Around 10:00 A.M., Maj. Gen. David R. *Jones's* division began arriving on the field and was ordered to deploy south of the Boonsboro Pike. As *Jones's* men went into position, *Lee* told them, "We will make our stand on these hills." When it arrived on the field, *Lee* posted Brig. Gen. John B. *Hood's* division to *Jones's* right and by the end of the day had over a hundred cannon in place behind Antietam Creek. More importantly, he had received a triumphant message from *Jackson* reporting, "Through God's blessing, Harper's Ferry and its garrison are to be surrendered."

Jackson also promised that five of the six divisions that had been engaged in that operation could be on the road that evening. This sealed *Lee's* decision. He would not leave Maryland without a fight.

Analysis

On the surface, it is hard to imagine a worse decision for *Lee* to have made than to accept battle at Sharpsburg. On September 15 he faced the prospect of battle with an enemy that was superior in numbers with what appeared to be only a single usable ford in his rear should a retreat became necessary. Moreover, the Army of Northern Virginia's access to that ford could be interdicted by a successful Federal attack south of Sharpsburg. To make matters worse, *Lee* had no choice but to also defend the Dunker Church plateau north of town, for if the Federals were able to post artillery upon it, they would be able to pour an enfilade fire into Lee's position and destroy his line. Not surprisingly, few aspects of *Lee's* military career have received more criticism than his decision to fight at Sharpsburg.

In fact, *Lee's* decision to stand at Sharpsburg on September 15 was an eminently sound one. First, *Lee* did not only have a single ford available to him on September 15. At that time and until the Federals crossed the upper Antietam Creek during the afternoon of the sixteenth, the turnpike that ran north from Sharpsburg to Hagerstown was open to *Lee*, which gave him access to the Potomac crossing at Light's Ford near Williamsport. In addition, this road gave *Lee* the ability to resume offensive operations after concentrating his army at Sharpsburg and by doing so reclaim the operational initiative. Moreover, *Lee* crossed the Potomac looking to break the Northern will to continue the war before the mobilization of Northern resources and manpower reached a point where the odds against the South became overwhelming. To retreat back across the Potomac after having been soundly defeated at South Mountain would have left no doubt that the North had won the campaign, with the consequence that Northern morale would receive a critical boost. In addition, to end the campaign at that point would relinquish the strategic initiative to the Federals. The first half of 1862, in which the North had possessed the initiative and managed to conquer huge swaths of territory in the West and reach the gates of Richmond, provides ample evidence to suggest that *Lee* was correct to assume this would have been suicide for the Confederacy.

STOP 1B   *Lee* Deploys and Plans, September 16, 1862

What Happened   After spending the night in the Jacob Grove house in Sharpsburg–the only night he would spend indoors during the
entire campaign–*Lee* spent September 16 concentrating his
command at Sharpsburg and considering his options. He
saw little in the foggy morning to suggest the Federals were
preparing a major offensive that day, which, combined with
the prospect of *Jackson's* pending arrival, inspired *Lee* to make
plans for taking the offensive himself. Around 8:00 A.M., as
Stuart was conducting a reconnaissance north of Sharpsburg
to see if a march in that direction would be feasible, *Jackson*
personally arrived at Cemetery Hill and met with *Lee* and
Longstreet. After hearing that *Jackson's* old division, now commanded by Brig. Gen. John R. *Jones*, and a division commanded by Brig. Gen. Alexander *Lawton* were crossing the Potomac
at Shepherdstown, *Lee* informed *Jackson* of his hope to march
north toward Hagerstown, for which he had already laid the
groundwork by shifting the division commanded by *Hood*,
perhaps his most aggressive division commander, from a
position south of Sharpsburg to one north of the town. Although his men were dead tired, *Jackson* agreed with the
plan. Then, however, Federal artillery on the other side of
Antietam Creek opened up, and reports arrived of Federal
forces crossing the Middle Bridge. When it became clear that
this was not the prelude to an assault, *Lee* resumed planning
a move north. Around 3:00 P.M., he called *Longstreet* and *Jackson* to the Grove house to discuss the idea, but then reports
arrived of Federal forces approaching the lower Antietam
Creek and of a large Union force crossing the creek over the
Upper Bridge and a nearby ford that would soon be in a position from which it could block a Confederate march to Hagerstown. *Lee* abandoned his hopes for taking the offensive
and resigned himself to a defensive battle at Sharpsburg.

Vignette   After the war, *Longstreet* was critical of *Lee's* decision to give
battle at Sharpsburg and, to buttress his case, provided a
vivid picture of the Federals' arrival on the opposite bank of
the Antietam. "Larger and larger grew the field of blue until
it seemed to stretch as far as the eye could see," he wrote,
"and from the tops of the mountains down to the edges of
the stream gathered the great army of McClellan. It was an
awe-inspiring spectacle as this grand force settled down in
sight of the Confederates, then shattered by battles and scattered by long and tiresome marches."

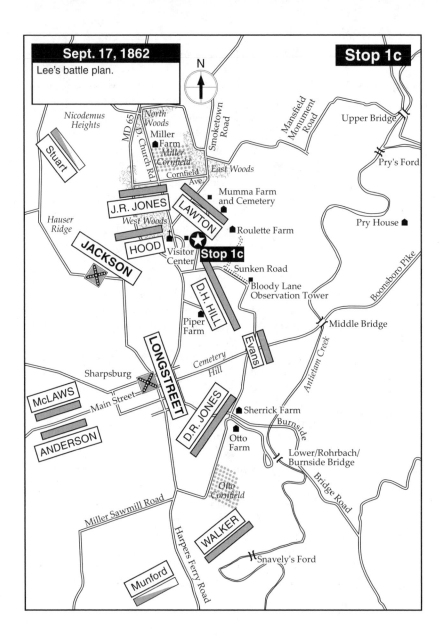

Nicodemus Heights

North Woods

Miller Farm

Miller Cornfield

Cornfield Ave

East Woods

Mumma Farm and Cemetery

Mansfield Monument Road

Upper Bridge

Pry's Ford

Stuart

MD 65

D. Church Rd.

Smoketown Road

J.R. JONES

LAWTON

Hauser Ridge

West Woods

Roulette Farm

Pry House

JACKSON

HOOD

Visitor Center

Stop 1c

Sunken Road

Bloody Lane Observation Tower

Boonsboro Pike

Antietam Creek

D.H. HILL

Piper Farm

Evans

Middle Bridge

LONGSTREET

Cemetery Hill

Sharpsburg

McLAWS

Main Street

D.R. JONES

Sherrick Farm

Burnside

ANDERSON

Otto Farm

Lower/Rohrbach/ Burnside Bridge

Miller Sawmill Road

Otto Cornfield

Bridge Road

WALKER

Snavely's Ford

Harpers Ferry Road

Munford

STOP 1C   *Lee's* Battle Plan, September 17, 1862

What Happened   By the evening of September 16, *Lee* had determined that al-though the Federals were menacing both ends of his line, the greatest danger (as well as the greatest opportunity for escaping Sharpsburg) was to the north. He deployed his forc-es accordingly by directing J. R. *Jones's* and *Lawton's* divisions to take up positions north of town and by instructing *Jack-son* to assume personal command of that sector of the field.

Around 4:30 P.M. *Hood's* division became engaged with the lead elements of a Federal force that had advanced into the East Woods. This firefight continued until dark. When it was over, *Hood* was given permission to pull his command back from the East Woods, and *Lawton's* division took its place.

By dawn on September 17, with *Stuart's* cavalry connecting his left with the Potomac, *Jackson* had formed a northward facing battle line with J. R. *Jones's* and *Lawton's* divisions. Supporting *Lawton's* right, and extending the line to Cemetery Hill was D. H. *Hill's* division. Directly facing the Middle Bridge, which carried the Boonsboro Pike over the Antietam, was Brig. Gen. Nathan *Evans's* command, composed of a single brigade. D. R. *Jones's* division extended the line from Cemetery Hill to Harpers Ferry Road, with a small force under the command of Brig. Gen. Robert *Toombs* posted forward to defend the Lower Bridge. Brig. Gen. John *Walker's* division covered Snavely's Ford just downstream from the Lower Bridge with Col. Thomas T. *Munford's* cavalry covering its flank. Just west of Sharpsburg, Maj. Gen. Lafayette *McLaws's* and Maj. Gen. Richard H. *Anderson's* divisions rested in reserve after arriving from Harpers Ferry. Seventeen miles away at Harpers Ferry, Maj. Gen. Ambrose P. *Hill* was under orders to march his division to Sharpsburg with all possible haste. Although he was confident of success as his army prepared to fight a defensive battle on September 17, *Lee* understood that the Army of the Potomac was not to be taken lightly and that after having over a full day to prepare his attack, McClellan would make it a heavy one. When *McLaws* encountered his commanding general early on September 17, *Lee* advised him, "We have I believe a hard day's work before us."

Analysis

Despite his heavy disadvantage in numbers, *Lee* had reason for optimism as he contemplated the coming battle at Sharpsburg. The Army of Northern Virginia was confident, skillfully led, and battle-tested. The rolling and broken terrain on the west side of the Antietam Creek was also exceedingly well-suited for the conduct of an aggressive defensive battle. It would enable *Lee* to conceal his strength, deployment, and movements and create command and control problems for the Federals. The difficult terrain would instill caution in a prudent commander when he planned and conducted attacks and would lead an impulsive commander into tactical problems. In either case, it would create situations where the Federals would be vulnerable to counterattacks. A combination of a stout defense and timely counterattacks would have the effect, *Lee* could reasonably hope, of bloodying and frustrating the Federal Army to the point that its commanders would concede a tactical defeat by going over to the defensive. Not only could such a setback have the depressive effect on northern morale that was the objective of *Lee's* strategy, it might also make it possible for his army to move north from Sharpsburg toward Hagerstown and to reach a point where they could return to a campaign of maneuver.

Moreover, *Lee* had the advantage of operating on interior lines. In addition to occupying a much shorter line than McClellan, *Lee* also possessed a network of roads, the most important being the Hagerstown Pike, which provided him with excellent lateral communications that the terrain rendered invisible to the Federal high command and were uninterrupted by Antietam Creek. These allowed *Lee* to shift forces back and forth along his line with far greater speed than McClellan could. This, combined with the fact that *Lee* was fighting on the defensive, gave the Confederate commander a significant advantage when it came to command and control at Antietam.

Further Reading   Harsh, *Taken at the Flood*, 298–368; Sears, *Landscape Turned Red*, 160–62, 164–65, 168, 174–76.

The Sharpsburg Bridge over the Antietam.
From a war-time photograph. BLCW 2:634

STOP 2   Pry House

Directions   From the Visitor Center parking lot, *turn left* onto DUNKER
                      CHURCH ROAD and *proceed* to MD 65. *Turn left* onto MD 65 and
                      continue 0.8 mile (along the way MD 65 becomes N. CHURCH
                      STREET) to the intersection with E. MAIN STREET (MD 34). *Turn
                      left* and *proceed* 2.1 miles on MD 34 until you see a large sign
                      on the left side of the road for the "Pry House Field Hospi-
                      tal Museum." *Turn left* onto the gravel driveway leading to
                      the Pry House, *proceed* to the end of the driveway, and *turn
                      right* into the parking area. Exit your car and *follow* the grav-
                      el road and path around to the northwest side of the Pry
                      House, where the visitor's entrance to the house is. You will
                      see to your left a cleared area on the bluff above Antietam
                      Creek. *Walk* over to a point on the bluff where the Save His-
                      toric Antietam Foundation has cleared a vista toward the
                      battlefield. From this point, you should be able to see the
                      Bloody Lane Observation Tower and, to the right of it, the
                      visitor's center and New York monument (the tall shaft with
                      the eagle on top).

Orientation   You are looking west across Antietam Creek toward Sharps-
                      burg Heights. The hamlet of Keedysville is approximate-
                      ly one mile behind you. In September 1862 the hill below
                      you was clear and this vantage point provided a fairly good
                      sense of the terrain on the other side of the creek. It was
                      probably near here that *Lee* caught his first glimpse of the
                      terrain around Sharpsburg early on the morning of Septem-
                      ber 15. This position did not, however, offer a view of the
                      extreme flanks of the battlefield. The East Woods obscured
                      much of the field north of Sharpsburg, while the terrain pre-
                      vented observers here from seeing what was going on at the
                      Lower Bridge. McClellan compensated for this somewhat by
                      setting up a system of signal stations. One of these stood on
                      Red Hill, the northern slope of which is on the other side of
                      the Pry House and MD 34 and will be visible if you look over
                      your left shoulder. The high ridge with the modern towers
                      you may be able see in the distance behind Red Hill is South
                      Mountain.

STOP 2A   The Federals Arrive, September 15, 1862

What Happened   After his victory at South Mountain on September 14, Mc-
Clellan ordered a vigorous advance into the Cumberland
and Pleasant valleys on the fifteenth. Maj. Gen. Joseph Hooker would lead the army's northern wing through Turner's
Gap toward Boonsboro, while the army's southern wing,
commanded by Maj. Gen. William Franklin, would pass
through Crampton's Gap and save the garrison at Harpers
Ferry. The center wing, commanded by Maj. Gen. Ambrose
Burnside, would march through Fox's Gap and, depending
on circumstances, support Franklin's efforts, move north to
assist Hooker, or march directly to Sharpsburg to cut off the
Confederates at Boonsboro from the Potomac.

At daylight Hooker learned *Lee's* forces were in full flight
toward the Potomac and began an energetic pursuit. To
the south, however, Franklin advanced cautiously through
Crampton's Gap until he encountered a Confederate battle line positioned across Pleasant Valley. As Franklin re-
connoitered the enemy position, the sound of artillery fire
was clearly audible from Harpers Ferry—as was its cessation
around 8:00 A.M., indicating that whatever chance there had
been to save the garrison was gone. Meanwhile, after leaving McClellan's headquarters on the morning of September
15, Burnside went to Fox's Gap to implement his commander's orders for a vigorous advance. Upon reaching the gap,
however, Burnside found Brig. Gen. Jacob Cox had let the IX
Corps go into bivouac to recuperate from the previous day's
fighting. Without informing McClellan, Burnside decided to
let Cox's men continue to rest. Shortly before noon, McClellan learned of the situation. Upon personally reaching Fox's
Gap, McClellan found the IX Corps still in bivouac. He then
issued orders for Burnside's men to clear the road so that
Brig. Gen. George Sykes's division of Maj. Gen. Fitz John Porter's V Corps could lead the march west from Fox's Gap. Several hours had been lost, and a key part of McClellan's pursuit plan had been undone.

Meanwhile, the division spearheading Hooker's advance,
Maj. Gen. Israel B. Richardson's, reached Keedysville, deployed along the Boonsboro Pike, and by 2:00 P.M. had
pushed skirmishers forward to the Antietam. Sykes's division arrived shortly thereafter and deployed to Richardson's
left. Upon reaching Keedysville during the afternoon, Mc-
Clellan met with Hooker, Sumner, and Porter and looked
over the Confederate position. Hooker reported the Confederates had between 30,000 and 50,000 troops holding a
strong position on the other side of the creek, but that good

crossing points had been located above the Middle Bridge. Burnside and Cox then arrived and joined McClellan and the other general officers as they discussed the situation and looked over the field. It quickly became clear to McClellan that only Richardson's and Sykes's commands would be available for action that afternoon, and an attack across the creek by only two divisions was unlikely to succeed. Thus, he decided to spend the rest of the day and the night of September 15–16 concentrating his command and that he would use one of the crossings Hooker had found to get at the rebels on September 16. Franklin would remain in Pleasant Valley to guard the army's line of communications to Washington.

Vignette Upon reaching the field near Keedysville on the afternoon of September 15, Cox later wrote, "I rode up with General Burnside, dismounted, and was very cordially greeted by General McClellan. . . . He introduced me to the officers I had not known before, referring pleasantly to my service with him in Ohio and West Virginia, putting me upon an easy footing with them in a very agreeable and genial way. We walked up the slope of the ridge before us, and looking westward from its crest the whole field of the coming battle was before us. . . . [O]n our left was the village of Sharpsburg, with fields inclosed by stone fences in front of it. At its right was a bit of wood (since known as the West Wood), with the little Dunker Church standing out white and sharp against it. Farther to the right and left the scene was closed in by wooded ridges with open farm lands between, the whole making as pleasing and prosperous a landscape as can easily be imagined. We made a large group as we stood upon the hill, and it was not long before we attracted the enemy's attention. A puff of white smoke from a knoll on the right of the Sharpsburg road was followed by the screaming of a shell over our heads. McClellan directed that all but one or two should retire behind the ridge, while he continued the reconnaissance, walking slowly to the right. I noted with satisfaction the cool and business-like air with which he made his examination under fire. The Confederate artillery was answered by a battery, and a lively cannonade ensued on both sides, though without any noticeable effect. The enemy's position was revealed, and he was evidently in force on both sides of the turnpike in front of Sharpsburg, covered by the undulations of the rolling ground which hid his infantry from our sight."

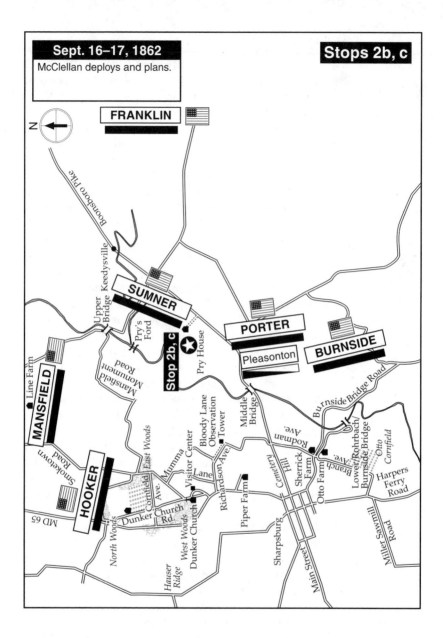

Sept. 16–17, 1862
McClellan deploys and plans.

Stops 2b, c

FRANKLIN

SUMNER

PORTER

BURNSIDE

MANSFIELD

HOOKER

Stop 2b, c

Pleasonton

Boonsboro Pike

Upper Bridge Keedysville

Pry's Ford

Pry House

Mansfield Monument Road

Line Farm

Smoketown Road

MD 65

North Woods

East Woods

West Woods

Hauser Ridge

Cornfield

Dunker Church

Dunker Church Rd.

Mumma Ave.

Visitor Center

Bloody Lane

Observation Tower

Lane

Richardson Ave.

Piper Farm

Middle Bridge

Cemetery Hill

Sharpsburg

Main Street

Rodman Ave.

Branch Ave.

Sherrick Farm

Otto Farm

Burnside Bridge Road

Lower/Rohrbach Burnside Bridge

Otto Cornfield

Harpers Ferry Road

Miller Sawmill Road

STOP 2B   McClellan Deploys His Command, September 16, 1862

What Happened   By dawn on September 16, McClellan had the I, II, V, IX, and XII Corps on hand. Upon its arrival the previous day, the IX Corps had been posted south of Sykes's division and formed the Union left. McClellan's center straddled the Boonsboro Pike, with Sumner's corps north of the road and Porter's command south of it. Hooker's I Corps was positioned north of the II Corps around the fork of Antietam Creek and Little Antietam Creek. Serving as a general reserve was Maj. Gen. Joseph K. F. Mansfield's XII Corps. Before he could begin moving his command into positions from which they could attack *Lee*, McClellan first had to determine what the situation was on the other side of the creek, something a heavy morning fog made impossible. When the fog lifted at midmorning and it was clear the Confederates were still at Sharpsburg, McClellan decided to ride over to his left to check into affairs south of the Boonsboro Pike. After personally reconnoitering the area, McClellan directed Burnside to post the IX Corps in a position from which it could attack the Lower (also known as the Rohrbach and, today, Burnside) Bridge on September 17. McClellan then returned to his headquarters in Keedysville and ordered Hooker to take his corps across the Antietam. Shortly after 3:30 P.M., Hooker's command began crossing the Antietam at Pry's Ford and the Upper Bridge. McClellan then arrived on the scene and was greeted by Hooker, who was alarmed at the fact that his corps was then the only significant Federal force on the west side of the Antietam and argued that if it was not significantly reinforced, the enemy would "eat me up." McClellan responded by telling Hooker that the XII Corps would be sent to his assistance. McClellan then rode back to the east side of the creek and established his field headquarters at the Pry House. He arrived here in time to see Hooker's men enter a stand of woods, which would later be dubbed the East Woods, and have a sharp engagement with the Confederates that ended shortly after dark.

Analysis

McClellan was clearly eager after South Mountain to gratify President Lincoln's hopes that he would "destroy the rebel army, if possible." He developed a sound plan for September 15 and assigned its execution to three trusted subordinates. Hooker fulfilled McClellan's expectations; Burnside and Franklin did not. If not for the lethargy in Fox's Gap, *Lee's* movements on September 15 would have been severely complicated by the combination of Hooker's column pressing his army's rear and Burnside's command either menacing its flank or supporting the effort to save Harpers Ferry. Moreover, McClellan would have had more than two divisions at Keedysville before night fell on September 15. As it turned out, by the time McClellan personally reached the Antietam that day, it was too late to attempt anything other than a frontal assault across the creek against an enemy of unknown strength holding what all recognized to be a good defensive position. At Malvern Hill in July, *Lee* had launched frontal assaults against a Union army he believed to be in a fragile state, only to see the attacks brutally repulsed. To anyone who knew what had happened at Malvern Hill, as did McClellan, the folly of making a similar attack at Antietam with only two divisions would have been so evident as to not even invite comment.

On September 16, as he had the day before, McClellan stayed his hand and did not attack the enemy at Sharpsburg. It is possible McClellan thought *Lee* would leave Maryland without a fight. However, it is more likely that his actions on the sixteenth were motivated by a simple desire to have his own forces properly marshaled before making an attack, for his actions clearly indicate he anticipated a major battle on the seventeenth. Of course, McClellan's failure to attack on September 16 would give *Lee* time to get all but one of his divisions to the battlefield by the morning of September 17, which ensured the fight at Antietam would be a tough one.

Camp gossip. From a photograph. BLCW 1:ix

STOP 2C   McClellan Plans and Manages the Battle, September 17, 1862

What Happened   What McClellan's exact battle plan was at Antietam is some-
what unclear, for the general offered varying explanations
of it in postbattle writings and testimony before a congressional committee. This much, at least, is clear: McClellan intended for Hooker to begin the battle by pressing the Confederate left north of Sharpsburg early on September 17.
Meanwhile, Burnside's corps was to take up a position from
which it could cover the Army of the Potomac's southern
flank, force a crossing of the lower Antietam, and then push
west to crush the Confederate right and seize *Lee's* line of escape back across the Potomac. Sumner's and Porter's corps
would open the battle at the center of the Union line. Mc-
Clellan initially held the XII Corps at Keedysville as a general reserve, but sent it to Hooker's assistance late on the sixteenth. That same day, McClellan directed Franklin to march
the VI Corps to Keedysville. On his arrival on the morning of
the seventeenth, Franklin would take Mansfield's place as
the army's reserve and enable McClellan to send Sumner's
corps across the Antietam to join the fight north of Sharpsburg. McClellan would base the commitment of Sumner's
corps and the timing of Burnside's attack on events and directed both commanders to have their corps ready to move
early on the seventeenth. McClellan's plan was designed to
ensure that, if *Lee* had the numbers that intelligence wrongly suggested, there would be two or three Union corps in
position to block a Confederate counterstrike against the
Union center. If Hooker or Burnside got in serious trouble,
McClellan could relieve the pressure on them by using the
corps holding his center to press *Lee's*. Alternately, if Hooker's or Burnside's attacks were successful, these corps could
cross the creek and deliver a decisive blow against the Confederate center.

McClellan would spend most of the battle on this side of
the creek due to the fact that there was no place on the west
side of the Antietam from which he could effectively manage the battle on exterior lines he was compelled to fight
by the terrain and *Lee's* position. If he had placed himself on
the west side of the Antietam north of Sharpsburg, it would
have compromised his ability to directly manage his reserve and communicate with Burnside. Nonetheless, he did
cross the creek during the afternoon to mediate a dispute
between Sumner and Franklin north of Sharpsburg. He was
willing to do so because at that time quiet had settled over
Burnside's section of the field after the IX Corps managed
to get across the Antietam, but McClellan immediately re-

turned to his command post on this side of the creek after meeting with Sumner and Franklin.

Vignette

A staff officer who was at McClellan's side for much of the battle later wrote that, after watching the initial attacks by Hooker's command from the high ground behind the Pry House, McClellan and his staff called for their horses and "rode rapidly to a commanding knoll on the eastern side of the Sharpsburg turnpike, about the centre of our line of battle and nearly opposite the town of Sharpsburg, . . . I had leisure to remark upon the head-quarters group immediately about me. In the midst was a small redan built of fence-rails, behind which sat General Fitz John Porter, who, with a telescope resting on the top rail, studied the field with unremitting attention, scarcely leaving his post during the whole day. His observations he communicated to the commander by nods, signs, or in words so low-toned and brief that the nearest of bystanders had but little benefit from them. When not engaged with Porter, McClellan stood in a soldierly attitude intensely watching the battle and smoking with the utmost apparent calmness, conversing with surrounding officers and giving his orders in the most quiet undertones. General [Randolph B.] Marcy, his Chief of Staff was always near him, and through him orders were usually given to the aides-de-camp to be transmitted to distant points of the field. Several foreign officers of the French, Prussian, and Sardinian service were present. Everything was as quiet and punctilious as a drawing-board ceremony."

Further Exploration

The Pry House is owned by the National Park Service. Its first floor contains an excellent museum, administered by the National Museum of Civil War Medicine in Frederick, with exhibits on Civil War medicine and the Pry House that particularly focus on the experience and role of both at Antietam. The museum opened in 2005 and is open from April to December.

Further Reading

Harsh, *Taken at the Flood*, 308–15, 344–54; Rafuse, *McClellan's War*, 301–27; Sears, *Landscape Turned Red*, 158–60, 169–74.

It was not yet 4:00 P.M. on September 16, 1862, when Maj. Gen. Joseph Hooker's Union I Corps began crossing the Antietam at the Upper Bridge and Pry's Ford. Shortly after Hooker's lead division, commanded by Brig. Gen. George G. Meade, crossed the creek, McClellan appeared on the scene and, in response to a personal request from Hooker, agreed to send Maj. Gen. Joseph F. K. Mansfield's XII Corps from its position in reserve at Keedysville to the I Corps's assistance. Meade then pushed his lead brigade, commanded by Brig. Gen. Truman Seymour westward until it struck Smoketown Road. There, Seymour turned southward and around 4:30 P.M. moved into a woodlot that would come to be known as the East Woods, where he encountered Brig. Gen. John Bell *Hood's* division. For nearly two hours Seymour's and *Hood's* men exchanged fire until darkness fell around 6:30. As the fighting died down in the East Woods, Hooker established his headquarters at the Joseph Poffenberger farm and deployed his corps as a light rain began to fall. During the night, he learned that Mansfield's command had crossed the Antietam and had gone into bivouac about a mile north of the East Woods.

The first phase of the battle of Antietam began shortly before dawn on September 17. Around 5:15 A.M. Seymour's men began exchanging a steady fire with Confederate forces in their front, and within fifteen minutes Federal artillery and Confederate artillery had joined the fight. Meanwhile, Hooker decided to make a full-scale attack southward with his corps to seize the Dunker Church plateau next to where the Hagerstown Pike and Smoketown Road intersected. Hooker also directed Mansfield to move his command to the battlefield, but would not await its arrival before beginning his attack.

Maj. Gen. Thomas J. "Stonewall" *Jackson* initially assigned the task of defending the Dunker Church plateau to divisions commanded by Brig. Gen. Alexander *Lawton* and Brig. Gen. John R. *Jones*, supported by Maj. Gen. Daniel H. *Hill's* division. *Hood's* division stood in reserve in the West Woods. Hooker's attack carried his forces into a thirty-acre cornfield owned by David R. Miller located between the Hagerstown Pike and the East Woods. There around 6:00 A.M., his men first made contact with *Lawton's* command. In what would become known as the Bloody Cornfield, the battle quickly took on a degree of ferocity that would rarely, if ever, be matched in American military history. By 7:00 A.M., however, Hooker had gained possession of the Cornfield and effectively shattered *Lawton's* and *Jones's* divisions.

Jackson responded to the situation by calling up his reserves. Around 7:00 A.M., *Hood's* division returned to the field and launched a vicious assault that drove Hooker's exhausted troops back through the Cornfield. This occurred just as Mansfield's lead division, commanded by Brig. Gen. Alpheus S. Williams, was arriving on the field. Williams's division and elements from Hooker's badly battered corps were then able to bring the Confederate counterattack to a bloody halt in a bitter and brutal fight. The Federals were prevented, however, from resuming their drive south by the arrival of reinforcements from D. H. *Hill's* division.

Unfortunately, just after his corps arrived on the field, Mansfield was mortally wounded. Consequently, when Brig. Gen. George Greene's division reached the East Woods around 8:15 A.M., there was limited coordination between his and Williams's efforts. Greene then decided to push two of his brigades forward, roughly following Smoketown Road. This compelled *Hill's* men to pull back to the West Woods, which enabled Greene to advance to Mumma farm and force Confederate artillery off the Dunker Church plateau around 9:00 A.M. Hooker had finally achieved his corps' tactical objective and, in the process, compelled *Lee* to strip other parts of his line to prevent the total destruction of his left. Hooker would not get much time to savor his success. After riding forward to the Dunker Church, he was struck in the foot by a bullet and forced to leave the field.

STOP 3   North Woods

Directions

Return to your car. At the end of the Pry House driveway, *turn right* onto BOONSBORO PIKE (MD 34) and *proceed* 2.1 miles to its intersection with S. CHURCH STREET and N. CHURCH STREET (MD 65). *Turn right* onto N. CHURCH STREET and *travel* 0.8 mile to DUNKER CHURCH ROAD. *Turn right* and *stay on* DUNKER CHURCH ROAD as it *forks left* at the entrance to the Visitor Center parking lot. After driving 1.1 miles on DUNKER CHURCH ROAD, *turn right* onto MANSFIELD AVENUE. *Continue* on MANSFIELD AVENUE for 0.1 mile to the parking area on the left. After exiting your car, *cross* MANSFIELD AVENUE and *walk* about 50 yards to a small post marked "2."

Orientation

You are standing at what was in 1862 the southern edge of what became known as the North Woods. Behind you, on the other side of MANSFIELD AVENUE, is Poffenberger Ridge. To your front and left is the East Woods. Straight ahead of you in 1862 was a plowed field, a pasture, and beyond that, David R. Miller's thirty-acre cornfield. On this side of DUNKER CHURCH ROAD (which in 1862 was known as the Hagerstown Pike), you can see the top of the buildings at the Miller farm, which are just behind the ridge to your right front. Just beyond the southern border of the Miller Cornfield is a line of monuments along modern CORNFIELD AVENUE, which was not there at the time of the battle. Beyond that you should be able to clearly see the Visitor Center, which sits on the plateau about 1,000 yards from where you are standing. An open pasture was south of the Cornfield in 1862. The farm buildings south of CORNFIELD AVENUE were not, however, there at the time of the battle. On the other side of DUNKER CHURCH ROAD, behind the tall obelisk monument in your right front is the West Woods. If you look to your right, you will see a distinctive rise on the other side of DUNKER CHURCH ROAD and MD 65. That is Nicodemus Heights.

STOP 3A   Hooker Moves into Position, September 16–17, 1862

Directions   *Remain in place* and face south toward the Visitor Center.

What Happened   After crossing the Antietam late in the afternoon of September 16, the lead element of Hooker's I Corps, Brig. Gen. Truman Seymour's brigade of Brig. Gen. George Meade's division, pushed westward from the creek and upon reaching Smoketown Road, turned south and entered the East Woods. There, around 4:30 P.M., Seymour encountered Brig. Gen. John Bell *Hood's* division and engaged in a brief firefight that lasted until dark. At 10:00 P.M., *Hood* fell back to the West Woods, with a division commanded by Brig. Gen. Alexander *Lawton* taking his place on the Confederate front line.

Meanwhile, Hooker deployed his command. By dawn on September 17, he had posted Meade's division – minus Seymour's brigade, which remained in the East Woods – in the North Woods, approximately where their monuments today line Mansfield Avenue behind you. Brig Gen. Abner Doubleday's division was posted to the right and rear of Meade's line to extend the corps's front to the Hagerstown Pike and cover its flank. To Meade's left, Brig. Gen. James Ricketts's division extended the Federal line eastward and supported Seymour's position by deploying across the Smoketown Road north of the East Woods. Hooker posted artillery on Poffenberger Ridge. Further artillery support would come from long-range Parrott guns posted east of the Antietam. Meanwhile, approximately a mile to the northeast on the Smoketown Road, the two divisions of Mansfield's XII Corps were in bivouac at the George Line farm, where they had arrived at approximately 2:30 A.M. after a night march from Keedysville that was especially tough on the large number of green troops in its ranks.

Vignette   As his men settled into their positions after dark on September 16, Hooker decided to visit his frontline troops. "The night becoming dark and drizzly, I sought shelter in [J. Poffenberger's] barn, a few yards to the left of the Hagerstown pike (facing the south)," he later wrote. "Desultory firing was kept up between the pickets almost throughout the night, and about 9 o'clock P.M. I visited them in order to satisfy myself concerning this firing, and found that the lines of pickets of the two armies were so near each other as to be able to hear each other walk, but were not visible to each other. I found Seymour's officers and men keenly alive to their proximity to our enemy, and seemed to realize the responsible character of their services for the night. Indeed, their conduct inspired me with the fullest confidence, and on returning to the barn I immediately dispatched a courier informing the commanding general of my surroundings, and assuring him that the battle would be renewed at the earliest dawn."

Major-General Joseph
K. F. Mansfield. From a
photograph. BLCW 2:640

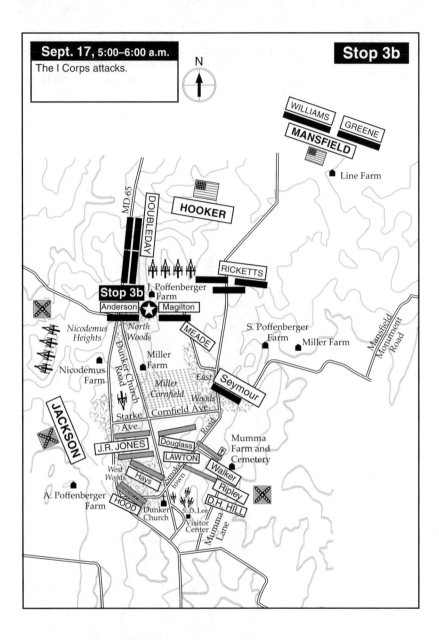

Sept. 17, 5:00–6:00 a.m.
The I Corps attacks.

N

Stop 3b

WILLIAMS
GREENE
MANSFIELD

Line Farm

MD 65
DOUBLEDAY
HOOKER

RICKETTS

Stop 3b
J. Poffenberger Farm
Anderson ★ Magilton

Nicodemus Heights
North Woods

Nicodemus Farm

Miller Farm

MEADE

S. Poffenberger Farm
Miller Farm

Mansfield Monument Road

Dunker Church Road

Miller Cornfield
East Woods
Seymour

JACKSON

Starke Ave.
Cornfield Ave.
Smoketown Road

Mumma Farm and Cemetery

J.R. JONES
Douglass
LAWTON
West Woods
Hays
Walker
Ripley
D.H. HILL

A. Poffenberger Farm
HOOD
Dunker Church
S. D. Lee
Visitor Center
Mumma Lane

STOP 3B The I Corps Attacks, 5:00–6:00 A.M.

What Happened At approximately 5:00 A.M. on the morning of September 17, Hooker rode forward to near this point to examine the ground in front of him. By 5:15, as the sun began to rise, Seymour's brigade in the East Woods had begun a spirited engagement with a brigade from *Lawton's* division led by Col. James A. *Walker*. A few minutes later Federal artillery on Poffenberger Ridge and east of the Antietam opened fire.

To resist Hooker's attack, *Jackson* had posted *Lawton's* division in the pasture east of the Hagerstown Pike about 700 yards south of here, with its front extending east and south across the Smoketown Road to a cemetery located on the Samuel Mumma farm. To *Lawton's* left, a division commanded by Brig. Gen. John R. *Jones*, was posted on the west side of the Hagerstown Pike in two lines of two brigades each. Connecting the Confederate left to the Potomac was Brig. Gen. Fitz *Lee's* brigade of cavalry, operating under the direct supervision of Maj. Gen. James E. B. *Stuart* and supported by about fourteen guns, commanded by Capt. John *Pelham*. These guns were posted on Nicodemus Heights and, supported by a brigade from *Jones's* division commanded by Brig. Gen. Jubal *Early*, could fire into the flank of any Union force attacking south toward the Dunker Church. To the south, on the high plateau across the Hagerstown Pike from the Dunker Church, *Jackson* had four batteries of artillery under the command of Stephen D. *Lee*. To support his position, Jackson had *Hood's* division, posted in the West Woods in reserve, and Maj. Gen. Daniel H. *Hill's* division, most of which was posted in a farm lane just south of the Dunker Church plateau. Fully aware that Federal possession of the Dunker Church plateau would render the entire Confederate position along Sharpsburg Heights untenable, *Jackson* prepared to make a tough fight for it.

At approximately 5:30 A.M. Hooker decided to launch an attack against *Jackson's* position and sent a message to Mansfield to move his corps forward from the Line farm, but decided not to await its arrival before beginning his attack. Seymour, Hooker decided, would continue his fight in the East Woods until Ricketts's division moved up to take over the battle from him. Ricketts would then drive south and west through the East Woods, following Smoketown Road. Meanwhile, Doubleday's division would advance southward along the Hagerstown Pike. Meade's other two brigades would remain in the North Woods to serve as a general reserve.

As his tactical objective, Hooker selected the Dunker Church, the only landmark clearly visible through the morning haze, located at the convergence of the Hagerstown Pike, along which Doubleday's division advanced, and Smoketown Road, along which Ricketts's men advanced. The church was also selected due to the fact that S. D. *Lee's* artillery was posted nearby and—and from their position there, in combination with *Pelham's* guns on Nicodemus Heights—was able to subject the Federal advance to a murderous crossfire.

Analysis

Hooker's plan for a converging attack on the Dunker Church plateau was a good one. Although he could not know it from his position, that piece of terrain was the key to the Confederate position north of Sharpsburg. His decision to launch his attack before Mansfield's men came up has been criticized, however. Clearly, one factor behind this decision was Hooker's eagerness to gain laurels for himself, the surest route to which was to act on his innate aggressiveness on the morning of September 17. Probably more compelling, however, in shaping Hooker's decision was the situation on the ground. When he decided to attack, the battle had already begun in the East Woods and there was no point in letting this go on in isolation. Hooker's decision to attack without waiting for Mansfield's men to come up is also suggestive of McClellan's intentions as he communicated them to Hooker. After conducting a reconnaissance of the Confederate position west of the Antietam on September 15, Hooker concluded *Lee* had 30,000 to 50,000 troops with him in front of Sharpsburg and was well aware that this had been increased by the arrival of *Jackson's* command. To believe that his single corps could crush the Confederate left, if that was the task McClellan assigned to him, was, in this light, unrealistic. However, if McClellan's intention was for Hooker to simply exert pressure north of Sharpsburg, see how *Lee* reacted, and respond accordingly, then opening the fight with only a single corps made sense.

Hooker probably anticipated that Mansfield's command would arrive on the field at a point in time when the results of the I Corps's attacks were evident, and intended to let the situation at that point determine how he would employ the XII Corps. As it turned out, despite the ferocity with which *Jackson's* men resisted his attacks, Hooker's plan and its execution enabled him to achieve his tactical objective. The I Corps's attacks severely battered and bloodied *Jackson's* command; then Mansfield arrived on the field to stabilize the situation and push forward to seize the Dunker Church plateau. Moreover, Hooker's attacks compelled Robert E. *Lee* to weaken his line elsewhere, creating opportunities for truly decisive success south of Sharpsburg.

Further Reading   Carman, "Maryland Campaign," chap. 13, 32–41, 43–46, chap. 15, 53–56; Sears, *Landscape Turned Red*, 176–84; U.S. War Department, *War of the Rebellion*, vol. 19, ser. 1, pt. 1:217–19, 955–56.

STOP 4   East Woods

Directions   Return to your car. *Exit* the parking area and *resume driving* east along MANSFIELD AVENUE for 0.4 mile until it ends at SMOKETOWN ROAD. *Turn right* onto SMOKETOWN ROAD and *proceed* 0.1 mile to CORNFIELD AVENUE. *Turn right* onto CORNFIELD AVENUE and immediately *pull over* into the parking area on your right. Exit your vehicle, *walk* to the northwest corner of the parking area, and face north.

En route. You will pass an upturned cannon and monument to Maj. Gen. Joseph F. K. Mansfield on your left. The former marks the approximate spot on the battlefield where the XII Corps commander was mortally wounded only a few minutes after arriving on the field.

Orientation   The East Woods were much larger at the time of the battle of Antietam, extending south to SMOKETOWN ROAD and west to the eastern edge of the Miller Cornfield. If you look to your left rear, you will see a copse of trees on this side of SMOKETOWN ROAD, which marks the approximate location of the southwest corner of the East Woods in 1862. If you look to your left down CORNFIELD AVENUE, about 10 yards back from the road and midway between you and the cannon is a small marker that indicates the western edge of the East Woods. The old Hagerstown Pike (modern DUNKER CHURCH ROAD) is about a quarter mile west of where you are standing. If you look to your left front, you will see the thirty-acre Miller Cornfield, bordered by a wood fence to the north and south. In front of you on the other side of the Cornfield you will note a rise. In September 1862 that was a cleared field. About a mile and a half up SMOKETOWN ROAD in the direction from which you just came was the location of the Line farm, where the XII Corps bivouacked before marching to the battlefield on September 17. About 0.4 mile down SMOKETOWN ROAD in the other direction from here, just beyond the large cupola (the Maryland monument) visible to your left rear, is the Dunker Church.

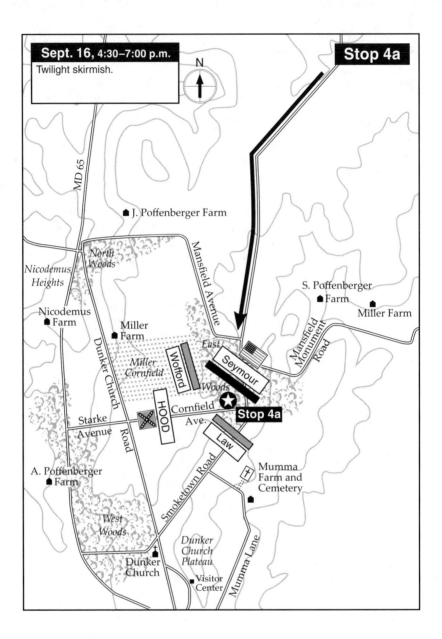

J. Poffenberger Farm

North Woods

Nicodemus Heights

Mansfield Avenue

S. Poffenberger Farm

Miller Farm

Nicodemus Farm

Miller Farm

Dunker Church Road

Miller Cornfield

Wofford

East Woods

Seymour

Mansfield Monument Road

Starke Avenue

HOOD

Cornfield Ave.

Stop 4a

Law

Mumma Farm and Cemetery

A. Poffenberger Farm

Smoketown Road

West Woods

Dunker Church Plateau

Dunker Church

Mumma Lane

Visitor Center

STOP 4A   Twilight Skirmish, September 16, 1862, 4:30–7:00 P.M.

What Happened   After crossing the Antietam about a mile and a half east of
                      here at the Upper Bridge and Pry's Ford between 3:00 and
                      4:00 P.M. on September 16, the three divisions of Hooker's
                      corps advanced west from the creek with Seymour's bri-
                      gade of Meade's division in the lead. Seymour's men turned
                      south after reaching Smoketown Road and had begun mov-
                      ing toward the East Woods when they encountered ele-

ments of the 9th Virginia Cavalry. Seymour quickly drove off the Confederate cavalry and pushed into the East Woods. Upon learning of Seymour's advance, Brig. Gen. John Bell *Hood* ordered Col. William T. *Wofford's* and Col. Evander *Law's* brigades from his division to move toward the East Woods, with *Wofford's* men pushing against its western edge and Law's entering the woodlot from the south. *Hood's* men quickly made contact with Seymour's and a sharp firefight commenced. This engagement continued until around 6:30 P.M., when it became too dark for either side to see anything but muzzle flashes. Seymour remained in the East Woods the rest of the night. At *Hood's* request, *Jackson* let his division pull back to the West Woods around 10:00 P.M. and Brig. Gen. Alexander *Lawton's* division took over the defense of this part of the field.

Analysis

Although a minor engagement, the skirmish between Seymour's and *Hood's* men has been viewed as a critical event by some historians who have argued that it compromised the Federal effort north of Sharpsburg on September 17 by giving away the element of surprise. This argument is without merit. *Lee's* army would have had to be completely—and uncharacteristically—asleep at the switch not to notice an entire Federal corps crossing the Antietam, and in fact news of Hooker's crossing reached *Lee* almost as soon as it happened. The main significance of the engagement in the East Woods on September 16 was Seymour's remaining in close contact with the enemy after it was over. This ensured the fight on September 17 would begin in the East Woods.

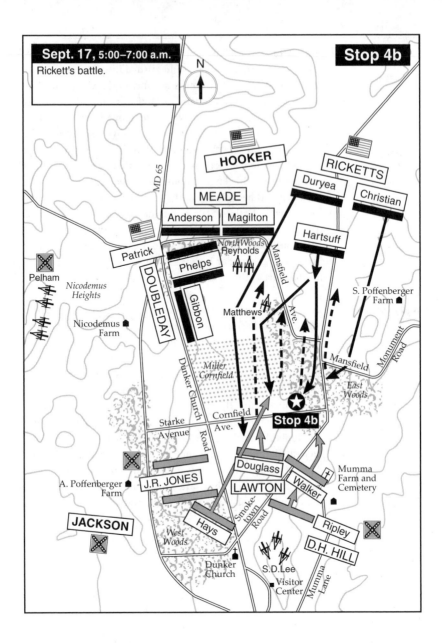

Sept. 17, 5:00–7:00 a.m.
Rickett's battle.

Stop 4b

N

HOOKER

RICKETTS

Duryea

Christian

MEADE

Anderson   Magilton

Hartsuff

MD 65

Patrick

North Woods
Reynolds

DOUBLEDAY

Phelps

Pelham

Nicodemus
Heights

Gibbon

Matthews

Mansfield Ave.

S. Poffenberger
Farm

Nicodemus
Farm

Monument Road

Dunker Church Road

Miller
Cornfield

Mansfield

East
Woods

Starke
Avenue

Cornfield
Ave.

Stop 4b

A. Poffenberger
Farm

Douglass

J.R. JONES

LAWTON

Walker

Mumma
Farm and
Cemetery

Smoketown Road

JACKSON

Hays

Ripley

West
Woods

D.H. HILL

Dunker
Church

S.D. Lee

Visitor
Center

Mumma
Lane

STOP 4B   Ricketts's Battle, September 17, 1862, 5:00–7:00 A.M.

What Happened   The battle of Antietam began in the East Woods around
                      5:15 A.M. on September 17. For about forty-five minutes, Sey-
                      mour's and *Walker's* men were the only infantry significant-
                      ly engaged on the entire field. This changed about 6:00 A.M.
                      when Brig. Gen. Abram Duryea's brigade from Ricketts's di-
                      vision joined the fight as part of the general advance of the
                      I Corps ordered by Hooker. As Seymour's men battled in the

East Woods, Ricketts moved forward his command in accordance with Hooker's orders to take over the fight from Seymour and advance along Smoketown Road toward the Dunker Church. In preparation for his advance, Ricketts had placed Gen. George Hartsuff's brigade in the lead with Col. William Christian's brigade supporting his left. Duryea's brigade was assigned the task of supporting Hartsuff's right. Before his command pushed into the East Woods, Hartsuff decided to ride forward to conduct a personal reconnaissance. By then, Col. S. D. *Lee's* artillery on the Dunker Church plateau was pouring a terrific fire into the East Woods and Hartsuff was severely wounded.

Hartsuff's brigade and Christian's remained in place while news of Hartsuff's wounding made its way to his successor in command, Col. Richard Coulter. Duryea's brigade, however, continued moving south and passed through a gap between the North and East Woods to the fence line at the northern edge of the Miller Cornfield. There, about 5:45 A.M., Duryea halted his command and began forming them into line. When they finished deploying, Duryea ordered his men to resume their advance south into and through the tall corn. When Duryea's men cleared the cornfield and began advancing into the open pasture to the south, they encountered a brigade of six Georgia regiments commanded by Col. Marcellus *Douglass* and elements from *Walker's* brigade. The two sides then engaged in a vicious firefight that lasted for about a half hour and ended with Duryea losing about a third of his men and falling back through the cornfield.

As Duryea's command pulled back to lick its wounds, Coulter finally managed to get his brigade moving forward. His right regiments, the 12th Massachusetts and 11th Pennsylvania, advanced through the southeast corner of the Cornfield, driving *Lawton's* skirmishers out of it, and reached a point about 50 yards south of the Cornfield. There, Coulter's men encountered Brig. Gen. Harry T. *Hays's* Louisiana brigade, which had just moved forward from its reserve position in the West Woods. Meanwhile, on Coulter's left the 13th Massachusetts and 83rd New York pushed through the East Woods and then wheeled right to a point at the western edge of the woods. At this point, *Hays* ordered an all-out counterattack that, aided by elements from *Douglass's* command, drove the right and center of Coulter's command back into the East Woods. By then, however, three regiments from Ricketts's final brigade had arrived, now commanded by Col. Peter Lyle after Christian mentally collapsed while under Confederate artillery fire and fled the field.

Lyle directed his command to deploy in line, cross Smoke-town Road, and form behind a fence on the edge of the East Woods on Coulter's left.

Upon arriving at the fence, Lyle's men were greeted by canister fire from a Confederate battery located midway be-tween the Mumma farm and Smoketown Road. As Coulter's right and center melted under the weight of *Hays's* and *Doug-lass's* counterattack, Lyle's brigade managed to maintain their position and helped bring *Hays's* attack to a halt. But upon watching Coulter's men retire and seeing fresh Con-federate troops moving their way—the vanguard of *Hood's* division—Lyle's men decided to join their comrades as they pulled back through the East Woods. Ricketts's drive to the Dunker Church had been brought to a bloody halt with over a third of the men in the division killed, wounded, or miss-ing. However, in conjunction with Doubleday's division, by 7:00 A.M. Ricketts's men had inflicted a terrible beating on the Confederates that left their position north of Sharps-burg hanging by a thread.

Analysis   The fact that Ricketts's command did not enter the fight in a single advance and Duryea's command had to carry the fight north of Sharpsburg alone for a half-hour reflects how problems of command and control affected tactics in the Civil War. Ricketts no doubt fully intended for his entire division to advance together astride Smoketown Road. The loss of two brigade commanders, however, in combination with the terrain, foiled this. When a brigade commander was wounded during the Civil War, command automatical-ly devolved upon his senior regimental commander. Given the time it often took for news of a commander's wounding to pass along the chain of command, for the new brigade commander to make the command adjustments in his own regiment, and for him to get a good enough grasp on the sit-uation to issue and execute orders, it is not surprising that it took some time after Hartsuff's wounding for Coulter to get things sorted out in his command and resume the of-fensive. The fact that Hartsuff's and Christian's men also had to negotiate the East Woods, while Duryea's men made their advance over open terrain before reaching the Corn-field, further compromised Ricketts's effort to make a sin-gle, concerted advance. Consequently, *Douglass's*, *Walker's*, and *Hays's* men were able to repulse Duryea and then deal with Coulter's and Lyle's attacks. Had all three of Ricketts's brigades gone into action together as intended, it is hard to see how his advance along Smoketown Road could have been held up the way it was.

Vignette   One man later wrote of his experience as a member of *Douglass's* brigade during the clash with Duryea, "As soon as it was light the enemy was seen approaching. By order of Colonel Douglass their fire was reserved until the enemy approached within a distance of 100 yards. The enemy also did not fire until they attained a position this near to us. The officer in command addressed the men and acted in [e]very respect as though on parade–the words of command could be heard distinctly. Colonel Douglass then ordered his command to fire, so as to get the first fire, and at short range–He ordered the second volley, both of which were discharged before we received the enemy's fire. At each discharge, wide gaps were made in the enemy's ranks, and the groans of the wounded were horrible. Our men bore their suffering in silence. . . . Colonel Douglass repeatedly passed up and down the line, encouraging the men, directing them to keep cool and aim well. And, as they would deliver their fire, and the destruction which followed could be seen he would say 'That's right my brave boys–pour it into them again.'"

Further Reading   Carman, "Maryland Campaign," chap. 13, 13–41, chap. 15, 53–68, 85–90; Sears, *Landscape Turned Red*, 184–90, 203–6, 210–13, 272–73; U.S. War Department, *War of the Rebellion*, vol. 19, ser. 1, pt. 1:217–18, 258–59, 923, 955–56, 975–77.

On the skirmish line.
BLCW 1:465

STOP 5   The Hagerstown Pike

Directions   Return to your car and *resume driving* west along CORNFIELD
                      AVENUE 0.3 mile to its intersection with DUNKER CHURCH
                      ROAD. *Turn right* onto DUNKER CHURCH ROAD. You will im-
                      mediately see a cannon next to the fence on the left side
                      of the road; *pull into* the pull over on the right side of the
                      road across from it. Exit your car and carefully *cross* DUNK-
                      ER CHURCH ROAD to a point at the fence next to the cannon.
                      Turn around and face east toward DUNKER CHURCH ROAD.

Orientation   Directly in front of you, on the other side of DUNKER CHURCH
                      ROAD, which in 1862 was known as the Hagerstown Pike, is
                      the thirty-acre Miller Cornfield. The Miller farm is clearly vis-
                      ible if you look to your left front. On the other side of DUNK-
                      ER CHURCH ROAD north and south of the Cornfield (whose
                      borders are indicated by wood fences) in 1862 were open
                      fields. If you look to your right, you will see where CORN-
                      FIELD AVENUE and STARKE AVENUE (neither of which were
                      here at the time of the battle) intersect DUNKER CHURCH
                      ROAD. The modern farm buildings to your right front were
                      not here at the time of the battle. The woodlot on this side
                      of DUNKER CHURCH ROAD on the other side of STARKE AVENUE
                      is the West Woods. The Dunker Church plateau, the objec-
                      tive of the Federal attack and Confederate defense on the
                      morning of September 17, is about 600 yards south of where
                      you are standing. Nicodemus Heights is on the other side of
                      the modern HAGERSTOWN PIKE north and west (your left rear)
                      from where you are now standing.

STOP 5A   Doubleday's Attack, 6:00–6:30 A.M.

What Happened   On the morning of September 17, Stonewall *Jackson* had J. R.
                            Jones's and *Lawton's* divisions deployed on either side of the
                            Hagerstown Pike. West of the road, *Jones's* men were de-
                            ployed in two lines. In the first line, about 225 yards south
                            of modern STARKE AVENUE were two brigades command-
                            ed by Col. Andrew J. *Grigsby*; about 200 yards farther south
                            was a second line of two brigades under the combined com-
                            mand of Brig. Gen. William E. *Starke*. A battery of three guns
                            commanded by Capt. William *Poague* was posted on a slight
                            knoll just in front of *Grigsby's* line. On the east side of the
                            Hagerstown Pike and separated from *Grigsby's* right by about
                            a 120-yard gap, *Jackson* posted two brigades of *Lawton's* divi-
                            sion, which extended the Confederate line to the Mumma
                            Cemetery on the other side of Smoketown Road.

                            Around 6:00 A.M. Doubleday's attack began. As Ricketts
                            advanced into the Cornfield and East Woods, Doubleday
                            ordered three brigades from his division forward from the
                            Poffenberger farm. After passing through the North Woods,
                            Doubleday's men moved to the Hagerstown Pike, which they
                            were to guide on as they advanced south. Spearheading the
                            assault was Brig. Gen. John Gibbon's all-Western "Black Hat"
                            brigade. Following Gibbon was Col. Walter Phelps Jr.'s bri-
                            gade of New Yorkers and U.S. Sharpshooters, and Brig. Gen.
                            Marsena Patrick's brigade of New Yorkers. Doubleday's final
                            brigade, Lt. Col. William Hoffman's, was left behind to cover
                            the Federal flank and artillery on Poffenberger Ridge.

                            In the open field north of the Miller farm, Gibbon de-
                            ployed his lead regiment, Lt. Col. Edward Bragg's 6th Wis-
                            consin in line with two companies in front as skirmishers.
                            To support Bragg's advance, Gibbon posted Capt. Joseph
                            B. Campbell's Battery B, 4th U.S. Artillery about 100 yards
                            south of the North Woods. Bragg's men then advanced
                            astride the Hagerstown Pike with their left wing pushing
                            past the Miller farm and into the Miller Cornfield just as Du-
                            ryea's brigade of Ricketts's division was pulling back after
                            their engagement with *Lawton's* men.

Vignette   Leading Company F of the 6th Wisconsin into battle at An-
                            tietam was Capt. Werner von Bachelle, who, one man lat-
                            er wrote, "had a fine Newfoundland dog, which had been
                            trained to perform military salutes and many other remark-
                            able things. In camp, on the march, and in the line of battle,
                            this dog was his constant companion. The dog was by his
                            side when he fell. Our line of men left the body when they
                            retreated, but the dog stayed with his dead master, and was

found on the morning of the 19th of September lying dead upon his body. We buried him with his master. So far as we knew, no family or friends mourned for poor Bachelle, and it is probable that he was joined in death by his most devoted friend on earth."

"Captured by Stonewall Jackson himself." BLCW 2:360

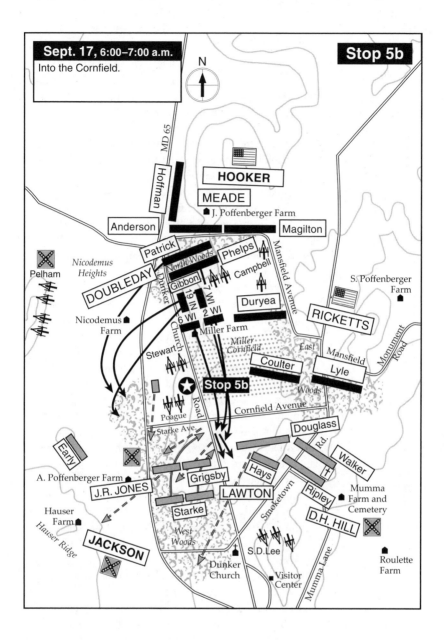

STOP 5B   Into the Cornfield, 6:00–7:00 A.M.

Directions   *Remain in place. Turn right* and face toward the Indiana monument, the tall obelisk near the corner of CORNFIELD AVENUE and DUNKER CHURCH ROAD.

What Happened   Seeing Bragg's men encounter stiff resistance from Confederate forces west of the Hagerstown Pike, Gibbon directed two of his regiments, the 19th Indiana and 7th Wisconsin to cross the road, while the 6th and 2nd Wisconsin advanced through the Cornfield. As Gibbon was doing this, Doubleday ordered Phelps to support the attack into the Cornfield and directed Patrick to assist Gibbon's units west of the road. As the right wing of Gibbon's command and Patrick established a foothold in the northern part of the West Woods, Gibbon's left and Phelps's brigade pushed through the Cornfield and encountered the three left regiments of *Douglass's* brigade of *Lawton's* division, positioned about 200 yards south of the Cornfield. *Lawton's* men put up a tough fight but, already bloodied from their earlier fight with Duryea's men, were soon compelled to retreat toward the West Woods. *Lawton* was carried off the field wounded, *Douglass* was dead, and of *Lawton's* fifteen regimental commanders, eleven were casualties.

As *Lawton's* command and *Jones's* first line crumbled and left the field, the 6th and 2nd Wisconsin pushed into the open pasture south of the Cornfield. *Starke* responded by ordering his two brigades to oblique to the right and advance to the Hagerstown Pike. From behind the fences lining the pike, *Starke's* men poured a murderous fire into the right flank of Gibbon's advance and compelled Gibbon's men to fall back to the Cornfield. After being joined there by two regiments from Phelps's brigade, Gibbon's men moved forward and renewed the fight with *Starke*, as Campbell moved forward a two-gun section from his battery, commanded by Lt. James Stewart. After deploying just west of the turnpike, Stewart began firing into *Starke's* left flank while skirmishers from Gibbon's and Patrick's commands moved forward from the northern end of the West Woods and began firing into *Starke's* rear. Seeing the toll the combined weight of this fire was taking on his men, *Starke* realized he could not keep up the fight and ordered his men to fall back to the West Woods. Of the 1,150 men of *Starke's* command that had entered the battle, 470 had been killed or wounded. *Starke* himself was wounded three times and would be dead by noon. Gibbon's and Phelps's commands were in scarcely better shape. Nonetheless, they once again turned southward to resume the drive toward the Dunker Church.

Vignette

The experience of combat in the Cornfield was vividly recounted by Maj. Rufus Dawes of the 6th Wisconsin: "At the front edge of the corn-field was a low Virginia rail fence. Before the corn were open fields, beyond which was a strip of woods surrounding a little church, the Dunkard church. As we appeared at the edge of the corn, a long line of men in butternut and gray rose up from the ground. Simultaneously, the hostile battle lines opened a tremendous fire upon each other. Men, I can not say fell; they were knocked out of ranks by dozens. But we jumped over the fence, and pushed on, loading, firing, and shouting as we advanced. There was, on the part of the men, great hysterical excitement, eagerness to go forward, and a reckless disregard of life, of everything but victory. . . . We all joined together, jumped over the fence, and again pushed out into the open field. There is a rattling fusillade and loud cheers. 'Forward' is the word. The men are loading and firing with demoniacal fury and shouting and laughing hysterically, and the whole field before us is covered with rebels fleeing for life, into the woods. Great numbers of them are shot while climbing over the high post and rail fences along the turnpike. We push on over the open fields half way to the little church. The powder is bad, and the guns have become very dirty. It takes hard pounding to get the bullets down, and our firing is becoming slow."

Further Reading   Carman, "Maryland Campaign," chap. 15, 68–85; Sears, *Landscape Turned Red*, 180–85.

Brigadier-General William E. Starke, c.s.a. From a tintype. BLCW 2:628

STOP 6   The Cornfield

After returning to your car, do a *U-turn* and drive back down
DUNKER CHURCH ROAD to the intersection with CORNFIELD AV-
ENUE and STARKE AVENUE. *Turn left* onto CORNFIELD AVENUE
and then *pull into* the parking area on your left. Exit your car
and *walk* down CORNFIELD AVENUE to the rose marble Texas
Monument on the right side of CORNFIELD AVENUE across the
road from the monument to the 14th Brooklyn. *Stop* here
and face east, with CORNFIELD AVENUE just to your left.

Orientation   You are standing just south of the Miller Cornfield, which is
to your left on the other side of CORNFIELD AVENUE. The Miller farm is to your left rear. The old Hagerstown Pike (now
DUNKER CHURCH ROAD) is just behind you; the remnants of
the East Woods are to your front left (and in 1862, extended south across your front to Smoketown Road), while the
North Woods are to your left in the distance. If you look
over your right shoulder beyond the modern farm buildings
you will see the West Woods on the other side of DUNKER
CHURCH ROAD and how they extend south several hundred
yards. Nicodemus Heights is on the other side of the modern HAGERSTOWN PIKE, north and west of the Miller farm.
The high ground on which the Visitor Center sits, the objective of the Federal attack and Confederate defense on the
morning of September 17, and Dunker Church is about 500
yards south from where you are standing, and is clearly visible to your right.

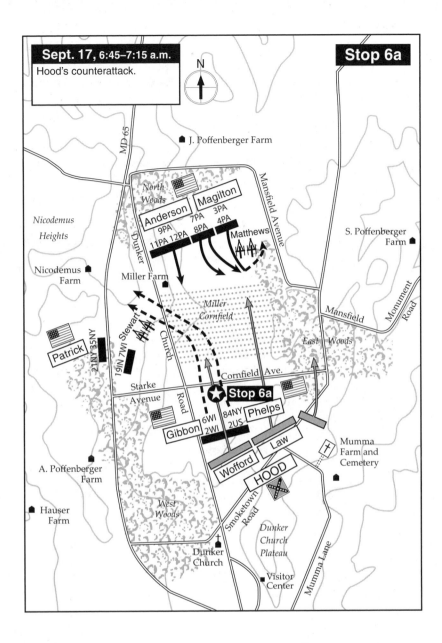

J. Poffenberger Farm

MD 65

Mansfield Avenue

North Woods

Anderson   Magilton

9PA   7PA   3PA
11PA 12PA   8PA   4PA

Matthews

Nicodemus Heights

S. Poffenberger Farm

Nicodemus Farm

Miller Farm

Miller Cornfield

Mansfield

Monument Road

East   Woods

Patrick

21NY 35NY

19IN 7WI Stewart

Church

Cornfield   Ave.

Dunker

Starke Avenue

Road

Stop 6a

6WI   84NY
Gibbon   2WI   2US   Phelps

Law

Mumma Farm and Cemetery

Wofford

HOOD

A. Poffenberger Farm

West Woods

Smoketown Road

Dunker Church Plateau

Mumma Lane

Hauser Farm

Dunker Church

Visitor Center

STOP 6A

Hood's Counterattack, 6:45–7:15 A.M.

What Happened

After their clash with the Federals in the East Woods the previous evening, *Jackson* had let Brig. Gen. John Bell *Hood's* division go into reserve in the West Woods. Having not had a hot meal in days, *Hood's* men began September 17 by preparing their breakfast. This task was not yet completed when *Hood* received orders from *Jackson* at about 6:00 A.M. to join the battle for the Cornfield. Screaming the "rebel yell" as they rushed forward from the West Woods, Brig Gen. William *Wofford's* Texas Brigade slammed into Gibbon's and Phelps's exhausted commands just as they had resumed their drive south toward the Dunker Church and quickly drove them back into and through the Cornfield. Meanwhile, to *Wofford's* right, Col. Evander *Law's* brigade men swept away the elements of Ricketts's division that were still in the eastern section of the Cornfield and pushed forward toward the fence at its northern end.

As *Hood's* men crashed into and drove back Doubleday's and Ricketts's men, Lt. Col. Robert Anderson's and Col. Albert L. Magilton's brigades from Meade's division were already moving forward from the North Woods toward the Cornfield. *Wofford* ordered his men to halt at the southern edge of the Cornfield in order to dress their lines, but Lt. Col. Philip *Work's* 1st Texas, in *Hood's* words, "slipped the bridle and got away." The Texans drove forward into the Cornfield, just as Anderson's brigade, with Capt. Dunbar B. Ransom's battery in support, reached its northern edge. Steadying their rifles on the lower rails of the fence bordering the Cornfield, Anderson's men waited until the Texans were 30 yards away and then opened fire. As fire from Anderson's infantry and Ransom's battery slammed into their front, the Texans also began taking fire from Gibbon's and Patrick's brigades and Lt. James Stewart's two gun section of artillery, which were posted west of the Hagerstown Pike. The western end of the Cornfield became a slaughter pen. Canister and small arms fire at point-blank range tore huge holes in *Work's* ranks and made it impossible for the rest of *Wofford's* command to come to their assistance.

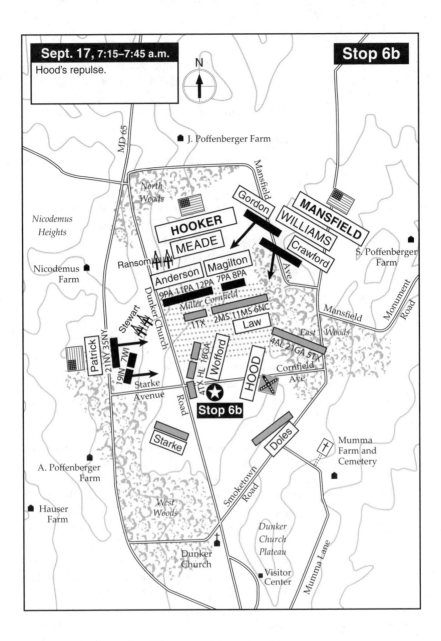

N

J. Poffenberger Farm

North Woods

Nicodemus Heights

MD 65

Mansfield Ave.

Gordon

MANSFIELD

WILLIAMS

HOOKER

MEADE

Crawford

S. Poffenberger Farm

Nicodemus Farm

Ransom

Anderson   Magilton

9PA 11PA 12PA   7PA 8PA

Miller Cornfield

Mansfield Road

Monument Road

Stewart

Dunker Church

1TX   2MS 11MS 6NC

Law

East Woods

4AL 21GA 5TX

21NY 35NY

Patrick

Wofford

4TX HL 18GA

HOOD

Cornfield Ave.

19IN   7WI

Starke Avenue

Stop 6b

Starke

Doles

Mumma Farm and Cemetery

A. Poffenberger Farm

Smoketown Road

Hauser Farm

West Woods

Dunker Church Plateau

Mumma Lane

Dunker Church

Visitor Center

STOP 6B	*Hood's* Repulse, 7:15–7:45 A.M.
Directions	*Remain in place* and *turn left* to face toward the Cornfield.
What Happened	As *Wofford's* men pushed into the Cornfield, Capt. Ezra W. Matthews's Union battery was firing double canister into the Cornfield from a position on the high ground north of it in a frantic effort to stop *Law's* advance. To support Matthews, Magilton reoriented his advance to move by the flank

toward the East Woods. *Law's* men, however, opened such an intense fire into Magilton's ranks that two of his regiments immediately broke and left the field. The 7th and 8th Pennsylvania Reserves did not, however, and a fierce battle ensued between them and *Law's* men. It was at this point that Brig. Gen. Alpheus Williams's division of Maj. Gen. Joseph F. K. Mansfield's XII Corps began arriving on the field. Even though many of his men had been in the service less than a month, Williams did not hesitate to order them into the battle. The commander of Williams's lead brigade, Brig. Gen. Samuel Crawford quickly advanced the 125th Pennsylvania to a position from which they were able to steady Magilton's left as he battled *Law*. Meanwhile, Mansfield led other elements from Crawford's brigade into the East Woods. Almost immediately thereafter, however, Mansfield was mortally wounded and command of the corps passed to Williams. Brig. Gen. George H. Gordon's brigade from Williams's division was the second one to arrive and began pushing through the gap between the North Woods and East Woods into the open area north of the Cornfield and toward a gap that had opened between *Wofford's* and *Law's* brigades.

By this point, after firing a few rounds into *Wofford's* left from their position on a rock ledge west of the Hagerstown Pike, four regiments from Patrick's and Gibbon's commands had begun advancing toward the road. With Gibbon and Patrick menacing his left and rear, the arrival of Williams's command, and Anderson's men still pouring a heavy fire into his front, *Wofford* had no choice but to pull his shattered command back to the West Woods. Fortunately, at this point some of *Starke's* men returned to the fight and began firing into the right flank of the Federals along the Hagerstown Pike, which forced them to pull back and relieved the pressure on *Wofford's* left. With his nearly fought-out command also in danger of being overwhelmed, *Law* had to order his men to retreat from the Cornfield as well.

Analysis

Hood's division saved the Confederate position north of Sharpsburg from an early collapse and punished Hooker's corps so much that it was no longer capable of major offensive operations. It did so, however, at a horrible cost. Shortly after he returned to the West Woods, an officer asked *Hood* where his division was and was told, with only slight exaggeration, "Dead on the field." In *Law's* brigade, over half the soldiers in the 6th North Carolina, 2nd Mississippi, and 11th Mississippi had been killed or wounded. Of the 854 men that *Wofford* led out of the West Woods, 560 had been shot. No regiment suffered worse losses than the 1st Texas. Eight of its color bearers were shot down in rapid sequence in the Cornfield; at the end of the day, over 80 percent of the regiment, 186 of 226 men, were dead, wounded, or missing. This was the highest percentage of casualties that would be suffered by any regiment in any engagement during the Civil War. *Hood* later complained that his men had not received any support until after the fight in the Cornfield was over. This, however, was largely a consequence of the ferocity with which *Hood's* men entered the battle. This saved the Confederate left, but also made it difficult to manage the battle—as illustrated by *Wofford's* losing control of the 1st Texas during the advance toward the Cornfield. It is also difficult to see how *Hood* could have achieved much more than he did with additional support, given the arrival of the Union XII Corps and the crossfire the Federals were able to pour into the Cornfield.

General John B. Hood, c.s.a. From a photograph. BLCW 4:275

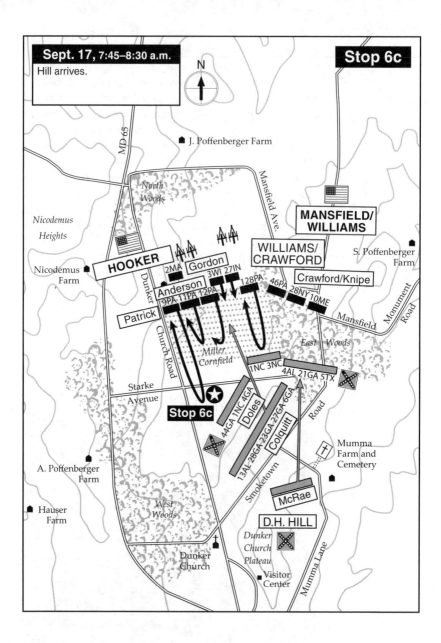

N

STOP 6C   *Hill* Arrives, 7:45–8:30 A.M.

Directions   *Remain in place* and *turn right* to again face east down CORN-
FIELD AVENUE.

What Happened   As *Wofford's* men pulled back from the Cornfield, Anderson's
brigade pushed after them in pursuit. Then, upon reaching
the southern edge of the Cornfield, the Pennsylvanians encountered the left and center of Col. George P. *Doles's* bri-

gade of Maj. Gen. Daniel H. *Hill's* division and, after a brief engagement, pulled back through the Cornfield. Meanwhile, *Doles's* right advanced to a position on the southern edge of the Cornfield next to the East Woods and began assisting two regiments from *Hood's* command and a regiment from *Walker's* brigade still holding that part of the field in their fight with elements from the Union XII Corps.

Shortly thereafter, *Doles's* men found themselves battling the green troops of the 128th Pennsylvania, which was attempting to push south with their left in the East Woods and right in the open pasture north of the Cornfield. Almost as soon the Confederates opened fire, though, they wounded the Pennsylvanians' commander and his second in command, which threw the Federal ranks into disarray. Brigade commander Lt. Col. Joseph Knipe managed to get the Pennsylvanians, now commanded by Maj. Joel B. Wanner, once again moving south through the Cornfield. When Wanner's men emerged from the Cornfield, however, *Doles's* men greeted them with another ferocious volley that shattered their ranks and sent them retreating back through the corn.

Meanwhile, Gordon's brigade was still moving forward over the open ground north of the Cornfield after helping induce *Hood's* men to abandon the Cornfield. Fortunately for the Confederates, at this point another of *Hill's* brigades, Col. Alfred *Colquitt's* arrived on the field, with *Doles's* men shifting to the left to let *Colquitt's* five regiments come up on their right and push into the Cornfield. To bolster his right and support *Colquitt*, Hill also ordered Lt. Col. Duncan K. *McRae's* brigade forward. A savage battle between *Hill's* men and Gordon's brigade and the Federals still in the East Woods then erupted that did not end until the arrival of Brig. Gen. George Greene's Union division on the field.

Vignette

One of the officers who participated in the battles for the Cornfield and West Woods at Antietam as a member of Gordon's brigade was Capt. Robert Gould Shaw of the 2nd Massachusetts. After reaching the field, the regiment was posted on the right of Gordon's line, Shaw wrote shortly after the battle, "in a little orchard, and . . . got a cross fire on that part of the enemy's line [in the Cornfield], which, as we soon discovered did a great execution. . . . It was the prettiest thing we have ever done, and our loss was small at that time; in half an hour, the Brigade advanced through the cornfield in front, which, until then, had been occupied by the enemy; it was full of their dead and wounded. . . . Beyond the cornfield was a large open field, and such a mass of dead and wounded men, mostly Rebels, as were lying there, I never saw before; it was a terrible sight, and our men had to be very careful to avoid treading on them; many were mangled and torn to pieces by artillery, but most of them had been wounded by musketry fire. We halted right among them, and the men did everything they could for their comfort, giving them water from their canteens, and trying to place them in easy positions. There are so many young boys and old men among the Rebels, that it seems hardly possible that they can have come of their own accord to fight us, and it makes you pity them all the more, as they lie moaning on the field." A few months after he penned these words, Shaw accepted appointment as commander of the 54th Massachusetts, one of the first African American regiments raised by the North during the Civil War. One of the opening scenes in the 1989 movie *Glory*, which chronicles Shaw's experiences with this regiment, provides a dramatization of his service at Antietam.

Colonel Robert G. Shaw.
From a photograph.
BLCW 4:58

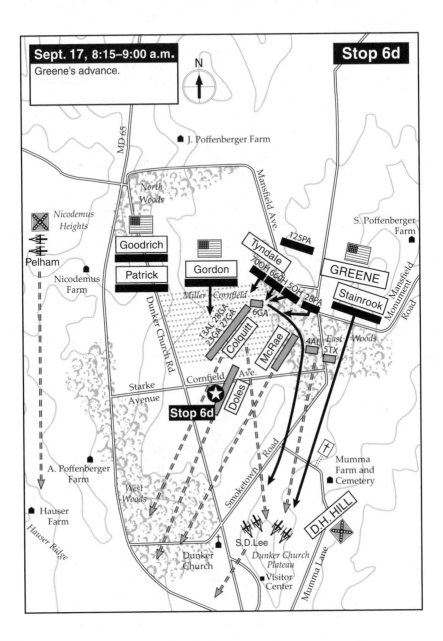

J. Poffenberger Farm

MD 65

North
Woods

Mansfield Ave.

S. Poffenberger
Farm

Nicodemus
Heights

125PA

Goodrich

Tyndale

Pelham

Nicodemus
Farm

Patrick

Gordon

70OH 66OH 5OH 28PA

GREENE

Stainrook

Miller Cornfield

13AL 28GA
23GA 27GA

6GA

Mansfield Monument Road

Colquitt

McRae

4AL
5TX

East Woods

Starke
Avenue

Cornfield Ave.

Dunker Church Rd.

Doles

Stop 6d

Mumma
Farm and
Cemetery

A. Poffenberger
Farm

West
Woods

Smoketown Road

Hauser
Farm

Hauser Ridge

S.D. Lee

D.H. HILL

Dunker
Church

Dunker Church
Plateau

Mumma Lane

Visitor
Center

STOP 6D   Greene's Advance, 8:15–9:00 A.M.

What Happened   At approximately 8:15 A.M., Greene's division from the Union XII Corps reached the battlefield. After dispatching one brigade to the end of the Federal line west of the Hagerstown Pike, Greene posted the rest of his command in the East Woods, with Lt. Col. Hector Tyndale's brigade on the right and Col. Henry Stainrook's on the left. Shortly thereafter, Capt. T. P. *Thomson* of the 5th North Carolina, the regiment holding *McRae's* right, saw Tyndale's lead regiment, Maj. Ario Pardee Jr.'s 28th Pennsylvania extending the Federal line beyond the Confederate right flank. "They are flanking us!" *Thomson* cried out. "See yonder's a whole brigade!" As word passed along the line that they were about to be enveloped, *McRae's* men panicked and retreated toward the West Woods and Sunken Road.

Meanwhile, the three Ohio regiments on Tyndale's right advanced to the western edge of the East Woods, where they spotted *Colquitt's* men near the northern end of the Cornfield only 30 yards away with their right flank completely exposed. The Ohioans immediately opened fire into the Confederate flank and then, with Pardee's Pennsylvanians on their left, charged into the Cornfield. After a brief and vicious fight, some of it hand-to-hand, *Colquitt's* men broke and gave *Hill* no choice but to order *Doles* to retreat from the Cornfield as well. Greene then pushed Tyndale and Stainrook forward following Smoketown Road to the Mumma farm, which Confederate artillerist Col. S. D. *Lee* took as his cue to remove his guns from the Dunker Church plateau. Greene then halted his advance to replenish his ammunition and allow artillery support to come up. At that point, a regiment from Crawford's brigade, the 125th Pennsylvania, suddenly pushed past them on Smoketown Road to seize a foothold in the West Woods.

The Dunker Church plateau, the terrain feature Hooker had identified as his objective over three hours earlier was in Federal hands. Unfortunately, Hooker would not get much time to savor his victory. Shortly before 9:00 A.M., the general was riding just south of the Cornfield when a bullet, probably fired by a Confederate sharpshooter, slammed through his foot and loss of blood quickly rendered him insensible. Consequently, at 9:00 A.M. the Federals north of Sharpsburg lacked an overall commander as the first significant lull in the fighting all morning settled over the field. Meanwhile, *Lee* had already directed Brig. Gen. John *Walker's* division to abandon its position guarding Snavely's Ford south of Sharpsburg, called up Maj. Gen. Lafayette *McLaws's* division from its position in reserve west of Sharpsburg, and ordered them both to the West Woods. Shortly after 8:30 A.M., *Lee* had also directed Capt. Thomas *Carter* to begin posting artillery on a ridge west of the Hagerstown Pike near the Reel farm to create a fall-back position for his forces north of Sharpsburg.

Vignette

A few days later, General Williams recalled that during the XII Corps's fight for the Cornfield, "the roar of the infantry was beyond anything conceivable to the uninitiated. Imagine from 8,000 to 10,000 men on one side, with probably a larger number on the other, all at once discharging their muskets. If all the stone and brick houses of Broadway should tumble at once the roar and rattle could hardly be greater, and amidst this, hundreds of pieces of artillery, right and left, were thundering as a sort of bass to the infernal music." In his battle report, Hooker wrote of the Cornfield, "In the time I am writing every stalk of corn in the northern and greater part of the field was cut as closely as could have been done with a knife, and the slain lay in rows precisely as they had stood in their ranks a few moments before. It was never my fortune to witness a more bloody, dismal battlefield."

Further Reading   Carman, "Maryland Campaign," chap. 15, 91–118, chap. 17, 188–90, 210–12, 251–52; Priest, *Antietam*, 54–70; Sears, *Landscape Turned Red*, 190–95, 197–213.

Overview of Sumner's Fight, 9:00 A.M.–2:00 P.M.

The second phase of the battle of Antietam began around 9:00 A.M. with the arrival of Maj. Gen. Edwin V. Sumner, commander of the Union II Corps, in the East Woods. The fighting that had started with Hooker's attack had ended with the Union in possession of the Dunker Church plateau. In response to reports from *Jackson*, *Lee* was rushing reinforcements to the north in an attempt to bolster this section of his line. The most important of the forces headed to *Jackson's* aid were Maj. Gen. Lafayette *McLaws's* division, which had begun the day in reserve west of Sharpsburg, and Brig. Gen. John *Walker's* division, which shortly after 8:00 A.M. was directed to leave its position covering Snavely's Ford on the lower Antietam south of Sharpsburg.

After reaching the East Woods accompanied by a division commanded by Brig. Gen. John Sedgwick, Sumner had short conversations with Williams and Hooker, conducted a reconnaissance of the field, and saw Greene's command at the Dunker Church plateau. He then decided to personally lead Sedgwick's division into the West Woods, hoping to reach a point from which he could roll up the Confederate left. As Sedgwick's command pushed into and through the woodlot, however, *McLaws's* division entered the woods from the south just in time to slam into and lap around the Union left. Within fifteen minutes, Sedgwick's division was decimated and fleeing from the West Woods.

Because Sumner placed himself with Sedgwick's division and pushed its advance so fast, he lost direct contact with Brig. Gen. William French's trailing division. After reaching the East Woods, French ordered his command to advance south toward the Mumma farm and shortly thereafter encountered a Confederate force commanded by Maj. Gen. Daniel H. *Hill* that was posted in a worn farm lane that would become known as the Sunken Road. French then launched a series of attacks against the Sunken Road that failed to make a dent in the Confederate line. Around 11:00 A.M., Maj. Gen. Israel Richardson's division arrived on the scene and took over the fight but initially enjoyed no more success than French had.

Meanwhile, units from Brig. Gen. George Greene's division of the XII Corps, which had reached the Dunker Church plateau earlier in the morning, pushed forward into the West Woods and secured a position in the woods that they were able to hold for nearly two hours before being driven out by Confederate counterattacks. Shortly thereafter, around 1:00 P.M., Richardson's command, aided by a mix-up in orders

The field of Antietam.
BLCW 2:636

and confusion among the Confederates at the Sunken Road, managed to seize possession of the road. The Federals were unable, however, to exploit their success even though there were fresh troops on the field. These were the two divisions of Maj. Gen. William B. Franklin's VI Corps, which McClellan had dispatched to the field north of Sharpsburg after Sedgwick's disaster. When Franklin's lead division arrived, one of its brigades made a spirited, albeit clumsily executed attack near the Dunker Church. Encouraged, Franklin decided to make another attack. When he found out what Franklin was doing, Sumner told him to stop, fearing another failed attack would lead to the total collapse of the Union position north of Sharpsburg. Franklin disagreed with Sumner's assessment of the situation and sent a staff officer back to McClellan requesting permission to attack. McClellan responded by riding over to the East Woods to talk to Franklin and Sumner, but Sumner's protests persuaded McClellan not to let Franklin attack at that point, although he told Franklin to prepare to make an attack later that evening.

Meanwhile, *Lee* directed *Jackson* and *Stuart* to see if they could find or create a route north of the Dunker Church to make it possible for the Army of Northern Virginia to march north toward Hagerstown and escape the box McClellan was squeezing it into. *Stuart* and *Jackson* promptly organized a force to carry out *Lee's* orders, but *Stuart* grossly mismanaged his part of the operation, getting his force into an artillery duel with the Federals in which the Confederates were badly outmatched and quickly overwhelmed. *Stuart* was compelled to abandon the mission, and this, in combination with McClellan's subsequent decision to postpone Franklin's attack until reinforcements reached the field the following morning, brought an end to major fighting north of Sharpsburg on September 17. Late in the afternoon, however, a Maine regiment made a pointless attack across Bloody Lane that accomplished nothing other than to add more names to the casualty list. Unfortunately for McClellan, the reinforcements he was waiting for to support Franklin in his attack would not be ready to do so until the nineteenth. This compelled the Federal commander to postpone the attack until that morning, by which time the Confederates had left Sharpsburg.

STOP 7   West Woods

Directions   Return to your car and *proceed* west on CORNFIELD AVENUE
to its intersection with DUNKER CHURCH ROAD. *Turn left* onto
DUNKER CHURCH ROAD; after driving 0.1 mile, *turn right* into
the Philadelphia Brigade Park. *Proceed* to the parking area
and exit your car. *Walk* over to the eastern side of the monument to the Philadelphia Brigade and face east (toward
DUNKER CHURCH ROAD).

Orientation   In 1862 the area you are standing in was bounded to the
west and south by the West Woods, but open to the north
and east. Through the trees to your left front is the Indiana Monument, which is just outside the southwest corner
of the Miller Cornfield. The structures on the other side of
DUNKER CHURCH ROAD in your left front were not here at the
time of the battle. The Dunker Church is located about 300
yards to the south through the trees to your right.

General Thomas J.
("Stonewall") Jackson,
C.S.A. From a photograph.
BLCW 1:121

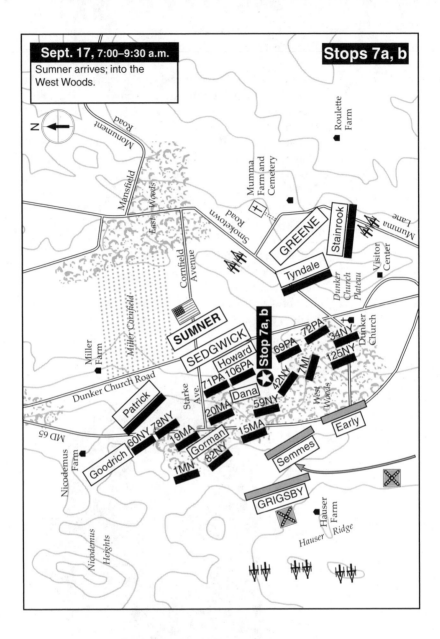

Sept. 17, 7:00–9:30 a.m.
Sumner arrives; into the West Woods.

Stops 7a, b

STOP 7A   Sumner Arrives, 7:00–9:00 A.M.

What Happened   At 6:00 A.M. on September 17, Maj. Gen. Edwin Sumner was awake and eagerly anticipating orders to lead his corps into the battle north of Sharpsburg. Although he had directed Sumner to be ready to do this the previous evening, McClellan was determined to let the situation develop more before committing any more troops to the battle north of Sharpsburg. McClellan was also reluctant to weaken the force holding his center before Maj. Gen. William Franklin's VI Corps reached the field to take Sumner's place. However, shortly after 7:00 A.M., the stiff resistance Hooker encountered convinced McClellan to authorize Sumner to take two of his divisions (the third was left behind until Franklin arrived) and go to Hooker's and Mansfield's assistance.

Sumner then led Brig. Gen. John Sedgwick's and Brig. Gen. William French's divisions across the Antietam at Pry's Ford. Sedgwick's was in the lead and Sumner placed himself personally at its head as it moved to the East Woods. There, Sumner directed Sedgwick to form his three brigades into two lines each facing west and learned the morning's fighting had left Hooker's corps so battered that not more than 300 men could be rallied. Williams's report on the condition of his corps was also grim, and he pointedly warned Sumner to take care of his flanks if Sumner chose to renew the attack. From these reports and a personal reconnaissance, Sumner concluded the I and XII Corps had driven the rebels from their initial positions but also had been rendered combat ineffective. He also deduced Greene's troops at the Dunker Church plateau probably marked the right flank of the enemy's position. If he could pass around this force to the north, Sumner surmised he would reach a point beyond the Confederate left from which he could then swing south and roll up the enemy flank.

Shortly after 9:00 A.M., Sumner directed Sedgwick to advance toward the West Woods and had orders sent to French to push his division forward to support Sedgwick's left. Unfortunately, in his zeal to get his men into action, Sumner pushed Sedgwick's division forward so fast that French's had already lost contact with it.

Vignette

"It was a beautiful sight," an officer in the II Corps later wrote of Sedgwick's advance toward the West Woods, "those three lines of battle, as they emerged from the first belt of woods, passed through the cornfield, ripe almost to harvest – and, moving steadily westward, crossed the Hagerstown pike. But, surely, they are not going to attack the enemy in that order! . . . Two hundred men moving by the flank, in single file, would extend from the head of the column to its rear. Should those troops advance in this order, all three lines will be almost equally under fire at once, and their losses must be enormously increased. And where are the brigades that are to support them on the right and left, and protect the flanks of this perilously dense column? French is out of reach. The shattered brigades of the Twelfth Corps are holding stiffly on to their ground, under cover, but are hardly in numbers or condition to undertake the offensive. . . . But Sumner does not wait. All his life in the cavalry, he has the instincts of a cavalry commander. The order is still forward."

STOP 7B   Into the West Woods, 9:00–9:30 A.M.

Directions   *Walk* around to the western side of the Philadelphia Brigade
monument and face west toward the woods.

What Happened   Leading Sedgwick's advance into the West Woods was Brig.
Gen. Willis Gorman's brigade, deployed in line with the
82nd New York in the center, the 1st Minnesota on the
right, and the 15th Massachusetts on the left. Meanwhile,
having gotten separated from the rest of the brigade, another of Gorman's regiments, Col. James A. Suiter's 34th New
York, was entering the West Woods just north of the Dunker Church. There, Suiter's men took up a position near the
125th Pennsylvania, a unit from the XII Corps.

About fifteen minutes after entering the West Woods,
Gorman's brigade reached the western edge of the woodlot
and found the only enemy in their front to be *Stuart's* horse
artillery, which had moved south from its initial position
on Nicodemus Heights to Hauser Ridge, and the remnants
of Col. Andrew J. *Grigsby's* infantry division at the Alfred Poffenberger farm. *Grigsby's* men were soon joined, however,
by Brig. Gen. Paul J. *Semmes's* brigade from Maj. Gen. Lafayette *McLaws's* division, which then advanced toward the position at the edge of the West Woods held by Lt. Col. John
Kimball's 15th Massachusetts. Federal small arms fire managed to bring *Semmes's* advance to a halt about 150 yards
from Kimball's position. A sharp firefight then ensued, during which nearly half of *Semmes's* command was killed or
wounded. Aided by canister fired into the Federal lines by
Stuart's artillery, *Semmes's* men inflicted severe punishment
on Gorman's command as well.

While Gorman's men battled the Confederates at the
western edge of the woods, Brig. Gen. Napoleon Dana's brigade moved into and through the West Woods behind them.
As they did so, Dana's left regiment, the 7th Michigan, became engaged with Confederate forces moving up from
the south. Dana responded by directing the regiment next
to the Michiganders, the 42nd New York, to support them,
while the other three regiments continued their advance to
a point approximately 40 to 50 yards behind Gorman. Meanwhile, Brig. Gen. Oliver Otis Howard's brigade was following
behind Dana. Shortly after his command crossed the Hagerstown Pike, one of Howard's regimental commanders noted that Union forces in the woods to the south appeared to
be pulling back in terrific haste and suggested the brigade
move obliquely to the left in response. The suggestion was ig-
nored, and Howard's men continued pushing forward until

they reached a point only 40 to 50 yards behind Dana. The stage was set for a disaster.

Analysis

Sumner's plan to attack into the West Woods was not without merit. The Confederates in the West Woods were at that time in desperate straits; had Sumner been able to effectively execute his plan, it may well have achieved a great, perhaps decisive success. Sumner, however, led his men forward without—despite Williams's warning—making sufficient provision for securing his flanks, which was especially important given the vulnerability of a force deployed as Sedgwick's division was to an attack on its flank. As if this were not enough, Sumner's decision to place himself with Sedgwick's command compromised his ability to effectively control his entire corps. Consequently, French would provide no assistance to Sedgwick's command. Had French done so, the course of events in the West Woods may well have been significantly more favorable for the Union. Moreover, Sumner knew that French's division contained a large number of new troops who could have hardly been expected to march with the speed of Sedgwick's veterans, and it should have been clear to him that the terrain would make effective command and control difficult in any case.

Major-General Edwin
V. Sumner. From a
photograph. BLCW 2:248

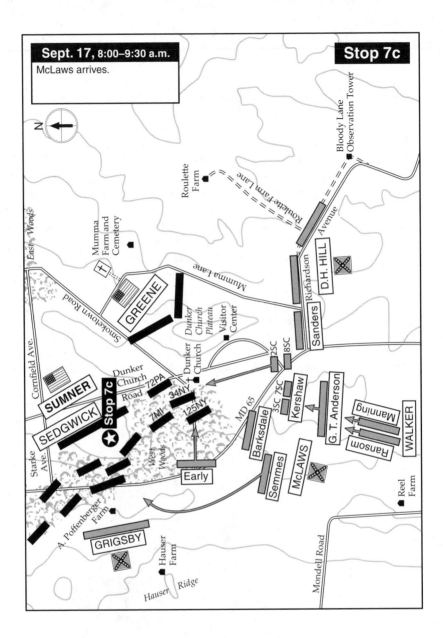

Sept. 17, 8:00–9:30 a.m.

McLaws arrives.

Stop 7c

STOP 7C *McLaws* Arrives, 8:00–9:30 A.M.

Directions *Walk* over to the paved path by the two National Park Service markers to your left front, and *follow* the path to a point between the two cannon that mark a position held by the Baltimore Artillery during the battle. *Turn left* and face south.

What Happened As Sumner led Sedgwick's men into and through the West Woods, *McLaws's* division was moving toward and through the woods from the south. After a grueling night march from Harpers Ferry, *McLaws's* men had reached the western outskirts of Sharpsburg shortly before sunrise that morning and had just laid down for some much-needed sleep when orders arrived directing them to move north to reinforce the Confederate left. Upon reaching the open area south of the West Woods, *McLaws* began deploying his command with *Semmes's* brigade on the left, Brig. Gen. William *Barksdale's* brigade to Semmes's right, Brig. Gen. Joseph *Kershaw's* brigade to Barksdale's right, and Lt. Col. Christopher C. *Sanders's* brigade on the far right. Unfortunately, at some point *Sanders's* command somehow pushed off so far to the right that it was effectively lost to *McLaws*. Then, *McLaws* was directed by *Jackson* to send a brigade to support the Confederates west of the West Woods. *Semmes's* was sent and, as described above, engaged Gorman's men at the western edge of the West Woods. Meanwhile, with his right on the Hagerstown Pike, *Kershaw* pushed into the West Woods at the double quick and, aided by an advance by Brig. Gen. Jubal *Early's* brigade command from the west, forced the 125th Pennsylvania and 34th New York as well as the 7th Michigan, which had nearly reached the Pennsylvanians' right, to begin falling back east through the woods and across the Hagerstown Pike.

Major-General Lafayette McLaws, c.s.a. From a photograph. blcw 3:333

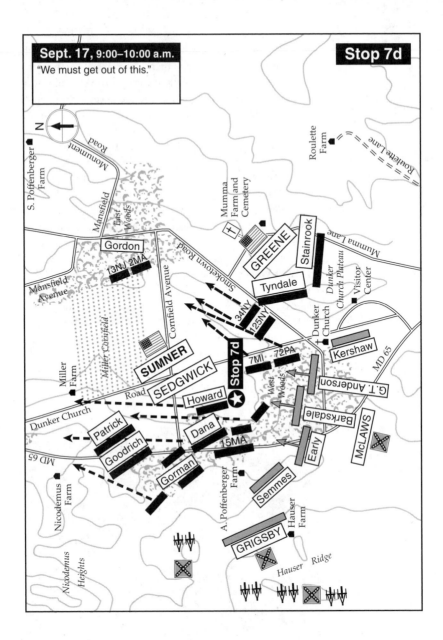

Sept. 17, 9:00–10:00 a.m.

"We must get out of this."

Stop 7d

STOP 7D "We must get out of this," 9:00–10:00 A.M.

What Happened As *Semmes* and Gorman's men battled at the western edge of the West Woods, *Barksdale* pushed his brigade north through the woodlot as Brig. Gen. George T. *Anderson's* brigade moved up onto the right of Barksdale and *Early*, whose brigade had fallen back from its scrape with the 125th Pennsylvania and had changed its front to the left to support *Barksdale's* left. The Confederates then fell upon the 72nd Pennsylvania, which had separated from the rest of Howard's brigade and had entered the woods just above the Dunker Church, and compelled the Pennsylvanians to fall back toward the East Woods along with the 125th Pennsylvania, 7th Michigan, and 34th New York. This left the rest of Sedgwick's men in an extremely dangerous position as the Confederates then slammed into and around their left flank. Taking fire from three directions and unable to respond effectively due to the angle at which they had been hit, the Federals were in serious trouble. "My God," Sumner exclaimed when he realized what was happening, "we must get out of this."

Howard and Dana attempted to change their fronts, but it was too late. Within minutes, both of their brigades were in full retreat. Their collapse left Gorman horribly exposed, with Kimball's 15th Massachusetts in an especially bad situation. Just as they appeared to be getting the upper hand in their fight with *Semmes*, evidence of Howard's and Dana's collapse reached Kimball's men in the form of a heavy fire into their left and rear. Kimball had no choice but to break off his fight with *Semmes* and retreat. Running a gauntlet of artillery and small arms fire, a surprising number of Kimball's men were able to maintain good order–and some even managed a brief rally–as they fled toward the North Woods. Less than half of the 600 men Kimball led into battle that morning, though, would be present for duty at the end of the day. No other Union regiment suffered such heavy losses at Antietam.

McLaws attempted to continue pressing his attack, with *Stuart's* artillery shifting north toward the Nicodemus farm to support him, but a series of delaying actions by Sedgwick's men, the presence of the Union I and XII Corps, and Union artillery eliminated any hopes *McLaws* might have had of inflicting more damage. Nonetheless, he had achieved a tactical success of the first order, wrecking a first-rate Union division and eliminating a grave threat to the Confederate position north of Sharpsburg. Of the 5,400 troops Sumner and Sedgwick led across the Hagerstown Pike, 2,200 were killed, wounded, or captured.

Analysis

McLaws's men arrived in the West Woods at the exact right time and in the exact right place. Had they arrived fifteen minutes later, Sumner might have already made his pivot southward and, presenting a full battle line, would have probably overwhelmed *McLaws's* exhausted men. Those who have described what happened to Sedgwick's command as an "ambush," though, incorrectly suggest that what happened in the West Woods was the product of a deliberate

Confederate plan. This was not the case—which is not to say the Confederate high command deserves no credit for what happened in the West Woods. *Lee* had skillfully managed his reserve, and what happened in the West Woods was a product of *Lee's* larger vision for how the battle would be conducted. Rather than conducting a static positional defense, the cornerstone of the Confederate battle plan was well-timed counterattacks against Federal movements that were poorly conceived, complicated by the terrain, or both. So although the Confederates enjoyed a remarkable degree of luck in the West Woods, that luck was a byproduct of skilled generalship, assisted materially by Federal tactical errors.

The consequences of this event would be momentous. The fact that the Confederates were able to overwhelm Sedgwick's veteran division after absorbing Hooker's and Mansfield's attacks did much to suggest that McClellan's perception of the strength of *Lee's* army, although in retrospect clearly exaggerated, was correct. Although he escaped with only a flesh wound in the hand (Sedgwick, though, was wounded three times), Sumner was emotionally shattered by what had happened in the West Woods and would spend the rest of September 17 convinced Union forces north of Sharpsburg, of which he was the senior commander, were on the verge of collapse. Consequently, while the Federals enjoyed a considerable advantage in numbers on that section of the field, Sumner would make a point of suppressing any impetus for employing it aggressively the rest of the day.

Vignette

The turn of events in the West Woods was vividly described by Roland Bowen in the 15th Massachusetts in letters to his family after the battle. "Good said I," he wrote of how he felt during the engagement with *Semmes's* men at the western edge of the woods. "We have got um now, all-though both sides are Allmighty cut up. But at the same instant I heard a cry from the rear, 'Fall back.' Turning round, said I, fall back Hell, ain't the rebels falling back themselves. So I went on fireing. Again some confusion. 'Fall back, we are flanked on our left, the rebs are getting in our rear.' What. Great god can't be possible. But I saw it was no joke, the bullets actually came from the rear. My God, such confusion. All hands ran for dear life. . . . The rebs saw their advantage and with Grape and Canister and Musketry they mowed us down . . . chased us like the Devil for about a half or ¾ of a mile when our batteries opened on them with grape and they give up the chase. They were very foolish for they might have drove us clean into Pennsylvania as well as not."

STOP 7E   Gordon's Charge, 9:45–10:15 A.M.

Directions   *Return* to the Philadelphia Brigade monument and, stand-
                        ing at its northeast corner, face toward the modern struc-
                        tures on the other side of DUNKER CHURCH ROAD just south
                        of CORNFIELD AVENUE.

What Happened   Upon receiving a message from Sumner requesting assis-
                        tance for Sedgwick's beleaguered command around 9:45
                        A.M., XII Corps commander Williams directed brigade com-
                        mander Brig. Gen. George Gordon to advance whatever
                        forces he had available toward the West Woods. Gordon
                        responded by ordering Col. Ezra Carman's 13th New Jersey
                        and Col. George Andrews's 2nd Massachusetts to push west
                        from the East Woods. When his command reached the West
                        Woods, Gordon instructed Carman that he must not fire on
                        any troops he might encounter in his advance, as they were
                        assumed to be part of Sedgwick's command. Carman imme-
                        diately passed on the instructions to his men and then ad-
                        vanced toward the West Woods. Upon reaching the fence
                        bordering the Hagerstown Pike, Carman's men began tak-
                        ing heavy fire from Confederates posted in the West Woods.
                        These belonged to Brig. Gen. John *Walker's* division, which
                        had just arrived on that part of the field. Unable to with-
                        stand the fire from *Walker's* Confederates, Carman issued or-
                        ders to pull back to the East Woods within a few minutes af-
                        ter reaching the fence. The 2nd Massachusetts also managed
                        to reach the Hagerstown Pike, but when Carman's men re-
                        treated, Andrews could not hold his position and also fell
                        back toward the East Woods.

Vignette   When Capt. Robert Gould Shaw of the 2nd Massachusetts
                        looked back on the battle in a letter to his mother a little
                        over a week later, he wrote of this attack against the West
                        Woods, "Of course there are mistakes made in every battle;
                        that day we were the victims of one; for Gordon's Brigade
                        was sent forward to support Sumner in [the West Woods,]
                        which he had already been driven out of. Instead of find-
                        ing friends there, we were met by a volley of musketry; we
                        didn't return fire for some time, thinking there was some
                        mistake, and when we did fire, we did very little execution,
                        and had to retire. Colonel Andrews saved us there, for if we
                        had gone as far as we were ordered, we should probably
                        have been overwhelmed. . . . It is sometimes very hard to dis-
                        tinguish between friend and foes, when the fire (especially
                        of artillery) is rapid, owing to smoke."

Further Reading   Carman, "Maryland Campaign," chap. 17, 181–251; Harsh, *Taken at the Flood*, 385–87, 389–92, 406–10; Sears, *Landscape Turned Red*, 216–17, 221–30, 274–76.

Charge of Irwin's Brigade (Smith's Division) at the Dunker Church. From a sketch made at the time. BLCW 2:646

STOP 8   Dunker Church

Directions   Return to your car, and *upon exiting* the Philadelphia Brigade Park, *turn right* onto DUNKER CHURCH ROAD. *Drive* 0.1 mile to the Dunker Church on the right-hand side of the road. *Pull over*, parking in front of or across the road from the church. Exit your car, *walk* up to the brick patio in front of the church, and *turn around* to face across DUNKER CHURCH ROAD toward the Maryland Monument, the large cupola with a green dome.

Orientation   Just in front of you is the intersection of SMOKETOWN ROAD and DUNKER CHURCH ROAD. To your right front is the Dunker Church plateau with the New York Monument on top of it (the monument on the other side of the road directly in front of you is the Ohio Monument). On the other side of the plateau, out of sight from you, is the Mumma farm. Directly behind you and to your left and right are the West Woods.

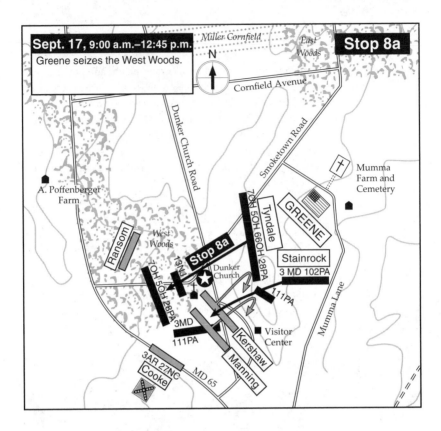

Sept. 17, 9:00 a.m.–12:45 p.m.
Greene seizes the West Woods.

Stop 8a

STOP 8A   Greene Seizes the West Woods, 9:00 A.M.–12:45 P.M.

What Happened   The 125th Pennsylvania from the XII Corps was the only Federal unit in the West Woods until, shortly after 9:00 A.M.,
the 34th New York came up in support, after veering off
from Brig. Gen. John Sedgwick's division of the II Corps as it
advanced toward the West Woods. Then, however, *McLaws's*
division forced both the 125th Pennsylvania and 34th New
York to pullback from the woods. Encouraged by this success, Brig. Gen. Joseph B. *Kershaw* ordered his brigade from
McLaws's division to attack Greene's position at the Dunker
Church plateau. A skirmish line, however, gave Greene's
men plenty of advance warning, and they easily repulsed
Kershaw's attack. Shortly thereafter, three regiments from
the brigade of *Walker's* division commanded by Col. Van
H. *Manning* crossed the Hagerstown Pike and tried to drive
Greene from the Dunker Church plateau. When they were
about halfway up the ridge, Greene's men unleashed a vi-
cious volley at short range that halted *Manning's* attack.

After repulsing *Manning's* charge, Greene decided around
10:30 A.M. to push forward into the West Woods with two

regiments from Col. Henry Stainrook's brigade on the left and three regiments from Lt. Col. Hector Tyndale's brigade on the right. Greene's men advanced nearly 200 yards into the West Woods before halting to form a line with Tyndale's men facing south and west and Stainrook's facing due south along the southern edge of the West Woods with their left at the Hagerstown Pike. Shortly thereafter, Col. Ezra Carman's 13th New Jersey reported to Greene, who ordered it to take up a position on the right of the units in the West Woods.

Greene and his 1,350 men would hold this position for nearly two hours. Unfortunately, Greene, who had seen Sedgwick's division advance into, but not his repulse from, the West Woods shortly after 9:00 A.M. was under the impression that it was within supporting distance of his right the entire time. Then, around 12:30 P.M., Confederate attacks hit both ends of Greene's line. Two regiments from *Manning's* brigade attacked Greene's southern regiments and managed to drive them back, while at the other end of Greene's line Carman was attacked by elements from Brig. Gen. Robert *Ransom's* brigade of *Walker's* division. Aided by depressions in the terrain, the cover of the woods, and the fact that Greene and Carman, assuming Sedgwick was nearby, had ordered their men not to fire in that direction, *Ransom's* men were able to hit the Yankees on their flank and menace their rear. With his flanks collapsing and no help in sight, Greene ordered his men to abandon the West Woods.

Vignette   After reaching the crest of the Dunker Church plateau, wrote one of Greene's men, "we awaited the advance of the enemy, who was advancing in column of regiments. We then received orders to fall back under cover of the hill, and awaited the advance of the enemy; when within a short range our troops were quickly thrown forward to the top of the hill, where we poured into their advancing columns volley after volley. So terrific was the fire of our men that the enemy fell like grass before the mower; so deadly was the fire that the enemy retired in great disorder, they not being able to rally their retreating forces. We charged them in a heavy piece of woods, driving them out of it, capturing a large number of prisoners (among them was a lieutenant-colonel and a lieutenant), and made terrible havoc in their ranks, covering the ground with the slain, many of them officers. We gained the woods, and held our position for two hours."

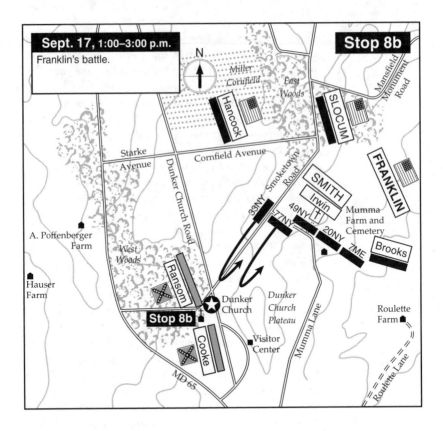

STOP 8B   Franklin's Battle, 1:00–3:00 P.M.

What Happened Shortly after Greene left the West Woods, the lead division
of Maj. Gen. William B. Franklin's VI Corps, commanded by
Brig. Gen. William F. "Baldy" Smith reached the field. Sumner—who by this point had, by dint of seniority, assumed
overall command of Federal troops north of Sharpsburg—immediately began deploying Smith's brigades in a manner designed to prevent the collapse of the entire Federal position,
which Sumner, badly shaken by his earlier experience in
the West Woods, considered a real possibility. Sumner posted one of Smith's brigades, led by Brig. Gen. Winfield Scott
Hancock, east of the Miller farm to support a line of Federal
batteries. Brig. Gen. William T. H. Brooks's brigade was ordered to form on the right of Brig. Gen. William French's
division, which was recuperating from its unsuccessful assaults on the Sunken Road. Finally, Col. William Irwin's brigade was posted astride the Smoketown Road with Hancock
on its right and Brooks on its left.

   After deploying his command near the Mumma farm, Irwin ordered the two regiments on his right, the 33rd and

77th New York, to advance toward the Dunker Church. When the two regiments were near the church, two North Carolina regiments in the West Woods belonging to Brig. Gen. Robert *Ransom's* brigade opened fire. This brought their advance to an immediate halt, but the New Yorkers quickly recovered and engaged in a brief, but sharp firefight with the Confederates in the woods before being ordered to fall back to the Mumma farm.

When he arrived in the East Woods, Franklin was not discouraged by Irwin's setback and began deploying Brig. Gen. Henry W. Slocum's division with an eye on making an attack against the West Woods. Upon learning of Franklin's intentions, Sumner immediately instructed him to stop what he was doing out of fear that if the attack failed it would destroy what Sumner believed to be the only effective force on the field. Franklin then asked Major Herbert Hammerstein of McClellan's staff, who happened to be nearby, to ride back to army headquarters and petition McClellan for permission to make the attack. Upon receiving Franklin's message, McClellan left his command post and rode across the Antietam to talk directly with Franklin and Sumner, arriving on the field shortly before 3:00 P.M. The normally pugnacious Sumner's gloomy predictions of doom if an attack by Franklin were to fail, however, persuaded McClellan not to let Franklin renew the attack north of Sharpsburg that afternoon.

Further Reading   Carman, "Maryland Campaign," chap. 17, 251–53, chap. 19, 1–32; Franklin, "Notes on Crampton's Gap and Antietam," 2:596–97; Sears, *Landscape Turned Red*, 231–32, 248–51.

STOP 9	Bloody Lane

Directions

Return to your car. *Proceed* north on DUNKER CHURCH ROAD (if you parked on the church side of the road, you will have to make a U-turn), and then immediately *turn right* onto SMOKE-TOWN ROAD. *Drive* 0.2 mile to MUMMA LANE and *turn right. Proceed* on MUMMA LANE 0.5 mile until it ends at RICHARDSON AVENUE. *Turn left* onto RICHARDSON AVENUE, *proceed* 0.1 mile, and *pull into* the parking area. Exit your car and *walk* over to the viewing platform where the National Park Service has put up two signs. If, after reading this section, you would like to study the fighting here in more detail, turn to the Bloody Lane Excursion.

En route. If you look to your left as you drive along SMOKE-TOWN ROAD, you will have a good view of the Miller Cornfield. After turning onto MUMMA LANE, you will pass the Mumma Cemetery on your left, which marked the right flank of *Jackson's* initial battle line north of Sharpsburg, and the Samuel Mumma farm, which Confederate troops set fire to on the morning of September 17 in order to deny its cover to Union forces. Also, note the high ground to your right on which the Visitor Center sits as you travel along SMOKE-TOWN ROAD and MUMMA LANE, the Dunker Church plateau.

Orientation

Directly in front of you is the historic trace of a farm road that in 1862 connected the Hagerstown Pike to the Boonsboro Pike. By the time of the battle of Antietam, travelers had worn the road down to the point where it provided a ready trench for Confederate defenders on this section of the battlefield. As a result of the battle, the Sunken Road also became known as Bloody Lane. If you look to your left, you will see where the historic road bends westward en route to rejoining modern RICHARDSON AVENUE and from there continues to its intersection with the Hagerstown Pike. The Dunker Church plateau is clearly visible to your left. To your right is the Bloody Lane Observation Tower, at which point the road turns southwest, once again rejoining the tour road, en route to the Boonsboro Pike. Constructed in 1896 by the U.S. War Department, the tower offers an excellent view of the battlefield in exchange for a climb up the stairs inside. On this side of the Sunken Road was located the farm of Henry Piper in 1862. At the time of the battle, the point where you are standing was in the middle of a twenty-five-acre cornfield, behind which there was a fifteen-acre apple orchard. Note how the ground both to the front and rear of the Sunken Road is much higher than the road itself, as well as the depression in the ridge in front of you through which the Roulette Lane runs.

STOP 9A   French Arrives, 7:30–9:30 A.M.

What Happened   After McClellan authorized Sumner to take two of his divisions across the Antietam to assist Hooker, the II Corps commander quickly pushed his forces to the creek crossings
with Sedgwick's in the lead. French's 5,700-man division
followed and crossed at Pry's Ford. French then posted Brig.
Gen. Max Weber's brigade on the left, Col. Dwight Morris's
in the center, and Brig. Gen. Nathan Kimball's on the right.
Unfortunately, due to the fact that his command included
an entire brigade of new troops (Morris's) and had only been
organized into a division on September 16, French was unable to keep pace with Sedgwick's veteran division.

As French pushed westward from the Antietam in a vain
attempt to catch up with Sedgwick, orders arrived from
Sumner directing him to form on Sedgwick's left. Consequently, French pushed forward to the East Woods around
9:15 A.M. in an attempt to locate Sedgwick. Seeing Greene's
two brigades at the base of the Dunker Church plateau, as
well as the smoldering embers of the Mumma farm (Confederate soldiers had deliberately set fire to it earlier that
morning), and possibly receiving a message from army headquarters to Sumner directing him to "push up on [Hooker's]
left through the ravine at the head of which the house was
burned this morning," French probably deduced he had
found Sedgwick. He then ordered his three columns to face
to the left and advance south across the Mumma farm, with
Weber's brigade in front, Morris's behind him, and Kimball's
in the rear. His evident intention was to reach a point from
which he could swing west to come up on what he assumed
was Sedgwick and Hooker's left as he was ordered to do.

As he pushed past the Mumma farm, however, Weber's
brigade began to receive fire from enemy skirmishers. These
were covering a Confederate force posted in the Sunken
Road just below a ridge, and French recognized that before he could reach what he thought was Sedgwick's left,
he would first have to make sure there was nothing on his
southern flank. Consequently, around 9:30 A.M., French directed Weber to push over the ridge and attack whatever
might be on the other side. As they passed through a cornfield and closed on the ridgeline, Weber directed his men to
fix bayonets and prepare to charge.

Analysis   In 1985 a group of high-ranking officers in the U.S. Army
participated in a tour of the Antietam battlefield. When
they reached the Sunken Road and discussed the events that
took place there, Gen. John A. Wickham, Chief of Staff of the

Army, expressed amazement at the willingness of Union soldiers to attack a well-positioned enemy in tight, linear formations that ensured they would take terrific casualties. The employment of tightly packed linear formations was a consequence of the fact that the state of weapons and communications technology at the time of the Civil War meant that there really was no better alternative. A more dispersed formation could not be effectively controlled and would not have the mass or firepower to break through an even modestly held defensive position. Not surprisingly, the first instinct of Civil War commanders was usually to try to find a way to maneuver around an enemy position or to find a way to attack it on the flank, and they employed frontal assaults when no better option was available. In French's case, there really was no alternative to attacking the Confederate position head on, unless he was willing to break contact with the rest of the Union force north of Sharpsburg and try to come up on the right flank of the Sunken Road. Given that French was out of direct contact with his superior officer after he reached the field and his brigades contained a large number of green troops, he could hardly have been expected to attempt such a risky and complicated maneuver.

Rallying behind the turnpike fence. BLCW 2:675

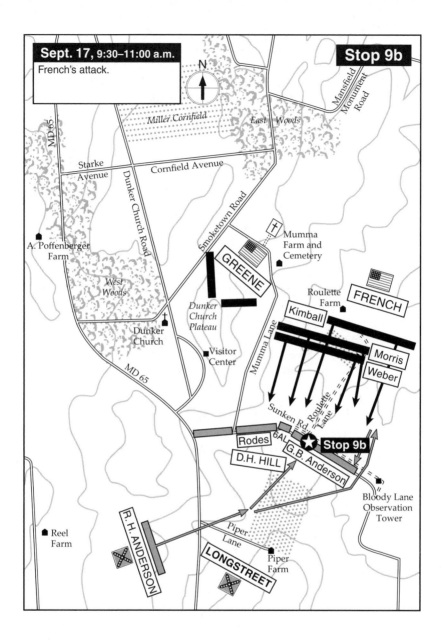

Sept. 17, 9:30–11:00 a.m.
French's attack.

N

Stop 9b

Miller Cornfield

East Woods

MD 65

Mansfield Monument Road

Starke Avenue

Cornfield Avenue

Dunker Church Road

Smoketown Road

A. Poffenberger Farm

West Woods

GREENE

Mumma Farm and Cemetery

Dunker Church Plateau

Dunker Church

Visitor Center

Roulette Farm

FRENCH

Kimball

Morris

Weber

MD 65

Mumma Lane

Sunken Rd.

Roulette Lane

Rodes

6AL

D.H. HILL

G.B. Anderson

Stop 9b

Bloody Lane Observation Tower

Reel Farm

R.H. ANDERSON

LONGSTREET

Piper Lane

Piper Farm

STOP 9B

French's Attack, 9:30–11:00 A.M.

What Happened   When French's men began their advance toward the Sunken Road, the Confederates had about 2,600 men posted in the road under the command of Maj. Gen. Daniel H. *Hill.* Holding the section of the lane directly in front of you was Brig. Gen. George B. *Anderson's* North Carolina brigade. The section of the lane facing northward was held by the five Alabama regiments commanded by Brig. Gen. Robert *Rodes.*

Between *Rodes's* left and the Hagerstown Pike, *Hill* had in position elements from *Colquitt's* and *McRae's* brigades that had made it back to the Sunken Road after fighting in the Miller Cornfield, as well as a brigade from *McLaws's* division commanded by Lt. Col. Christopher C. *Sanders*.

Upon reaching the crest of the ridge in front of the lane, French's lead brigade, commanded by Weber, was greeted by a blast of Confederate musket fire that stopped his attack cold. Undaunted, French threw Morris's brigade, and then Kimball's, against the Confederate position with the same results. None of French's men were able to reach the Sunken Road, although they were able to seize positions sheltered by the high ground overlooking the lane from which they easily repulsed a series of Confederate counterattacks.

As French's attack was coming to grief, both sides pushed reinforcements into the fight. On the Confederate side, Maj. Gen. Richard H. *Anderson's* division moved up from its reserve position west of Sharpsburg to the Piper farm to assist *Hill*. *Anderson*, however, was wounded almost as soon as he reached the field, with the consequence that the effort to reinforce *Hill's* position became very confused. The fact that, in order to reach the road, R. H. *Anderson's* men had to pass over high ground that was subjected to intense Union musket and artillery fire made reinforcing the road no easy task and helped complicate command and control within the road itself, which was exacerbated when G. B. *Anderson* was wounded.

Vignette

One of *Rodes's* subordinates, Col. John Brown *Gordon*, whose 6th Alabama held the bend in the Sunken Road, left a vivid description of the initial Union assaults against his position. "It was a thrilling spectacle," *Gordon* wrote of the Union advance. "Their gleaming bayonets flashed like burnished silver in the sunlight. With the precision of step and perfect alignment of a holiday parade, this magnificent array moved to the charge. . . . As we stood looking upon that brilliant pageant, I thought, if I did not say, 'What a pity to spoil with bullets such a scene of martial beauty!' But there was nothing else to do. . . . In a few minutes they were within easy range of our rifles, and some of my impatient men asked permission to fire. 'Not yet,' I replied. 'Wait for the order.' Soon they were so close that we might have seen the eagles on their buttons; but my brave and eager boys still waited for the order. Now the front rank was within a few rods of where I stood. It would not do to wait another second, and with all my lung power I shouted 'Fire!' My rifles flamed and roared in the Federals' faces like a blinding blaze of lightning accompanied by the quick and deadly thunder-bolt. The effect was appalling. . . . Before his rear lines could recover from the terrific shock, my exultant men were on their feet, devouring them with successive volleys. Even then these stubborn blue lines retreated in fairly good order. My front had been cleared; *Lee's* centre had been saved; and yet not a drop of blood had been lost by my men. The result, however, of this first effort to penetrate the Confederate centre did not satisfy the intrepid Union commander. Beyond the range of my rifles he reformed his men into three lines, and on foot led them to the second charge, still with unloaded guns. This advance was also repulsed."

The Sunken Road, or "Bloody Lane." From a photograph taken since the war. BLCW 2:668

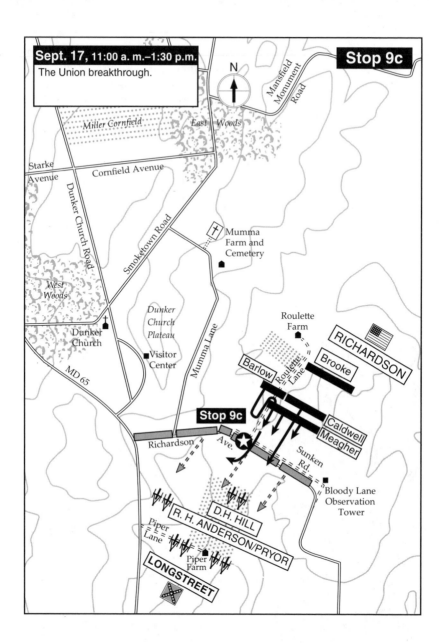

Sept. 17, 11:00 a. m.–1:30 p.m.
The Union breakthrough.

STOP 9C　　　　　　The Union Breakthrough, 11:00 A.M.–1:30 P.M.

What Happened　　　Relief for French's men arrived around 11:00 A.M. in the form
of three brigades belonging to Maj. Gen. Israel B. Richard-
son's veteran division. After going into position on French's
left, Richardson's lead command, the four regiments of Brig.
Gen. Thomas Meagher's Irish Brigade, renewed the assault
on the Sunken Road. Initially, Meagher's attack achieved no
more than French's earlier attacks had. But then a series of

mix-ups in the transmission of orders led to the abandonment of the road by all of Rodes's brigade, the three brigades of R. H. *Anderson's* division, and all but two of G. B. *Anderson's* regiments. This occurred just as the commander of the 29th Massachusetts from Meagher's brigade was ordering another charge against the road and Brig. Gen. John C. Caldwell's division was moving up to take over the battle.

Among the officers in Caldwell's command was Col. Francis Barlow, who commanded two New York regiments on the brigade's right. Barlow eagerly pushed his command forward and crested the ridge directly against the front of the last two Confederate regiments still in the lane, the 2nd and 14th North Carolina, at the point where the Roulette Lane joined the Sunken Road, though he was repulsed. Barlow then maneuvered his command so as to fire into their flank, and when the North Carolinians began to retreat from the road, Barlow pushed his brigade forward across the Sunken Road and into the Piper cornfield beyond.

Although their position in the lane had collapsed and scraping together infantry proved difficult, by the time Richardson's men captured the Sunken Road, *Hill* and Maj. Gen. James *Longstreet* had managed to assemble a formidable collection of artillery on the Piper farm. With an unlit cigar clenched between his teeth and a carpet slipper covering an injured foot, *Longstreet* personally held the horses of his staff as they took the place of wounded members of the Washington Artillery and helped direct their fire. Intense Confederate artillery fire, in combination with a series of fierce counterattacks—one personally led by a rifle-brandishing D. H. *Hill*—finally induced Richardson to pull back across the Bloody Lane. Once his men regrouped and were provided with artillery support, Richardson intended to renew the attack on the Confederates. Shortly thereafter, however, Richardson was mortally wounded. When his successor, Brig. Gen. Winfield Scott Hancock, arrived, it was clear the attack would not be renewed, even though two divisions of the VI Corps had reached the field and were nearby.

The VI Corps's contribution to the battle would consist of two attacks that the Confederates repulsed with little difficulty. The first was made by Irwin's brigade near the Dunker Church during the late morning; the second was made against the Confederates at the Piper farm by a single regiment, the 7th Maine, in the late afternoon. In all, losses in the fight for the Sunken Road ran about 30 percent of the forces engaged. Richardson's command lost 1,611 men, while French's casualties came to 1,750. Combined losses for *Hill's* and R. H. *Anderson's* divisions were 2,574.

Analysis

The fight for the Bloody Lane was one of the fiercest of the entire Civil War. Aided by the natural strength of the Sunken Road, the tenacious Confederates were able to hold off attacks by superior numbers for several hours and inflict such casualties that exploitation of the breakthrough was severely hampered. Ultimately, superior numbers and breakdowns in Confederate command decided the outcome of the fight, which created a terrific opportunity for the Federals. Unfortunately, although the fighting occurred in clear sight of McClellan's command post and Richardson's victory produced great excitement there, the commanding general was more concerned with the situation south of Sharpsburg at the time. He could have materially aided the effort at the Sunken Road by pushing across the Middle Bridge more than the small element of cavalry and infantry that was already across. But in his battle plan, the forces in his center, which were already much less than he originally intended, were not to be committed en masse until the results of Burnside's efforts were clear, which they were not at that point. Moreover, McClellan had in fact already ensured that more than enough fresh troops were available north of Sharpsburg to exploit the opportunity at the Sunken Road. Unfortunately, Sumner, the senior officer on that part of the field, remained badly demoralized as a consequence of Sedgwick's earlier disaster. Fearing that Union forces north of Sharpsburg were on the brink of disaster, Sumner's only thought was to use the troops McClellan had sent to strengthen his defensive position and had no intention whatsoever of resuming the offensive. Thus, the opportunity to make more of the success at Bloody Lane passed, and hopes for a truly decisive Union victory at Antietam passed exclusively to the shoulders of Ambrose Burnside.

Further Reading

Carman, "Maryland Campaign," chap. 18, 2–67; Grimsley, "In Not so Dubious Battle," 119–32; Sears, *Landscape Turned Red*, 235–54, 291–93; U.S. War Department, *War of the Rebellion*, vol. 19, ser. 1, pt. 1:323–24.

On the evening of September 16, 1862, McClellan instructed Maj. Gen. Ambrose Burnside to position the IX Corps in such a way as to be prepared to attack the Confederate right the following day. Burnside complied with McClellan's order and shortly after dawn had Brig. Gen. Jacob D. Cox preparing to force a crossing of the Antietam, with their attention focused mainly on the Lower (or Rohrbach) Bridge. (Even though McClellan's decision to discard the army's wing organization after South Mountain technically returned him to command of the IX Corps, Burnside nonetheless treated Cox as the corps's commander on the seventeenth.) Not until shortly after 9:00 A.M., however, did McClellan issue attack orders to Burnside, which arrived at IX Corps headquarters around 10:00 A.M.

Lee initially entrusted the responsibility for holding the Confederate right south of Sharpsburg to the divisions commanded by Maj. Gen. David R. *Jones* and Brig. Gen. John G. *Walker*. By the time Burnside received his attack orders, however, *Walker* had left the area to reinforce the Confederate defenses north of Sharpsburg. *Jones* remained with his division deployed in such a way as to connect with the Boonsboro Pike east of Sharpsburg, and cover Harpers Ferry Road, which exited Sharpsburg to the south. Cavalry under Col. Thomas T. *Munford* covered *Jones's* right flank. If the Federals could gain possession of the high ground along which Harpers Ferry Road ran, they would be in a good position from which to cut *Lee's* only line of retreat across the Potomac at Boteler's Ford. *Lee* recognized the danger, but McClellan's attacks north of Sharpsburg had left him no choice but to gamble that Maj. Gen. Ambrose P. *Hill's* division could cover the seventeen miles from Harpers Ferry quickly enough to reach the battlefield before the Federals took advantage of the weak Confederate right.

Jones entrusted the task of defending the crossings of the lower Antietam to a small force commanded by Brig. Gen. Robert *Toombs*. Aided by the strength of their position overlooking the Rohrbach Bridge, *Toombs's* men were able to frustrate Burnside's first two attempts to carry the bridge by direct assault. In an attempt to turn the Confederate position, Burnside sent Brig. Gen. Isaac Rodman's division south down the east bank of the Antietam in what proved to be a frustrating search for a crossing below the bridge. Finally, around 1:00 P.M., Rodman's division found Snavely's Ford and crossed the creek, while a third Union assault managed to carry the Rohrbach Bridge and drive *Toombs's* men from their position.

After taking a few hours to consolidate his bridgehead and bring up supplies for his troops, Burnside ordered the IX Corps forward. Just as Burnside's men had reached the outskirts of Sharpsburg and were poised to cut *Lee's* army off from Boteler's Ford, A. P. *Hill's* division reached the battle-field and overwhelmed the Federal left. Burnside and Cox responded by ordering their commands to pull back to the bluffs overlooking the bridge. As they did so, Burnside sent a message to McClellan asking the army commander to ful-fill his earlier promise of support. McClellan, however, had fewer troops than he had expected to have when he made this promise to Burnside and refused to commit the troops he had in reserve east of the Middle Bridge to the battle. In retrospect, McClellan could have done so with little risk, and they could have been sufficient to relieve the pressure on Burnside and might even have been able to deliver a de-cisive offensive stroke against *Lee's* center. However, with his senior commander north of Sharpsburg pessimistic about prospects on that front and now Burnside's sudden reverse, McClellan was not willing to risk his last reserve. Conse-quently, he told Burnside he could have no more infantry and instructed him to hold on to the bridge, which the IX Corps managed to do before nightfall brought an end to the battle.

Lieutenant-General
Ambrose P. Hill, c.s.a.
From a photograph.
BLCW 2:626

STOP 10   Burnside Bridge

Directions   Return to your car, then *exit* the Bloody Lane parking lot and
                         continue driving on RICHARDSON AVENUE 0.7 mile to its inter-
                         section with the BOONSBORO PIKE (MD 34). *Cross* the BOONS-
                         BORO PIKE *straight* onto RODMAN AVENUE and *proceed* 0.4 mile
                         to an overpass. Immediately *turn left* after crossing the over-
                         pass and *proceed* 0.5 mile to the parking area for Burnside
                         Bridge. *Park* your car and *proceed* to the stairway on the left
                         side of the parking area. *Walk* from there to the National
                         Park Service's overlook (there will be a sign reading "Point
                         Blank Range"), and face toward the bridge over Antietam
                         Creek. Note: This point on the battlefield is not handicapped
                         accessible. There is, however, a handicapped parking area
                         at the bottom of the hill leading up to the parking area.
                         After exiting your car from this area, *proceed* 50 yards along
                         the gravel path leading to the bridge and do the stop at this
                         point. If you would like to study the fighting here in more
                         detail, turn to the Burnside Bridge Excursion.

                         En route. RODMAN AVENUE follows the trace of a farm lane
                         that ran through the property of Joseph Sherrick and con-
                         nected the Boonsboro Pike with the Sharpsburg–Rohrers-
                         ville road. As you drive along RODMAN AVENUE, you will be
                         moving perpendicular to the line of advance of Brig. Gen.
                         Orlando Willcox's division of the IX Corps during the after-
                         noon of September 17. Just before you reach the overpass,
                         you will see on your left the Sherrick farm, which was here
                         at the time of the battle. If you look to your right at the over-
                         pass, depending on the time of the year, it is possible to see
                         a stone house and mill that were here at the time of the bat-
                         tle and saw heavy fighting during Willcox's advance.

Orientation   You are standing in what was a Confederate defensive position
                         in the contest for what was known in September 1862 as the
                         Rohrbach (or Lower) Bridge over the Antietam and as a conse-
                         quence of the battle became better known as Burnside Bridge.
                         In 1862 this bridge carried the Sharpsburg–Rohrersville road
                         over the Antietam. The road turned sharply to your right after
                         crossing to the east side of the creek en route to Rohrersville.
                         On the west side of the creek, just below the bluff on which
                         you are now standing, the road immediately made a sharp
                         turn to your left en route to Sharpsburg. Before the battle, this
                         bluff had been quarried for rock, which provided ready-made
                         rifle pits for defenders of this part of the lower Antietam. If
                         you look to your right and rear, you will see an open field and
                         hill. Just past the field, the terrain slopes down to the Anti-
                         etam at Snavely's Ford, which is approximately three-quarters
                         of a mile from where you are now standing.

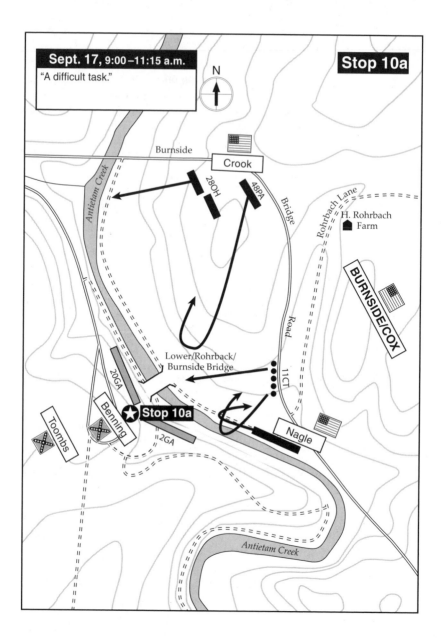

Burnside

Crook

28OH

48PA

Bridge

Rohrbach Lane

H. Rohrbach
Farm

Antietam Creek

BURNSIDE/COX

Road

Lower/Rohrback/
Burnside Bridge

11CT

20GA

Benning

★ Stop 10a

2GA

Toombs

Nagle

Antietam Creek

STOP 10A   "A Difficult Task," 9:00–11:15 A.M.

What Happened   By midmorning on September 17, responsibility for defending the lower Antietam rested solely upon Brig. Gen. Robert
Toombs's brigade of Maj. Gen. David R. *Jones's* division. When
the day began, Brig. Gen. John G. *Walker's* division was also
in the area, guarding Snavely's Ford. However, shortly after
8:00 A.M., *Lee* ordered *Walker* to move north of Sharpsburg
to join the battle on the Confederate left. This left only a lit-

tle over 500 Confederates to guard the lower Antietam. Fortunately, *Toombs* had a naturally strong position to defend. Steep, high bluffs overlooked nearly the entire Antietam at and below the Rohrbach Bridge, and aside from Snavely's Ford, the bridge was the only really practicable crossing point for large bodies of troops. Moreover, the area was less restricted at the time of the battle by trees that would have obstructed the Confederates' field of fire. While *Toombs* managed the overall defense of the lower Antietam, responsibility for directing the two Georgia regiments directly in front of the bridge rested with Col. Henry L. *Benning*.

Around 10:00 A.M., IX Corps commanders Maj. Gen. Ambrose Burnside and Brig. Gen. Jacob Cox received orders from McClellan to attack the Confederate position on the lower Antietam. Burnside and Cox immediately began executing the plan they had developed for seizing the bridge by ordering Col. Henry Kingsbury to deploy his 11th Connecticut in open order and rush forward toward the creek. Once there, Kingsbury's men were to lay down a covering fire against the Confederate defenders that would enable Brig. Gen. George Crook's brigade to charge across the bridge and establish a foothold on the western bank of the Antietam. Meanwhile, a reinforced division commanded by Brig. Gen. Isaac P. Rodman was directed to cross the Antietam at a ford that engineers from McClellan's staff reported to be less than a half mile below the bridge, turning the flank of the Confederates defending the bridge.

Although it took terrible casualties, elements of Kingsbury's command managed to reach the creek to engage the Confederates on the heights above. In the process, Kingsbury was mortally wounded, while some of his men made a futile attempt to wade the creek downstream from the bridge. The 11th Connecticut's heroics were for naught, though, as Crook's attack badly misfired. Part of the force that was supposed to charge the bridge lost its sense of direction and ended up reaching the Antietam about 300 yards upstream from the bridge. This left only a single regiment to make the decisive charge, which lacked the strength to even reach the bridge. As if this were not bad enough, Rodman's column found the crossing McClellan's engineers had identified inadequate for their needs and were compelled to continue moving downstream in search of a better crossing point.

Undeterred, Burnside and Cox prepared another assault. This time, instead of attacking the bridge head-on, they decided Brig. Gen. James Nagle's brigade from Brig. Gen. Samuel Sturgis's division would make its way to the Sharpsburg-Rohrersville road, which ran along the east bank of the creek, and then follow it to reach the bridge. Around 10:45 A.M., Nagle began his attack with Lt. Col. Jacob Duryea's 2nd Maryland in the vanguard. Duryea's men managed to reach the Sharpsburg-Rohrersville road and promptly commenced moving north toward the bridge in a column of four men abreast. However, by the time they got within 250 feet of the bridge, the fire from the opposite side of the creek into their front and left flank became too much to bear. With huge gaps torn in their ranks, Duryea's Marylanders and the regiments following behind them had to abandon whatever hope they had of reaching, much less making a successful assault across, the bridge.

Analysis

After the war, Confederate staff officer Henry Kyd *Douglas* asked, "Why the bridge? . . . which is now—is it sarcasm?—called Burnside's Bridge. . . . It was no pass of Thermopylae. Go look at it and tell me if you don't think Burnside and his corps might have executed a hop, skip, and jump and landed on the other side. One thing is certain, they might have waded it that day without getting their waist belts wet in any place."

In truth, as McClellan wrote after the battle, Burnside faced "a difficult task" on September 17. The only really practicable crossings of the creek in his sector were the bridge and Snavely's Ford, for the vegetation and high bluffs on either side of the creek would not allow an easy approach to the creek and quick push from the creek to the high ground above it anywhere else on the lower Antietam. Indeed, the fact that the Confederates only posted forces at the bridge and the ford on the morning of September 17 suggests that, after being in the area nearly two days, they believed the difficulty of crossing the lower Antietam anywhere else was prohibitive. As events proved, just reaching the bridge was difficult due to the open ground east of the bridge and the position *Benning's* men occupied. The narrowness of the bridge also made it relatively easy to defend it as long as the Confederates had sufficient ammunition. Moreover, as some of Kingsbury's men learned, wading the creek was no "hop, skip, and jump." Not only were the Federals under constant, point-blank fire as they approached and made their way across the creek, they also had to negotiate its slippery banks and alternately rocky and muddy bottom as well.

Although it is clear in retrospect that Burnside and Cox should have more closely supervised Crook's attack, it should be noted that Crook was a well-regarded young officer who would go on to have a distinguished military career, and few would have predicted that he would botch the task of preparing and executing his assault. In the case of the other major problem that morning, Rodman's troubled search for a crossing below the bridge, Burnside and Cox based their decisions on the recommendations of engineers from McClellan's staff. That these men would do a poor job (and to be fair, Confederate skirmishers on the west bank made the task of thoroughly reconnoitering the creek a difficult one) could hardly have been predicted. Engineering was one of the Union army's strengths, and the officers McClellan sent to assist Burnside were some of the most highly regarded in the country. It is certainly difficult to criticize Burnside and Cox for following their advice.

Major-General Ambrose
E. Burnside. From a
photograph. BLCW 3:109

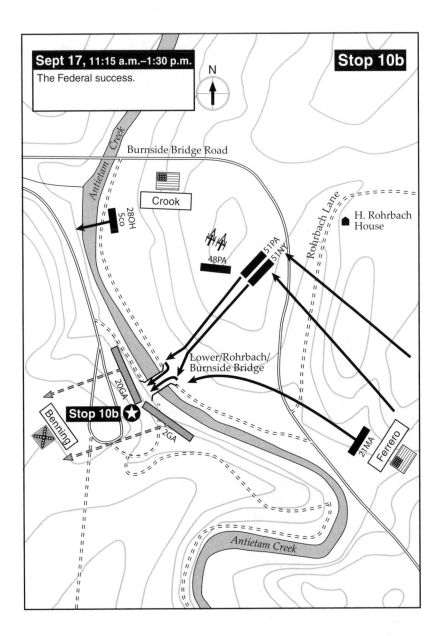

Sept 17, 11:15 a.m.–1:30 p.m.
The Federal success.

N

Stop 10b

Antietam Creek

Burnside Bridge Road

Crook

28OH
5co

48PA

51PA
51NY

Rohrbach Lane

H. Rohrbach
House

Lower/Rohrbach/
Burnside Bridge

20GA

Benning

Stop 10b ⭐

2GA

21MA

Ferrero

Antietam Creek

STOP 10B   The Federal Success, 11:15 A.M.–1:30 P.M.

Directions   *Remain in place* or *turn right* and *follow* the paved "Burnside
                      Bridge Walk" down to the bridge. After crossing the bridge
                      to the east bank of the Antietam, *turn around* and face to-
                      ward the creek.

What Happened   As the IX Corps regrouped in the wake of Nagle's failed as-
                      sault, a stream of couriers from McClellan's headquarters ar-

rived at Burnside's command post to impress upon him the commanding general's exasperation at the delay in getting across the creek. Burnside was himself frustrated and at one point snapped, "McClellan appears to think I am not trying my best to carry this bridge; you are the third or fourth one who has been to me this morning with similar orders."

Around 1:00 P.M., Burnside and Cox finished organizing yet another attempt at the bridge. This time, they turned to Brig. Gen. Edward Ferrero's brigade. Ferrero took two of his regiments, Col. Robert Potter's 51st New York and Col. John Hartranft's 51st Pennsylvania and guided them to a position on the ridgeline directly across from the bridge, while Burnside and Cox positioned artillery to provide covering fire as they charged the bridge. With the Pennsylvanians on the right and the New Yorkers on the left, Ferrero ordered his men forward. Despite the heavy covering fire provided by the Union artillery and their own growing exhaustion, the Georgians on the other side of the creek were still able to greet Ferrero's men with a heavy fire that, in combination with a fence blocking their direct line to the bridge, prevented the New Yorkers and Pennsylvanians from actually charging directly onto the bridge. Instead, both regiments pealed off to the side as they neared the entrance to the bridge. While Potter's men took cover behind the fence directly in front of and south of the bridge, Hartranft's men huddled behind a stone wall just north of the bridge. From behind this cover, the Federals opened fire against the Confederate positions on the other side of the creek. The combination of Union small arms and artillery fire, however, began to wear down *Benning's* Georgians, and within a few minutes of Potter's and Hartranft's men having reached their cover, the fire coming from the west side of the creek began to diminish. Sensing this, Potter's and Hartranft's men resumed their attack. With nearly every Federal soldier on the scene enthusiastically cheering them on, the two regiments pushed onto and rushed across the bridge side by side to reach the opposite side of the Antietam.

Unable to stop the Federal charge and low on ammunition, *Benning* ordered his men to withdraw. At about the same time, Rodman's command found Snavely's Ford and took only a few casualties crossing the Antietam, while some of Crook's men forded the stream a few hundred yards upstream from the bridge. Ferrero's men then turned to the right upon reaching the west bank of the Antietam and linked up with Crook's Ohioans, while three of Nagle's regiments followed Ferrero over the bridge and turned to the left to link up with Rodman. It had taken the IX Corps nearly three hours and about 500 casualties, but it was finally across the Antietam. *Toombs's* Georgians had fought magnificently and suffered 120 killed and wounded.

Vignette

After learning that his command had been assigned the task of attacking the bridge, Ferrero told his men, "It is General Burnside's special request that the two 51sts take the bridge. Will you do it?" Corporal Lewis Patterson of the 51st Pennsylvania replied, "Will you give us our whiskey, Colonel, if we take it?" Because of some recent infraction committed by its members, Ferrero had been denying the men of his command their liquor ration, but in light of the current situation, he was prepared to forgive past trespasses. "Yes, by God!" he asserted in response to Patterson. "You shall have as much as you want, if you take the bridge. I don't mean the whole brigade, but you two regiments shall have just as much as you want, if it is in the commissary or I have to send to New York to get it, and pay for it out of my own purse; that is if I live to see you through it. Will you take it?" The troops replied unanimously, "Yes!" True to his word, Ferrero made sure the men who stormed the bridge got their whiskey back.

Further Reading

Carman, "Maryland Campaign," chap. 21, 1–32; Harsh, *Taken at the Flood*, 400–401, 414–15; Murfin, *Gleam of Bayonets*, 270–78; Sears, *Landscape Turned Red*, 260–69.

McKinley Monument: As you return to the parking area, just south of it is a large monument with an eagle on top of it. This was erected in 1903 to honor the service of President William McKinley as commissary sergeant for the 23rd Ohio Infantry during the battle of Antietam. At the request of Rutherford B. Hayes, commander of the 23rd Ohio and another future president of the United States, McKinley was promoted to lieutenant for his service during the Maryland campaign. McKinley remained in the service for the rest of the war and finally achieved the rank of major. He was the last of the six veterans of the Civil War—and the only one who had not been a general officer—who served as president of the United States.

STOP 11   The IX Corps Attacks

Directions

Return to your car, *exit* the parking lot, and *follow* the park road as it picks up the trace of the historic Sharpsburg–Rohrersville road. The park road then leaves the historic road and *bends left* onto one-way BRANCH AVENUE. At 0.6 mile from the parking area for Burnside Bridge, *pull off* into the parking area on the left-hand side of the road. Exit your vehicle and *turn left*. *Walk* about 50 yards along the stone wall on your right and *stop* just before you reach the monument to the 36th Ohio. Face north toward the overpass.

En route. Note where the park road bends after leaving the parking area and the original Sharpsburg–Rohrersville road joins the modern road. Also note the John Otto farm on the left side of the park road and the Joseph Sherrick farm across modern BURNSIDE BRIDGE ROAD (which runs under the overpass) from the Otto farm.

Orientation

On the other side of the trees to your left rear is the high ridge along which Harpers Ferry Road runs. Cemetery Hill is the high ground to your left front. The overpass in front of you carries RODMAN AVENUE (which in 1862 was the Sherrick Farm Lane that connected the Boonsboro Pike with the Sharpsburg–Rohrersville road) over modern BURNSIDE BRIDGE ROAD, which crosses the Antietam a few hundred yards upstream from the historic bridge. The Boonsboro Pike is about three-quarters of a mile north of where you are now standing. In 1862 the Sharpsburg–Rohrersville road exited Sharpsburg where the modern BURNSIDE BRIDGE ROAD does, but then followed the park road through the ravine in front of you en route to the Lower Bridge. To your right front, on the other side of the ravine, is the Sherrick farm; to the right of that, on this side of the road, the top of the John Otto house should be visible to you through the trees.

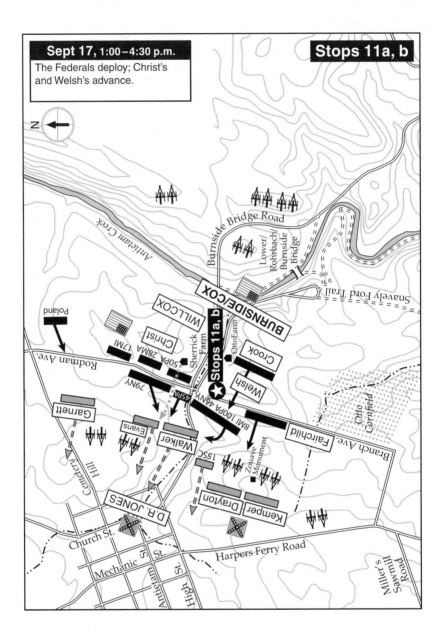

The Federals deploy; Christ's and Welsh's advance.

STOP 11A   The Federals Deploy, 1:00–3:00 P.M.

What Happened   After crossing the Antietam to relieve the elements from Sturgis's command that had seized and secured the union bridgehead on the west bank of the Antietam, Brig. Gen. Orlando Willcox deployed the two brigades of his divison on either side of the ravine through which the Sharpsburg–Rohrersville road ran. Col. Benjamin C. Christ's brigade formed up on the crest north of the road, while Col.

Thomas Welsh's formed on the south side of the road. Crook's brigade of the Kanawha Division was posted to the rear of Welsh and directed to support Willcox's 3,240-man command as it advanced toward Sharpsburg. To the left of Welsh, two brigades from Rodman's 3,700-man division were to push toward Sharpsburg with the tasks of supporting Willcox's left flank and seizing the Harpers Ferry Road on the high ridge south of town. Col. Hugh Ewing's brigade from the Kanawha Division would support Rodman's advance, while Sturgis's division remained on the heights overlooking the bridge as a general reserve.

All that *Lee* had available to resist this Union attack were five brigades of Maj. Gen. David R. *Jones's* division—in all, about 2,800 infantrymen, 430 artillerymen manning 28 guns—part of Brig. Gen. Nathan *Evans's* small brigade-sized division, and some cavalry commanded by Col. Thomas *Munford*. Two of *Jones's* brigades, Brig. Gen. Richard B. *Garnett's* and Col. Joseph *Walker's*, were posted on the eastern slope of Cemetery Hill between the Boonsboro Pike and the Sharpsburg–Rohrersville road. The other two brigades, Brig. Gen. Thomas F. *Drayton's* and Brig. Gen. James L. *Kemper's*, held the high ground between the Sharpsburg–Rohrersville road and the Harpers Ferry Road. About 750 yards forward and to the right of *Drayton* and *Kemper*, *Jones's* final brigade, commanded by *Toombs*, was along the western edge of the Otto cornfield recuperating from its gallant defense of the Rohrbach Bridge.

STOP 11B   Christ's and Welsh's Advance, 3:15–4:30 P.M.

What Happened   By 3:00 P.M., Willcox had finished deploying his division; fifteen minutes later, Cox issued orders for the IX Corps to begin its attack. On Willcox's right, Christ's brigade advanced over the Sherrick farm with Lt. Col. David Morrison's 79th New York leading the advance and deployed in a strong double line of skirmishers. As Christ's men advanced, they came under heavy fire from Confederate batteries posted on Cemetery Hill and the high ground along Harpers Ferry Road. Angling toward Cemetery Hill, Christ's men encountered tough resistance near the Sherrick farmhouse from a band of skirmishers from the 17th South Carolina of *Evans's* brigade. Morrison's men, however, were able drive off the South Carolinians and reach the Sherrick Farm Lane (modern Rodman Avenue). There, they halted to wait for the rest of the brigade to catch up. Meanwhile, in the course of their advance toward Cemetery Hill, Christ's right made contact with units from the V Corps that were south of the Boonsboro Pike. Although effectively supported by the Confederate artillery on Cemetery Hill, *Garnett* had nowhere near enough strength to resist the Federal advance. But just as *Garnett's* command began to break and fall back up Cemetery Hill, Christ decided to halt his entire command along the Sherrick Farm Lane before making his final push toward Sharpsburg.

On Christ's left, Welsh's brigade made its advance with the 100th Pennsylvania in front as skirmishers. Welsh, however, had difficulty keeping up with Christ due to the greater distance his brigade had to cover and the ruggedness of the terrain over which his regiments had to advance, which included the steep ravine just to your right through which the Otto Farm Lane ran. Like Christ's regiments, Welsh's brigade was pulled to the right as it advanced. Meanwhile, Morrison's New Yorkers resumed their advance by crossing the Sherrick Farm Lane and made contact with Col. Joseph *Walker's* brigade of South Carolinians in an apple orchard located on the north side of the Sharpsburg–Rohrersville road. There a fierce fight commenced between the Federals and *Walker's* men, who took advantage of the cover provided by a nearby stone house and mill.

As Morrison's men attacked the orchard, Welsh's right regiment, the 45th Pennsylvania, advanced astride the Sharpsburg–Rohrersville road and his left wing moved along the southern edge of the Sharpsburg–Rohrersville road to attack *Walker's* position from the south. Closely supported by Crook's brigade, Welsh's regiments south of the Sharpsburg–Rohrersville road also compelled the 15th South Carolina from *Drayton's* brigade to abandon the high ground on that side of the road. Meanwhile, Lt. John N. Coffin's two guns from the 8th Massachusetts Artillery unlimbered in Otto's yard and fired into the orchard. Supported by Coffin's fire, Christ's and Welsh's men swept *Walker's* South Carolinians from the orchard, stone mill, and stone house with a bayonet charge. As *Walker's* men fled the field, elements from Welsh's command pursued them to the edge of Sharpsburg.

The Old Lutheran Church, Sharpsburg.
From a war-time photograph. BLCW 2:665

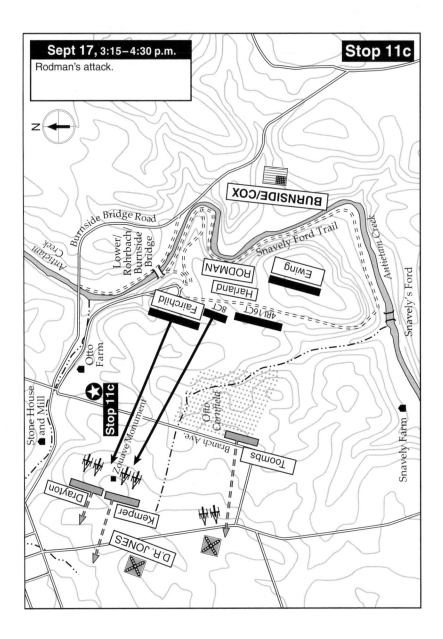

Sept 17, 3:15–4:30 p.m.
Rodman's attack.

Stop 11c

STOP 11C   Rodman's Attack, 3:15–4:30 P.M.

Directions   *Return* to the parking area and from there face south down BRANCH AVENUE.

What Happened   After crossing the Antietam, Rodman pushed forward to the high ground on the bluffs overlooking the creek. There, Rodman rested his men for two hours and, in preparation for an attack toward Sharpsburg, posted Col. Harrison S. Fairchild's brigade on the right and Col. Edward Harland's on the left. A brigade from the Kanawha Division commanded by Col. Hugh Ewing would serve as his reserve. Seeing Willcox's men begin their advance shortly after 3:15 P.M., Rodman ordered Fairchild and Harland forward. Rodman's tasks were to cover Willcox's left flank and seize Harpers Ferry Road. If the Federals could achieve the latter objective, they might cut *Lee's* army off from its only crossing of the Potomac at Boteler's Ford.

On the right, Fairchild advanced over the Otto property and toward the slope of the ridge on top of which Harpers Ferry Road ran, pausing occasionally to redress his lines and take shelter from the terrific Confederate artillery fire that greeted his advance. Near the crest of the ridge, Fairchild's men encountered five regiments from Brig. Gen. Thomas *Drayton's* and Brig. Gen. James *Kemper's* brigades—at most 600 men—posted behind a stone wall and wooden fence at the crest. When the Federals were about 50 yards away, a volley from the Confederate defenders briefly broke the momentum of the Union advance. Fairchild's men halted briefly to exchange fire with *Drayton's* and *Kemper's* men but after about ten minutes charged the rebel position. For a few moments, there was a desperate, hand-to-hand fight that ended with the Confederate line shattered. Despite orders to pause and reform their ranks, several of Fairchild's men pushed forward in pursuit of the fleeing rebels and reached Sharpsburg. Less than three weeks after the humiliation of Second Manassas, the Union army was tantalizingly close to cutting *Lee's* line of retreat and making the Army of Northern Virginia pay the ultimate price for bringing the war north of the Potomac. Fairchild's men paid a heavy price of their own in the process, losing 455 of the 940 men who entered the battle; no other Union brigade suffered a higher percentage of casualties at Antietam.

Vignette

David L. Thompson of the 9th New York left a vivid account of the advance against *Drayton's* and *Kemper's* position: "We were getting ready now for the charge proper, but were still lying on our faces. Lieutenant-Colonel Kimball was ramping up and down the Line. The discreet regiment behind the fence was silent. . . . [A] battery, however, whose shots at first went over our heads, had depressed its guns so as to shave the surface of the ground. . . . One of the enemy's grapeshot had plowed a groove in the skull of a young fellow and had cut his overcoat from his shoulders. . . . The suspense was only for a moment, however, for the order to charge came just after. . . . [A]s we rose and started all the fire that had been held back so long was loosed. In a second the air was full of the hiss of bullets and the hurtle of grape-shot. The mental strain was so great that I saw at that moment . . . the whole landscape for an instant turned slightly red. I see again, as I saw it then in a flash, a man just in front of me drop his musket and throw up his hands, stung into vigorous swearing by a bullet behind the ear. Many men fell going up the hill, but it seemed to be all over in a moment, and I found myself passing a hollow where a dozen wounded men lay. . . . All were calling for water, of course, but none was to be had. We lay there till dusk—perhaps an hour, when the fighting ceased. . . . We heard all through the war that the army 'was eager to be led against the enemy.' It must have been so, for truthful correspondents said so, and editors confirmed it. But when you came to hunt for this particular itch, it was always the next regiment that had it. The truth is, when bullets are whacking against tree-trunks and solid shot are cracking skulls like egg-shells, the consuming passion in the breast of the average man is to get out of the way. Between the physical fear of going forward and the moral fear of turning back, there is a predicament of exceptional awkwardness from which a hidden hole in the ground would be a wonderfully welcome outlet."

Further Reading   Carman, "Maryland Campaign," chap. 21, 31–44; Sears, *Landscape Turned Red*, 277–81.

Brigadier-General Isaac P. Rodman, mortally wounded at Antietam. From a photograph. BLCW 2:650

STOP 12   Otto Cornfield

Directions   Return to your car. *Continue* driving 0.3 mile along BRANCH
                        AVENUE to an upturned cannon on the right side of the road.
                        Pull off the road as far as possible and exit your vehicle. *Cross*
                        over to the left-hand side of the road to the marker that
                        reads, "12TH OHIO INFANTRY POSITION AND MONUMENT 395
                        YARDS NORTHEAST."

                        En route. If you look to your right shortly after passing a
                        small sign with an arrow on the right-hand side of the road
                        that reads "Drayton's Brigade," you will see a tall obelisk in
                        the distance. This is the monument to the 9th New York,
                        and it marks the approximate location of the position at
                        the fence held by *Drayton* and *Kemper* that Fairchild's men
                        overran.

Orientation   Turn right and face down BRANCH AVENUE, which bends to
                        the right a short distance in front of you and travels to its
                        intersection with HARPERS FERRY ROAD at the top of the ridge
                        to your right. If you look to your left, you will see a ravine
                        below you and an obelisk, the monument to the 16th Con-
                        necticut. In 1862 this was in a forty-acre cornfield that be-
                        longed to John Otto. The highest ridge in the distance be-
                        yond that is Red Hill. If you look to your right you will see
                        the high ridge along which HARPERS FERRY ROAD runs.

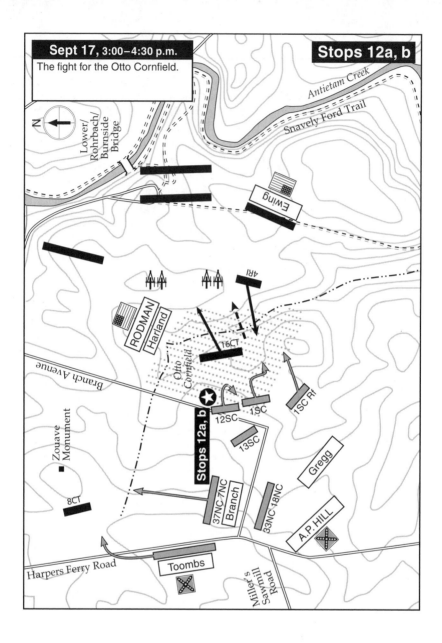

Sept 17, 3:00–4:30 p.m.
The fight for the Otto Cornfield.

Stops 12a, b

STOP 12A   A. P. *Hill* Arrives, 3:00–4:15 P.M.

What Happened   *Jackson* had left Maj. Gen. Ambrose P. *Hill's* Light Division at Harpers Ferry on September 15–16 the task of finishing up paroling the Union prisoners and gathering up the large stores of equipment captured there. At approximately 6:30 A.M. on September 17, *Hill* received orders from *Lee* directing him to join the rest of the army at Sharpsburg. Leaving one brigade at Harpers Ferry to finish gathering up captured

Union supplies, *Hill* had his other five on the road to Sharpsburg around 7:30. Six hours later, *Hill* personally arrived on the field and found *Lee* near his headquarters west of Sharpsburg. "General Hill," *Lee* remarked, "I was never so glad to see you, you are badly needed, put your force in on the right as fast as they come up."

Shortly thereafter, *Hill* rode south on Harpers Ferry Road and met with D. R. *Jones*, from whom he gathered information about the ground south of Sharpsburg and the troops on that part of the field. *Hill* also fortuitously learned there was a shorter route to the Confederate right than the one he had just taken. Instead of marching to the Shepherdstown Road after crossing the river, taking that road east to Sharpsburg, and then turning south on Harpers Ferry Road to reach the Confederate right, *Hill's* men would make their way to the Saw Mill Road and follow it to the battlefield. This road bypassed Sharpsburg to the south and connected with Harpers Ferry Road just south of that road's intersection with modern Branch Avenue—the exact point on the battlefield where *Hill's* men were needed. So serious was the crisis on the Confederate right that the men of the first of *Hill's* brigades to set out on the Saw Mill Road, Brig. Gen. Maxcy *Gregg's*, were not even given an opportunity to wring out their clothes after crossing the Potomac.

As *Gregg's* men neared the field, they found themselves under fire from Union artillery, which induced them to shift their line of advance to the right before crossing the road. As a consequence, they would approach the battlefield from a point beyond the Federal southern flank, rather than from the west. About 250 yards east of Harpers Ferry Road, *Gregg* halted his command and formed his regiments into line, with the 13th South Carolina on the left, 12th South Carolina in the center, and 1st South Carolina on the right. The 1st South Carolina Rifles served as the reserve. *Gregg* then ordered his brigade to advance north and east toward the Otto cornfield.

Analysis

Hill's march to Antietam has achieved legendary status in the annals of American military history, although it loses some of its luster upon closer examination. *Hill* received his orders to march from Harpers Ferry around 6:30 A.M. on September 17 and had his command on the march about an hour later. Once *Hill* got his command on the road, it took eight hours to cover the seventeen miles to Sharpsburg, a pace of little more than two miles per hour. *Hill* probably could have made better time and arrived in better condition—he lost over a third of his command en route—had he not chosen to take the difficult road that ran along the river rather than the easier road that ran to Shepherdstown via Halltown that the rest of *Jackson's* forces had taken. It is also curious that he did not have his men already prepared to march when *Lee's* orders arrived, for there was plenty of evidence to indicate a significant fight was going to take place at Sharpsburg by the evening of September 16. Nonetheless, whatever deficiencies there may have been in *Hill's* performance on September 17, it was all for the best as there was no other time and place on the field where *Hill* could have joined the battle and done more good for the Confederacy.

Vignette

As *Jones's* defensive positions were crumbling and it seemed that little stood between his line of retreat and Rodman's advance, a desperate Robert E. *Lee* looked to the south from his command post west of Sharpsburg and saw a large mass of troops moving toward the field. He turned to Lt. John A. *Ramsey* and asked, "What troops are those?" *Ramsey* offered his telescope to *Lee*, but the general responded by raising his injured hands and stating, "Can't use it." *Ramsey* then raised the telescope to his own eyes and initially saw troops carrying the U.S. flag. After reporting this to *Lee*, the general instructed him to look at another column to the west of it. *Ramsey* did so and reported, "They are flying the Virginia and Confederate flags." (Since the only brigade with Virginia units in *Hill's* division was the last in line, it was probably the South Carolina flag from *Gregg's* brigade that *Ramsey* actually saw.) "It is A. P. *Hill*," a visibly relieved *Lee* replied, "from Harpers Ferry."

STOP 12B   The 16th Connecticut, 3:45–4:30 P.M.

Directions   *Remain in place. Turn left* and face toward the 16th Connecticut monument.

What Happened   When the IX Corps began its advance shortly after 3:15 P.M., Harland's brigade was positioned slightly to the left and rear of Fairchild. Lt. Col. Hiram Appelman's 8th Connecticut was posted on the right, with Col. Francis Beach's 16th Connecticut next to Appleman's in the center and with Col. William H. P. Steere's 4th Rhode Island on the left. As the 8th Connecticut advanced up the long slope toward Harpers Ferry Road, Harland learned his orders for the advance had not reached his other two regiments. Harland then suggested to Rodman that Appleman halt so the rest of the brigade could catch up. Rodman rejected Harland's advice, told the brigade commander to continue leading the 8th Connecticut forward, and stated that he would ride back to bring up the two stray regiments.

Upon reaching the 16th Connecticut's position, Rodman spotted *Gregg's* Confederates advancing toward the Otto cornfield from the southwest and directed Beach to swing to the left and advance into the cornfield. The 16th Connecticut had been in the army less than a month, and it had received precious little instruction in the complicated movements that made a regiment an effective force on the battlefield. Nonetheless, Beach promptly led his 760 men forward into the cornfield, entering at its northeast corner.

Upon reaching the bottom of the hollow that ran through the field, Beach pushed skirmishers to its southwestern corner. It was from this direction that *Gregg's* command entered the cornfield. Upon reaching a stone fence that ran along the field's western border, the 13th South Carolina halted due to confusion over orders. Col. Dixon *Barnes's* 12th and Col. Daniel H. *Hamilton's* 1st South Carolina, however, pushed over the fence and into the cornfield. They quickly drove off Beach's skirmishers and charged the position held by the 16th Connecticut. The South Carolinians rushed forward with spirit but were repulsed by the rookies from Connecticut. *Barnes* attempted another charge, but by the time his second attack began, the 16th Connecticut had changed its front slightly and had the assistance of the 4th Rhode Island, which had come up on Beach's left. The Federals easily repulsed *Barnes's* second attack and forced the South Carolinians to fall back to the southwestern section of the cornfield.

In addition to assisting the repulse of the 12th South

Carolina, the arrival of Steere's command also had the effect of forcing *Hamilton's* 1st South Carolina to shift to the right to avoid being enveloped. After doing this, *Hamilton's* men opened fire. The response of Steere's command was hampered by the fact that the colors of the 1st South Carolina closely resembled the Union flag, which led the Federals to hold their fire at the opening of the fight. Nonetheless, Steere's men subsequently put up a stubborn fight and even managed to turn *Hamilton's* right flank. At this moment, Lt. Col. James *Perrin's* 1st South Carolina Rifles came up on *Hamilton's* right and found a position from which they could fire into the Union left flank. When *Perrin's* men opened fire, Beach's and Steere's exhausted commands broke and fled from the cornfield. The 16th Connecticut had suffered 42 killed, 143 wounded, and 20 captured, for a total loss of over 25 percent. Steere's losses came to 21 killed and 77 wounded.

Analysis

Given the difficulty of maneuvering and fighting in the Otto cornfield, even a veteran unit would have had a hard time holding on for very long in the face of *Gregg's* attack. Still, why the 16th Connecticut—a green regiment that had been mustered into the service less than a month earlier, had not received any training, and had loaded their muskets for the first time only the day before—ended up with responsibility for the left flank of the entire Union army is one of the mysteries of the battle. Who the particular officer responsible for this was and whether he was aware of the potential danger—and it is clear that someone should have been, as a Union signal station spotted *Hill's* command as it approached the field and sent a message to Burnside around 3:00 P.M. warning him, "Look out well to your left"—is unclear. Unfortunately, Rodman was killed in the battle and left no record of his decisions, although he did assume responsibility for the 16th Connecticut and 4th Rhode Island after Harland pointed out that they had fallen behind. By that point, however, it was too late to correct the problem before *Gregg* attacked. Regardless of why the 16th Connecticut was in the Otto cornfield, it was the worst place and time for them to be; their collapse after putting up a respectable fight helped transform what could have been the decisive Union attack of the battle into yet another crisis for the Union high command.

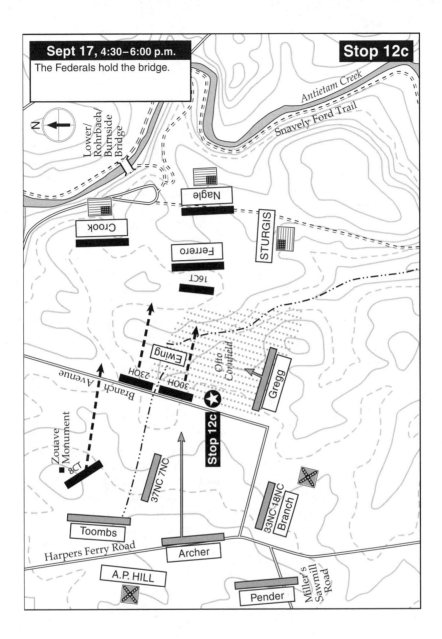

N

Antietam Creek

Snavely Ford Trail

Lower/Rohrbach/Burnside Bridge

Nagle

Crook

Ferrero

STURGIS

16CT

Ewing

230H

300H

Otto Cornfield

Gregg

Branch Avenue

Zouave Monument

8CT

37NC 7NC

Stop 12c

33NC 18NC

Branch

Toombs

Harpers Ferry Road

Archer

A.P. HILL

Pender

Miller's Sawmill Road

STOP 12C   The Federals Hold the Bridge, 4:30–6:00 P.M.

Directions   *Remain in place* and *turn left* to face north down BRANCH AVENUE.

What Happened   By the time the 16th Connecticut and 4th Rhode Island broke, Brig. Gen. Lawrence O'Branch's brigade of Hill's command had arrived on the scene. Branch then proceeded to attack the front, left, and rear of Appelman's 8th Connecticut, which was holding the left flank of the Federal forces on the high ground upon which Harpers Ferry Road ran. Appelman's men put up a tough fight, but with the Federal position in the Otto cornfield crumbling and the rest of *Hill's* division arriving on the field, they had no choice but to begin pulling back toward the Antietam.

Meanwhile, as the 16th Connecticut and 4th Rhode Island were falling apart, the 23rd and 30th Ohio from Ewing's brigade appeared on the high ground just east of the Otto cornfield. The Ohioans then pushed forward to the stone fence that bordered the western edge of the Otto property, where they immediately found themselves fighting off an attack by Brig. Gen. James J. *Archer's* brigade of about 400 Tennesseans and Georgians. The Ohioans opened a galling fire that threatened to halt the Confederate attack in its tracks. But then *Gregg's* South Carolinians resumed their advance and began menacing the flank and rear of the Federal position. Ewing attempted to adjust his lines in response but was unable to do so successfully and was forced to abandon his position at the stone wall. Seeing the Federals retreat, *Archer* charged into the cornfield. His men had advanced less than 100 yards when men from the 30th Ohio and 16th Connecticut that had rallied in the ravine forced *Archer* to pull back to the stone fence. The 12th South Carolina of *Gregg's* brigade then made yet another charge, which compelled the exhausted Federals to retreat back up the ridge east of the cornfield. *Barnes* pushed his men forward in pursuit to a fence bordering the cornfield, where, after *Barnes* fell mortally wounded, the South Carolinians halted.

Willcox's and Crook's commands remained in good shape, but with Rodman's division in tatters, Cox saw no alternative but to abandon his attack. Thus, he ordered Willcox and Crook to pull back and directed Sturgis to push his men forward to take the place of Rodman's shattered commands. This enabled the Federals to establish a position on the heights overlooking the bridge by nightfall that was too strong for the Confederates to overcome. In all, the fighting on September 17 had cost the IX Corps 2,349 casualties; 438 killed, 1,796 wounded, and 115 missing or captured. For his part, D. R. *Jones's* command had suffered 75 killed, 450 wounded, and 40 missing, while A. P. *Hill's* casualties came to 66 killed, 332 wounded, and 6 missing.

Further Reading   Carman, "Maryland Campaign," chap. 21, 44–47, 53–55, 57–85; Harsh, *Taken at the Flood*, 415–23; Sears, *Landscape Turned Red*, 280–90; U.S. War Department, *War of the Rebellion*, vol. 19, ser. 1, pt. 1:453.

STOP 13   *Lee's* Headquarters

Directions   Return to your car and *proceed* 0.3 mile on BRANCH AVENUE
to its intersection with HARPERS FERRY ROAD. *Turn right* onto
HARPERS FERRY ROAD and *proceed* 0.7 mile to the intersection
with MAIN STREET (en route, HARPERS FERRY ROAD becomes
S. MECHANIC STREET). *Turn left* and *proceed* 0.5 mile on MAIN
STREET (MD 34) until, just after passing Sharpsburg Elemen-
tary School, you see a small park on your right. *Pull over* here
and *park* on the side of the road. Exit your car and *walk* up
to the monument located in the center of the lot about 50
yards from the road. Be careful in exiting your vehicle, as
the pull off is very narrow.

Counting the scars in the colors. BLCW 3:284

STOP 13A   *Lee's* Council of War, September 17, 1862

Orientation   You are at the location of *Lee's* headquarters tent at Antietam, although Cemetery Hill, located approximately a mile
east of here, served as his main observation post for much of
the battle of September 17.

What Happened   As the sun set on September 17, *Lee* and his subordinates
were left to contemplate the wreckage of a battlefield where
they had lost approximately 31.4 percent of their army. In
contrast, McClellan had only lost about 24.4. percent of his
force—a remarkable number given the fact that the Federals
were on the offensive the entire day. The total casualties on
both sides came to over 22,700 killed, wounded, and missing, making September 17 the bloodiest single day in American military history. As their battered and exhausted men
settled in for a restless night around Sharpsburg, *Lee's* subordinates made their way to their commander's headquarters
and found him nearby on a knoll south of Shepherdstown
Road. As each man arrived, "General Lee," one officer later
recalled, "inquired quietly, 'General, how is it on your part
of the line?'"

While making his way to *Lee's* headquarters, *Longstreet*
came upon a house in Sharpsburg that was on fire. After doing what he could to help the distressed family, the general
continued on to *Lee's* headquarters. "My delay caused some
apprehension on the part of General Lee that I had been
hurt," *Longstreet* later wrote. "In fact, such a report had been
sent him. When I rode up and dismounted he seemed much
relieved, and, coming to me very hurriedly for one of his
dignified manner, threw his arms upon my shoulders and
said: 'Here is my old war-horse at last.'" *Lee* then asked *Longstreet* for a report on his command. "Longstreet, apparently
much distressed," one witness recalled, "replied to the effect that it was as bad as could be. . . . [H]is lines had been
barely held, and there was little better than a good skirmish
line along his front, and he volunteered the advice that General Lee should cross the Potomac before daylight." After receiving similar reports from D. H. *Hill* and *Jackson*, *Lee* turned
to *Hood*, who, one witness later recalled, "seemed completely unmanned and replied that he had no division." *Lee* exclaimed, "Great God, General Hood, where is the splendid
division you had this morning?" "They are lying," *Hood* replied, "on the field where you sent them, sir."

Nonetheless, after hearing his subordinates' reports, *Lee*
proclaimed, "Gentlemen, we will not cross the Potomac to-
night. You will go to your respective commands, strengthen

your lines, send two officers from each brigade toward the ford to collect your stragglers, and get them up. Many others have already come up. I have had the proper steps taken to collect all the men who are in the rear. If McClellan wants to fight in the morning, I will give him battle again!" Not one of *Lee's* subordinates challenged his decision.

Analysis

In retrospect, the evening of September 17 appears to have been the point at which *Lee's* audacity became foolhardiness. McClellan had come within a razor's edge of annihilating the Army of Northern Virginia that day and would have nearly a three-to-one advantage in manpower on September 18. Consequently, generations of historians have condemned *Lee's* decision not to retreat from Sharpsburg and risk the destruction of his army. Explanations of this decision have often revolved around the dubious thesis that *Lee* possessed special insight into the mind of his opponent that enabled him to discern that the Army of Northern Virginia was in little danger from a supposedly constitutionally timid commander like McClellan.

There were, in fact, compelling practical factors that shaped *Lee's* decision to remain at Sharpsburg on September 18. The first, and perhaps most important, was the simple fact that it would have been exceedingly difficult to get his army back across the river before daylight on September 18. During the fighting on September 17, the Army of Northern Virginia had lost a great deal of its organizational cohesion, and as a consequence *Lee's* subordinates were compelled to spend most of their remaining energy after the council of war just identifying the location of their units and trying to sort out their place in line. Moreover, there had been little to no preparation for a retreat. To get the entire army back to the single crossing at Boteler's Ford would require a clearly thought out plan, for a hasty retreat would result in a massive traffic jam that would leave *Lee's* army even more vulnerable than it was in the positions it held on September 18. To develop and execute such a plan before daylight on September 18 was probably impossible.

Just as important was *Lee's* concern about the moral effect of an immediate retreat across the Potomac. *Lee* staked the fate of the Confederacy on the hope that a series of Southern battlefield victories would demoralize and inspire a loss of will in the North that would lead to the election of officials amenable to Confederate independence. To retreat back across the Potomac so quickly after South Mountain and Antietam would, *Lee* could reasonably surmise, reinvigorate Northern morale, while Southern confidence in the Confederacy would lose some of the boost that had been bought in blood on the Peninsula and at Second Manassas. There is strong evidence that *Lee* was correct on this point. Southerners seeking to put a positive spin on the Maryland campaign pointed to *Lee's* ability to remain on the Maryland side of the Potomac on September 18 as evidence that the fights at South Mountain and Antietam had produced at worst a standoff that by no means negated the tangible accomplishment of the capture of Harpers Ferry and its garrison.

Route step. BLCW 2:530

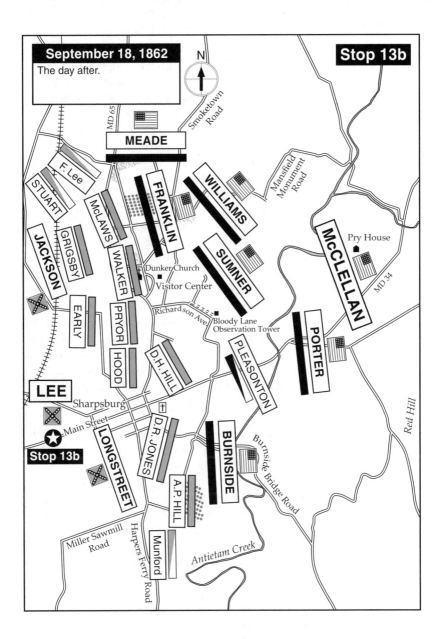

September 18, 1862
The day after.

N

Stop 13b

MD 65

MEADE

Smoketown Road

F. Lee

STUART

McLAWS

FRANKLIN

WILLIAMS

Mansfield Monument Road

JACKSON

GRIGSBY

WALKER

Dunker Church
Visitor Center

SUMNER

Pry House

McCLELLAN

MD 34

EARLY

PRYOR

Richardson Ave.
Bloody Lane
Observation Tower

PLEASONTON

PORTER

HOOD

D.H. HILL

LEE

Sharpsburg

Main Street

D.R. JONES

Red Hill

Stop 13b

LONGSTREET

A.P. HILL

BURNSIDE

Burnside Bridge Road

Miller Sawmill Road

Munford

Harpers Ferry Road

Antietam Creek

STOP 13B   The Day After, September 18, 1862

What Happened   Of course there was no way *Lee* could know McClellan would
decline to renew the battle on September 18. Indeed, during
the evening of September 17, McClellan approved a proposal by Franklin for an attack on the Confederate left at dawn
on the eighteenth. McClellan did this believing over 20,000
fresh troops would be on the field by daylight. A few hours
later, however, McClellan suspended Franklin's attack or-

der. He did so out of a realization that the reinforcements coming his way would not reach the battlefield by morning. He was also influenced by reports from staff officers that the ammunition for his long-range artillery was exhausted and that an attack in the morning would have to be made without their support.

Nonetheless, when dawn came on September 18, McClellan remained determined to renew the battle. Divisions commanded by Maj. Gen. Darius Couch and Brig. Gen. Andrew Humphreys arrived at midmorning, but only the former was in good enough condition to participate in an attack, as Humphreys's division was composed primarily of green troops who were exhausted by a hard night march from Frederick. McClellan then learned that the Pennsylvania militia he expected to come to his assistance, believing they had mobilized solely in defense of their state, had halted their march at Hagerstown and refused to march further south, and that the War Department, due to damage to the Baltimore and Ohio Railroad, would not be able to get a new supply of ammunition to the army until after dark. As if this were not enough, at midmorning, McClellan developed a severe case of dysentery that sapped his energy and undoubtedly contributed to his decision to hold off on renewing the battle until the nineteenth.

Meanwhile, an unofficial truce was established by the troops on both sides to allow the retrieval of the wounded and enable burial parties to begin their work. Despite his illness, McClellan issued orders on the evening of September 18 to Franklin to attack at dawn on the nineteenth. Franklin did as he was instructed, but when he moved forward at dawn on September 19, he found the enemy gone.

Analysis

Just as *Lee* has been criticized for remaining at Sharpsburg the day after the battle of Antietam, McClellan has been criticized for failing to take advantage of the fragile condition of *Lee's* army and his own vast advantage in manpower to complete the task of annihilating *Lee's* army on September 18. Clearly, McClellan missed a spectacular opportunity. Yet, I Corps commander Brig. Gen. George Meade expressed the views of many who had fought on September 17 when he informed McClellan that his command could "be depended upon . . . to resist an attack in our present strong position . . . though I do not think their morale is as good for an offensive as a defensive movement." Of course, it was not necessary for the I, II, XII, and IX Corps to do much more than put up a strong front to enable the approximately 24,000 fresh men of the V Corps, VI Corps, and Couch's division to deliver a decisive blow against the exhausted and fought-out 25,000 men who remained at arms in *Lee's* army without an undue degree of risk. This they had more than sufficient combat power to do.

All of this, however, is clearer in hindsight than it was in the aftermath of the bloodiest day in American military history. Certainly, the battle of September 17, in which the Confederates had not only been able to repulse every attack made against it but also had sufficient strength to deliver powerful counterblows both north and south of Sharpsburg suggested the Army of Northern Virginia remained a very dangerous foe. In sum, while McClellan clearly made the wrong decision when he did not renew the battle on September 18, it was not an unreasonable one. He had, after all, already won the campaign, and the information he had before him and the array of problems that arose on September 18 combined to make a compelling case for waiting until the nineteenth to renew the attack.

Further Reading   Carman, "Maryland Campaign," chap. 22, 1–10, chap. 25, 1–13; Gallagher, "Net Result of the Campaign," 5–10, 13–14, 20–21; Harsh, *Taken at the Flood*, 424–29, 437–48, 454–67; Murfin, *Gleam of Bayonets*, 290–91, 293, 295–302; Sears, *Landscape Turned Red*, 296–305.

STOP 14   National Cemetery

Directions   Return to your car. Make a *U-turn* back onto w. MAIN STREET
(MD 34) and *proceed* 1.0 mile to the National Cemetery on the
right. If there is no parking available on the right side of the
road in front of the cemetery, *continue* to the parking area
on the left-hand side of the road. After exiting your car, *enter*
the cemetery and either do the stop on the brick patio just
in front of the gate or *walk* over to the large monument at
its center.

Lieutenant-General
J. E. B. Stuart, C.S.A.
From a photograph.
BLCW 2:582

STOP 14A   *Lee* Retreats, September 18–21, 1862

What Happened   Remarkably, on the morning of September 18, *Lee* remained
determined to find some way to take the offensive. At mid-
morning he rode to *Jackson's* command post near the Dunker Church and asked *Jackson* and *Stuart* to look into collect-
ing fifty cannon and using them to smash the Federal right.
Neither *Jackson* nor *Stuart* liked the plan and both advised
Lee to solicit the advice of an artillery officer on the matter. *Lee* then returned to headquarters and directed Col.
Stephen D. *Lee* to report to *Jackson*, who led Colonel *Lee* over
to Nicodemus Heights, pointed to the enemy battle line and
said, "I wish you to take fifty pieces of artillery and crush
that force." Colonel *Lee* told *Jackson* he was willing to try, but
did not think it was a good idea. *Jackson* then sent him back
to army headquarters. Upon receiving Colonel *Lee's* report,
General *Lee* finally concluded that he had no choice but to
pull back across the Potomac. *Lee* hoped, however, that the
retreat back into Virginia would be only temporary. After re-
grouping on the Virginia side of the Potomac, *Lee* hoped to
recross the river at Light's Ford near Williamsport and move
from there into the Cumberland Valley well beyond McClellan's right flank. Thus, he sent *Stuart's* cavalry across the Potomac at Light's Ford to clear the crossing for the rest of the
army.

Around 9:00 P.M., *Lee's* army began pulling back toward
the Potomac and by 8:00 A.M. on the morning of September 19 the last of his infantry was crossing. Upon learning
the Confederates had evacuated their lines at Sharpsburg,
McClellan ordered Brig. Gen. Alfred Pleasonton's cavalry to
push to the Potomac in pursuit, but no significant Federal
force reached the river until the Confederates had completed their crossing. Later that day, elements from Maj. Gen.
Fitz John Porter's Union V Corps splashed across Boteler's
Ford and made a successful attack on *Lee's* rear guard that
led McClellan to authorize Porter to push four brigades
across the river the following morning. Shortly after Porter's men had crossed the river on September 20, however,
reinforcements that *Jackson* rushed back to Shepherdstown
launched a fierce counterattack that compelled Porter to
pull his men back across the Potomac.

Meanwhile, *Stuart's* effort to clear a path for the Army of
Northern Virginia's return to Maryland came to naught. After learning *Stuart* had pushed across the Potomac at Light's
Ford on September 19, McClellan ordered Pleasonton to take
two brigades of cavalry and a division of infantry to Williamsport. *Stuart* responded to the arrival of this force by pulling

back across the Potomac. *Stuart's* setback and the difficulties at Shepherdstown convinced *Lee* to give up his hopes of resuming the campaign. During the night of September 21, *Lee* sent a message to President Jefferson Davis reporting that the campaign had come to an end and that he needed time to repair his army. Satisfied with his success of compelling the rebels to abandon Maryland and alerted by the events at Shepherdstown and Williamsport to the fact that the Confederate army remained a dangerous animal, McClellan was content to give him that time.

Union cavalryman—The water-call. BLCW 3:441

STOP 14B   Antietam National Cemetery

What Happened   During the weeks that followed the battle of Antietam, the
town of Sharpsburg and the surrounding communities were
transformed into a huge network of hospitals for treating
the wounded and into burial grounds for interring the dead
from the fighting of September 17, 1862. In March 1865 the
state of Maryland established a burial site on this hill and in
September 1867 the cemetery was officially dedicated. Buried in Antietam National Cemetery are the remains of 4,776
Union soldiers (1,836 are unknown) who were killed at the
various battles fought in Maryland during the Civil War. At
the center of the cemetery is Old Simon, a monument over
forty-four feet tall to the private soldier of the Civil War,
which was formally dedicated on the 1880 anniversary of
the battle of Antietam.

Further Reading   Carman, "Maryland Campaign," chap. 22, 1–10, chap. 25,
1–13; Harsh, *Taken at the Flood*, 424–29, 437–48, 454–67;
Sears, *Landscape Turned Red*, 296–305.

To return to Antietam National Battlefield Visitor Center:
Return to your car. Make a *U-turn* back onto W. MAIN STREET
(MD 34) and *proceed* 0.2 mile to the intersection with N.
CHURCH/S. CHURCH STREET (MD 65). (If you were in the park-
ing area across the street from the National Cemetery, *turn
right* upon exiting.) *Turn right* onto N. CHURCH STREET (MD 65)
and *proceed* 0.8 mile to DUNKER CHURCH ROAD. *Turn right* onto
DUNKER CHURCH ROAD and *enter* the parking area.

General McClellan and
President Lincoln at
Antietam. From a
photograph. BLCW 2:659

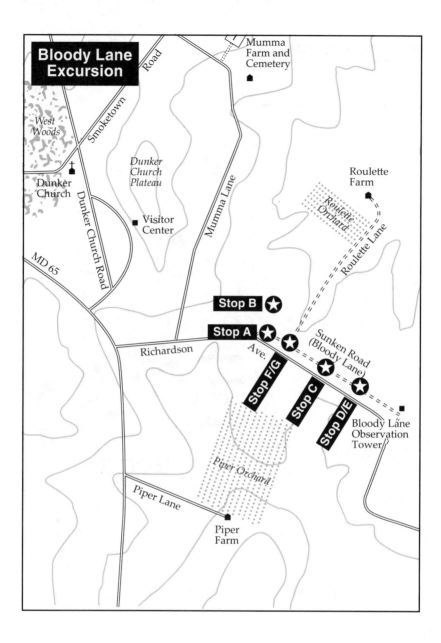

OPTIONAL EXCURSION 1: Bloody Lane

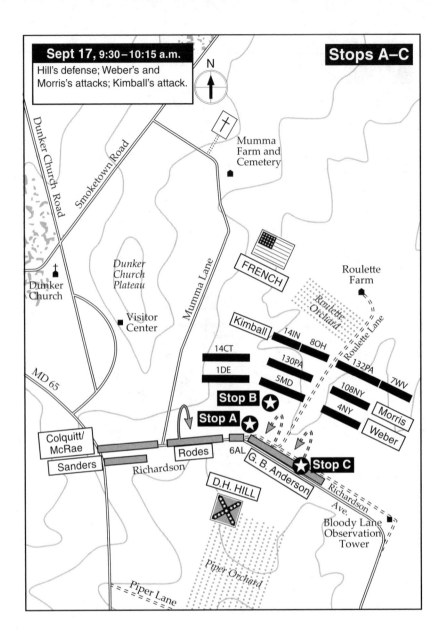

Sept 17, 9:30–10:15 a.m.
Hill's defense; Weber's and Morris's attacks; Kimball's attack.

N

Stops A–C

Mumma Farm and Cemetery

Dunker Church Road

Smoketown Road

Dunker Church Plateau

Dunker Church

Visitor Center

Mumma Lane

FRENCH

Roulette Farm

Roulette Orchard

Roulette Lane

Kimball

14IN

8OH

14CT

130PA

132PA

7WV

1DE

5MD

108NY

MD 65

Stop B ★

4NY

Morris

Stop A ★

Weber

Colquitt/ McRae

Rodes

6AL

Sanders

Richardson

G. B. Anderson

★ **Stop C**

Richardson Ave.

D.H. HILL

Bloody Lane Observation Tower

Piper Orchard

Piper Lane

STOP A   *Hill's Defense, 9:30 A.M.*

Directions   From the viewing platform, *walk* down to the road trace, *turn left*, and then *proceed* about 100 yards to the bend in the Sunken Road. There on the right you will see a monument to the 14th Indiana. *Turn right* and face toward the ridge in front of you, upon which sits a monument to the 5th Maryland Infantry.

Orientation

You are standing at the bend of the Sunken Road. On the other side of the rise in front of you are the Mumma and Roulette farms. On the other side of the ridge behind you is the Piper farm with the Hagerstown Pike beyond that. At the end of the dirt lane you passed as you walked to this point was the Roulette farm.

What Happened

When the battle of Antietam began, three of the five brigades in Maj. Gen. Daniel H. *Hill's* division were posted in the Sunken Road, while Brig. Gen. Roswell *Ripley's* brigade was positioned about 600 yards forward and Brig. Gen. George B. *Anderson's* brigade was astride the Boonsboro Pike. Then, in response to Hooker's attack, *Hill* pushed *Ripley's* brigade, then Col. Alfred *Colquitt's* and Lt. Col. Duncan K. *McRae's*, forward to join the fight for the Miller Cornfield. (*Ripley* was wounded shortly thereafter; consequently his brigade participated in the fight for the Miller Cornfield under the direction of Col. George P. *Doles*.) To compensate for their absence, *Hill* directed *Anderson* to shift to the left to occupy the leg of the Sunken Road to your right. Nonetheless, as Brig. Gen. William French's Union division of 5,700 men arrived on the field and began their advance toward the Sunken Road, *Hill* had only about 2,600 men on hand.

Holding the section of the road to your left, which travels west to the Hagerstown Pike, was Brig. Gen. Robert E. *Rodes's* Alabama brigade. This brigade had begun the day posted in the Sunken Road, and when *Colquitt* and *McRae* moved forward, *Hill* directed Rodes's men to follow them. But when it became evident that the fight for the Cornfield had turned against the Confederates, *Hill* ordered *Rodes* back to the Sunken Road. There, he was joined by battered elements of *Colquitt's* and *McRae's* commands that had escaped the Cornfield, as well as by a brigade commanded by Lt. Col. Christopher C. *Sanders* from Maj. Gen. Lafayette *McLaws's* division. These brigades extended the line from *Rodes's* left to the Hagerstown Pike. The section of the road to your right that runs to the observation tower was held by *Anderson's* 1,174-man brigade of North Carolinians. Col. Charles *Tew's* 2nd North Carolina connected with the right of Col. John *Gordon's* 6th Alabama at a point between the Roulette Lane and the bend in the road where you are now standing. To support their position, *Hill* placed artillery on the ridge behind you.

STOP B   Weber's and Morris's Attacks, 9:30–10:00 A.M.

Directions   *Turn left* and *walk* along the road trace about 30 yards to the
break in the fence on your right where the monument to
the 133rd Pennsylvania is located. *Pass through* the break in
the fence and *walk* toward the sand-colored 14th Connecticut monument for 50 yards. Then, *turn right* and *walk* about
50 yards to the dark grey monument to the 5th Maryland.
Upon reaching this monument, *stop* and *turn right* to face toward the Sunken Road in the direction of the 14th Indiana
and 8th Ohio monuments.

What Happened   Around 9:30 A.M., Brig. Gen. Max Weber's brigade of French's
division fixed bayonets and approached the crest of the hill
overlooking the Sunken Road with the 1st Delaware Infantry
on the right, 5th Maryland Infantry in the center, and 4th
New York on the left, with the latter two units advancing on
either side of the Roulette Lane. None of Weber's men had
yet experienced heavy combat. From the moment they began their advance, Weber's men came under fire from Confederate batteries near the Piper home and west of the Hagerstown Pike. Then, as they passed over the Mumma farm,
the 1st Delaware briefly had to contend with a South Carolina regiment that was in a position from which it could fire
into their flank. Once the South Carolinians were driven off,
Weber ordered his men to fix bayonets and charge up the
ridge that separated them from the Sunken Road. When Weber's men crossed the ridge, they were greeted by a blast of
musket fire. Over a quarter of the men in the 1st Delaware,
including the entire color guard, were killed or wounded,
and the rest of the regiment fell back in disorder through
the Mumma cornfield. The 5th Maryland likewise lost about
one fourth of its men before laying down to exchange fire
with *Hill's* Confederates. On the other side of the Roulette
Lane, the 4th New York also lost heavily and was stopped
cold by *Anderson's* North Carolinians. Some of *Anderson's*
men then attempted a counterattack, but this was easily re-
pelled. Nonetheless, in only about five minutes, Weber's brigade had suffered over 400 casualties and not made a dent
in the Confederate position. Among those struck was Weber, who turned command of the brigade over to Col. John
W. Andrews of the 1st Delaware.

As Andrews's men regrouped and exchanged fire with the
Confederates in the road, the three brand new regiments of
Col. Dwight Morris's brigade moved forward to renew the at-
tack. Morris would also attack with two regiments, the 14th
Connecticut and 130th Pennsylvania, to the right of the Rou-

lette Lane and one regiment, the 108th New York, to the left of the lane. After passing through the shattered ranks of the 1st Delaware, the 14th Connecticut was only able to advance about 50 to 65 yards beyond the Mumma cornfield before *Rodes's* men forced it to pull back to the relative shelter of the cornfield. The 130th Pennsylvania managed to reach the 5th Maryland's position on the crest of the ridge overlooking the Sunken Road north of the Roulette Lane, but could go no farther due to intense Confederate artillery and small arms fire. South of the lane, the 108th New York managed to advance to the position held by the 4th New York, but was halted there as well by severe musket fire.

Encouraged by the failure of Weber's and Morris's assaults, Maj. Gen. James *Longstreet* ordered the men in the left leg of the Sunken Road to make a counterattack. *Rodes* promptly complied, as did *Sanders*. However, the order to charge did not reach *Rodes's* rightmost regiment, the 6th Alabama, and the elements of *Colquitt's* brigade posted to his left were unwilling to advance far from the shelter of the Sunken Road. Consequently, *Rodes's* and *Sanders's* attackers found themselves horribly exposed upon leaving the road and received what one man described as "a galling and destructive shower of balls" from French's men. When it became evident that the attack would accomplish nothing and their men were suffering heavily, *Rodes* and *Sanders* fell back to the Sunken Road.

STOP C   Kimball's Attack, 10:00–10:15 A.M.

Directions   *Retrace* your steps back to the 133rd Pennsylvania monu-
                      ment, *turn left* after passing through the break in the fence,
                      and *walk* along the Sunken Road in the direction of the ob-
                      servation tower for about 200 yards until you reach the mon-
                      ument to the 132nd Pennsylvania on your left. *Turn left* and
                      face toward the ridge on the other side of the monument.

What Happened   While Weber and Morris were making their attacks, a mem-
                      ber of Sumner's staff reached French with orders to press
                      his advance. At the time, French's final brigade, Brig. Gen.
                      Nathan Kimball's, was straightening out its alignment after
                      reaching the Roulette farm. Kimball had posted the 14th In-
                      diana and 8th Ohio to the right of the Roulette Lane and the
                      132nd Pennsylvania and 7th West Virginia to its left. Kim-
                      ball's command was, with the exception of the brand-new
                      132nd Pennsylvania, composed entirely of veteran units.
                      Even before Kimball ordered the brigade forward, those
                      rookies had an extremely uncomfortable experience. As they
                      were maneuvering and deploying on the Roulette farm, a
                      Confederate artillery shell smashed into Roulette's beehives.
                      A swarm of angry bees descended on the Pennsylvanians,
                      and it took several minutes for their officers to restore or-
                      der and get their men ready for action. Shortly thereafter,
                      Kimball received orders from French to attack. Advancing
                      astride the Roulette Lane at the double-quick with fixed bay-
                      onets, Kimball's attack against the Sunken Road was greet-
                      ed by a hail of musket fire from *Rodes's* and *Anderson's* com-
                      mands that brought the attack to a bloody halt short of the
                      road. After recoiling to the crest of the ridge and hitting the
                      ground, Kimball's men joined the remnants of Weber's and
                      Morris's commands in exchanging fire with the Confeder-
                      ates at short range.

                      After only an hour of combat, French had wrecked his di-
                      vision without making the slightest dent in the Confeder-
                      ate position. Nonetheless, *Hill's* men were growing increas-
                      ingly uneasy. The Union troops on the ridge overlooking
                      the Sunken Road where it sloped down to the Roulette Lane
                      were in a good position from which they could pour an en-
                      filade fire into the right flank of the Confederates to the
                      left of the lane and the left flank of those to the right of the
                      lane. Moreover, from their position filling the gap between
                      French's right and Greene's left, Capt. John A. Tompkins's
                      battery from the 1st Rhode Island Artillery was able to pour
                      an effective fire into the Confederate position. Help for *Hill's*
                      beleaguered command, however, was on the way.

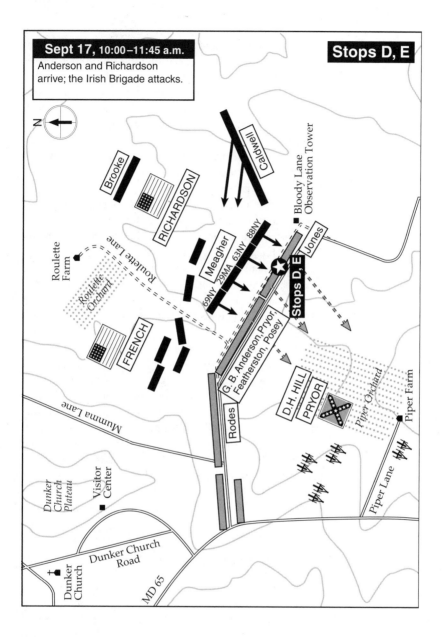

Sept 17, 10:00–11:45 a.m.
Anderson and Richardson arrive; the Irish Brigade attacks.

Stops D, E

N

Caldwell

Brooke

RICHARDSON

Roulette Lane

Meagher
29MA 63NY 88NY
69NY

Roulette Farm

Roulette Orchard

FRENCH

Bloody Lane
Observation Tower

Jones

Stops D, E

G. B. Anderson, Pryor, Featherston, Posey

Rodes

D.H. HILL

PRYOR

Piper Orchard

Piper Farm

Mumma Lane

Visitor Center

Dunker Church Plateau

Piper Lane

Dunker Church Road

Dunker Church

MD 65

STOP D   *Anderson* and Richardson Arrive, 10:00–11:15 A.M.

Directions   *Resume* walking south along the Sunken Road toward the observation tower for about 150 yards to a row of markers on your left next to the monument to the 2nd Delaware. *Stop here and turn left.*

En route. Note the mortuary monument (the upturned cannon) on your right to G. B. *Anderson*, who was mortally wounded in the fighting at the Bloody Lane.

What Happened   As Kimball's attack was coming to grief, Maj. Gen. Richard H. *Anderson's* division of 3,300 infantry and four batteries of artillery, commanded by Capt. Carey F. *Grimes*, arrived at the Piper farm. This gave the Confederate defenders in this sector of the battlefield a numerical advantage to go with the advantage their position and the greenness of much of French's division had given them. *Grimes* immediately posted his guns on a ridge northwest of the Piper barn, where they were able to assist in the repulse of Kimball's assault. Then, however, *Grimes* came under a smothering combined fire from Tompkins's artillery, Federal infantry on the ridge overlooking the Sunken Road, and long range Union artillery east of the Antietam that partially silenced his batteries. This fire also took a serious toll on the brigades of *Anderson's* command as they arrived at the Piper farm and tried to move forward to the Sunken Road. After running a gauntlet of Union small arms and artillery fire where they went into position to the right of G. B. *Anderson*, Brig. Gen. Ambrose P. *Wright's* brigade, which was the first of R. H. *Anderson's* brigades to reach the road, was worn down to only about 250 men, with both its commander and second in command wounded. Nonetheless, the brigade's new commander, Col. Robert *Jones* thought he saw an opportunity to attack the left flank of the Federals in front of him and decided to seize it. Upon seeing *Jones's* command emerge from the Sunken Road, however, the regiment holding the Union flank, the 7th West Virginia, coolly changed its front and drove off the Confederate attackers. As if this were not enough, at about this time, G. B. *Anderson* was struck in the ankle and foot and was forced to leave the field with a wound that turned out to be fatal.

To make matters worse for the Confederates, R. H. *Anderson's* division lost cohesion when its commander was wounded only minutes after arriving at the Piper farm, and his successor, Brig. Gen. Roger A. *Pryor*, was not up to the job of managing a division under fire. Moreover, the advantage in numbers the Confederates enjoyed in this section of the field as a result of R. H. *Anderson's* arrival would be short-lived. Around 11:00 A.M., the last of Sumner's divisions reached the field. This was the 4,029-man division commanded by Maj. Gen. Israel B. Richardson, which McClellan had released around 9:00 A.M. Unlike French's command, Richardson's was a first-rate veteran division. After crossing the Antietam around 9:30 A.M., Richardson had turned left and pushed forward with Brig. Gen. Thomas Meagher's Irish Brigade on the right, Brig. Gen. John C. Caldwell's brigade on the left, and Col. John Brooke's brigade in reserve. Richardson's line of march initially threatened to overlap the right flank of the Confederates in the Sunken Road. Then, however, Richardson found himself compelled to shift to the right to connect with French's beleaguered command. As a consequence, Richardson's command would repeat French's practice of making frontal assaults against the Sunken Road.

Lieutenant-General
Daniel H. Hill, C.S.A.
From a photograph.
BLCW 2:214

STOP E   The Irish Brigade Attacks, 11:15–11:45 A.M.

What Happened   The first of Richardson's brigades to assault the Sunken
Road was Meagher's Irish Brigade. Taking advantage of the
shelter provided by the terrain, Meagher deployed his command into line several hundred yards from the Confederate
position, with Lt. Col. James Kelly's 69th New York on the
right. To Kelly's left was Lt. Col. Joseph H. Barnes's 29th Massachusetts, a regiment that was not Irish but, in the words
of one chronicler of the battle, "intensely American in its
make up," with officers descended from some of Massachusetts's oldest families. To the left of Barnes was the 63rd New
York, while the 88th New York held the far left. Meagher directed his men to advance to the crest of the ridge in front
of the road, fire two volleys, and then charge the enemy position and carry it with the bayonet, counting on what he
later labeled "the impetuosity and recklessness of Irish soldiers in a charge" to bring success.

Like Weber's, Morris's, and Kimball's attacks, Meagher's
initially proved to be an exercise in futility. Musket fire
from the Confederates posted in the road slammed into the
ranks of the Irish Brigade as it crossed the ridge in front of
the Sunken Road. Meagher continued to push forward but
could not overcome fierce Confederate fire and was eventually compelled to order a halt, whereupon his men began a
sharp exchange of fire with the Confederates in the Sunken
Road. Meagher personally posted himself with Kelly's New
Yorkers on the right and after seeing them fire five or six
volleys, ordered a resumption of the attack. Some of Meagher's men managed to get within fifty yards of the road but
were once again brought to a bloody halt.

As Meagher battled G. B. *Anderson's* and *Jones's* brigades,
three more brigades from R. H. *Anderson's* division managed
to reach the Sunken Road. The fire from Meagher's three
Irish regiments began to slacken as casualties mounted. The
ranks of the 69th New York became so thin that Confederates in the Sunken Road called out to their color bearers to
"bring them colors in here." The two regimental color bearers defiantly took a few steps forward and called out, "Come
and take them you damned rebels." Looking on was Lt. Col.
Barnes, who was in a position where the terrain sheltered
his Massachusetts regiment from Confederate fire coming
from the Sunken Road, but where they could fire into the
Piper cornfield. Sensing the Confederates might in fact take
up the challenge issued by Kelly's color bearers and make
another attack out of the Sunken Road, and seeing how
thinned the ranks of the 69th New York on his right and the

63rd New York on his left were, Barnes called out to his men to give three cheers and attack the enemy.

Barnes's bold advance surprised the rebels, some of whom were in fact attempting a counterattack. Suddenly, not only was the Confederate attack aborted, but at about the same time, Brig. Gen. Carnot *Posey* also decided to pull his brigade back from the road in an attempt to alleviate the confusion in the Confederate ranks. Seeing *Posey's* men leave and startled by Barnes's attack, the other two brigades from R. H. *Anderson's* division broke and fled from the Sunken Road, carrying with them all but two of G. B. *Anderson's* regiments. As this was going on, Meagher pulled his four regiments back, and Caldwell's men passed through their lines to take over the battle. The Irish Brigade had pushed the Confederates at the Sunken Road to the brink of disaster, but paid an awful price. Although Barnes's losses were relatively light, the 63rd and 69th New York both suffered over 50 percent casualties, while the 88th New York had lost a third of its strength.

Major-General Israel B. Richardson. From a photograph. BLCW 2:642

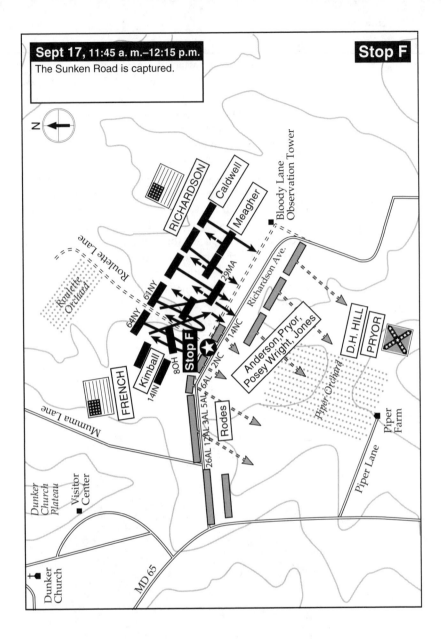

STOP F

The Sunken Road Is Captured, 11:45 A.M.–12:15 P.M.

Directions

Walk back to where the Roulette Lane and Sunken Road intersect.

What Happened

As the men of the Irish Brigade were engaged, Caldwell's brigade moved up to a position where he could attack the right flank of the Confederates in the Sunken Road and began slowly wheeling his command to do so. But then Richardson personally directed Caldwell to cease his movement and to shift over to the right, to relieve Meagher and take over the fight from his position. Caldwell did so with the 61st and 64th New York under the combined command of Col. Francis Barlow on the right, the 7th New York and 81st Pennsylvania in the center, and the 5th New Hampshire on the left.

Without effective command and control of the reinforcement of the Sunken Road position, the Confederate forces in the road at this time were badly intermingled, and the room for movement dramatically diminished. By the time Caldwell's men came up, Barnes's advance and Posey's attempt to alleviate the confusion had triggered the beginning of a collapse of the Confederate position in the road, in which all but the 2nd and 14th North Carolina of G. B. *Anderson's* brigade began pulling back to and through the Piper cornfield.

Meanwhile, Barlow pushed his two regiments over to the crest of the ridge overlooking the road at a point directly in front of the 2nd and 14th North Carolina, who fired a fierce volley that forced the New Yorkers to pull back behind the ridge. Barlow then shifted to the left and found a position from which, after pushing his left forward, he could enfilade the right flank of the North Carolinians, which had been exposed by the retreat of their comrades. Making matters worse for the North Carolinians, the brigade on its left was also abandoning the Sunken Road. In response to Richardson's attacks, *Rodes* had directed Lt. Col. J. N. *Lightfoot*—who assumed command of the regiment holding the bend in the Sunken Road, the 6th Alabama, after *Gordon* was wounded—to pull back a bit in order to counter enfilade fire they were receiving from the Federals on the crest to their right. Somehow *Lightfoot* gained the impression that his maneuver was to be part of a general movement by the entire brigade and told the commander of the regiment to his left to join him as he pulled back. Within minutes, *Rodes's* entire brigade was abandoning the Bloody Lane. As Barlow's men began pouring a horrific fire into their flank, the 2nd and 14th North Carolina finally evacuated the Sunken Road and fell back through the Piper property. Along with units from Kimball's command, Barlow pushed into the road and claimed over 300 prisoners. The other regiments of Caldwell's command then advanced over the Sunken Road and pushed into the Piper cornfield. The Bloody Lane was finally in Union hands.

Vignette

When a staff officer reached Colonel *Tew* of the 2nd North Carolina in the aftermath of G. B. *Anderson's* wounding with news that *Tew* was now in command of the brigade, *Tew* rose from the ground and, one man later recalled, "standing erect, lifted his hat and made . . . a polite bow, and fell immediately from a wound in the head." When the Federals later overran the Sunken Road, some came across *Tew's* seemingly lifeless body lying in the road and attempted to take his sword as a prize. Despite his grievous wound, *Tew* retained enough sense and strength to cling to his sword tightly enough to initially frustrate their efforts, although by the time night fell the sword was in Union hands.

Confederate dead (of D. H. Hill's
Division) in the Sunken Road.
From a photograph. BLCW 2:669

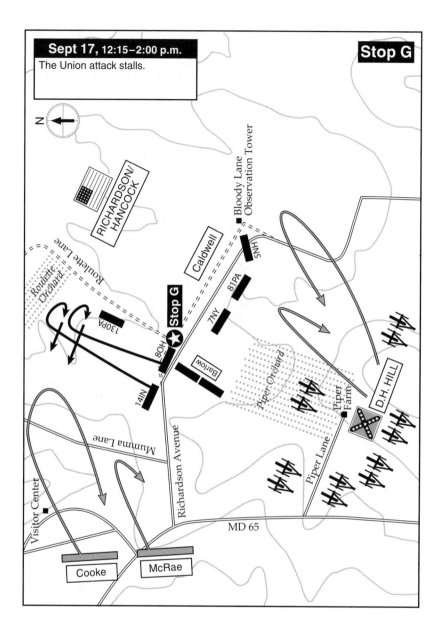

STOP G
The Union Attack Stalls, 12:15–2:00 P.M.

Directions
Turn around and *walk* back to the viewing platform. Upon reaching the platform face toward the entrance to the Roulette Lane.

What Happened
After passing over the Sunken Road, Barlow caught sight of a considerable enemy force moving to his right and changed his front to face in that direction. What Barlow saw was a

Confederate counterattack that had been conceived by *Longstreet* out of a desire to relieve the pressure on *Hill's* and *Anderson's* men in the Sunken Road. To make this attack, *Longstreet* selected *Sanders's* small brigade, now commanded by Lt. Col. William *MacRae*, and two regiments from *Walker's* division that were posted west of the Hagerstown Pike under the combined command of Col. John R. *Cooke. Cooke* was already pushing forward in an attempt to seize two Union cannon covering the withdrawal of Brig. Gen. George Greene's division of the Union XII Corps from the West Woods and had captured one of the guns when he received *Longstreet's* orders. He then redirected his advance southward across the Dunker Church plateau toward the Mumma cornfield, while *MacRae's* men advanced on his right. Kimball responded to *Cooke's* movement toward the Federal right and rear by redeploying the 8th Ohio and 14th Indiana so that they faced north. *Cooke* pushed into the Mumma cornfield and a fierce contest ensued between his and Kimball's men that ended with the Confederates pulling back. Of the 675 men in *Cooke's* command, less than half escaped death or injury. *MacRae's* command fared no better. By turning north after crossing the Sunken Road, Barlow had placed his men in a superb position from which to fire into *MacRae's* command as it attempted to support *Cooke*. Only 50 of the 250 men in *MacRae's* command were available for duty when the day was over.

Meanwhile, at the other end of the Federal line, Col. Edward Cross of the 5th New Hampshire also found himself under attack. This attack was made by a force D. H. *Hill* scraped together from elements of R. H. *Anderson's* division that were still on the Piper property. As *Hill* maneuvered this force in an attempt to reach a position from which it could attack the Union left flank, a battery from the Washington Artillery, posted in the Piper orchard, fired double charges of canister into the Federals as they pushed over the Sunken Road into the Piper cornfield. Due to the Confederate fire and high corn, the Federal units that had crossed the Sunken Road quickly lost much of their cohesion and became disoriented. Nonetheless, Cross was able to quickly discern what *Hill* was trying to do and shift his front so that it faced south in response. Although Cross's move thwarted *Hill's* hopes of finding an exposed Union flank, the Confederates persisted in their advance and soon found themselves in a fierce firefight with Cross's men that ended with the Confederate attack successfully repulsed. Undeterred, *Hill* rounded up another 200 Confederates and led them in another unsuccessful counterattack against the Federals.

Hill's efforts, however, bought time for *Longstreet* to bring up more artillery. At about 1:00 P.M., Richardson ordered his men to pull back across the Sunken Road to the cover of the ridge on the other side as the Confederates swept their front with artillery fire. When his men were back across the road, Richardson was mortally wounded by a Confederate spherical case shot and had to leave the field. Brig. Gen. Winfield Scott Hancock arrived shortly thereafter to take command of the division with orders simply to hold his position. The fight for Bloody Lane was over.

Analysis

The failure of the Union army to exploit its success at the Sunken Road has attracted considerable criticism from students of this battle. At 1:00 P.M., the Confederate position was indeed in desperate straits. It has been argued that a strong Federal push, which Richardson was trying to organize when he was wounded, could have driven a deep wedge into and might have effectively destroyed the Confederate position north of Sharpsburg. The failure of the Federals to exploit this opportunity has largely been laid at the feet of McClellan, from whose command post Richardson's breakthrough was clearly visible. It should be noted, however, that when the Confederate position at the Bloody Lane collapsed, McClellan had already ensured that there was no shortage of relatively fresh Union troops north of Sharpsburg. In response to Sedgwick's disaster in the West Woods, McClellan had ordered Franklin's VI Corps across the Antietam. Yet as Franklin's divisions arrived on the field, Sumner, the senior commander on the ground, had no intention of resuming the offensive, as he was convinced that the Federal position north of Sharpsburg was teetering on the brink of disaster, and McClellan was not willing to overrule him to order another assault.

It also is evident that by the time Richardson achieved his breakthrough, McClellan was probably satisfied that if decisive success was to be achieved, it would not come north of Sharpsburg. Three corps had been thrown at the Confederates there at horrific cost, and the rebels were reported to still be defiant and dangerous. Moreover, even had the attack against the Sunken Road been renewed, *Lee* still had space between his position north of Sharpsburg and the Potomac River over which he could fall back, shortening his lines, and still preserve his line of retreat across the river. It would be incredibly difficult to make such a retreat and get his entire army across Boteler's Ford to safety on the other side of the Potomac if the Federals vigorously pressed him, but it would be possible to save some of it. A successful attack by Burnside, however, might cut *Lee's* entire army off from the ford altogether. And as *Lee's* and McClellan's men anxiously watched each other across blood-soaked woods and fields north of Sharpsburg on the afternoon of September 17, Burnside came perilously close to doing just that.

Further Reading   Carman, "Maryland Campaign," chap. 18, 2–67; Krick, "It Appeared As Though Mutual Extermination Would Put a Stop to the Awful Carnage," 223–58; Sears, *Landscape Turned Red*, 235–54.

Looking for a friend. BLCW 4:195

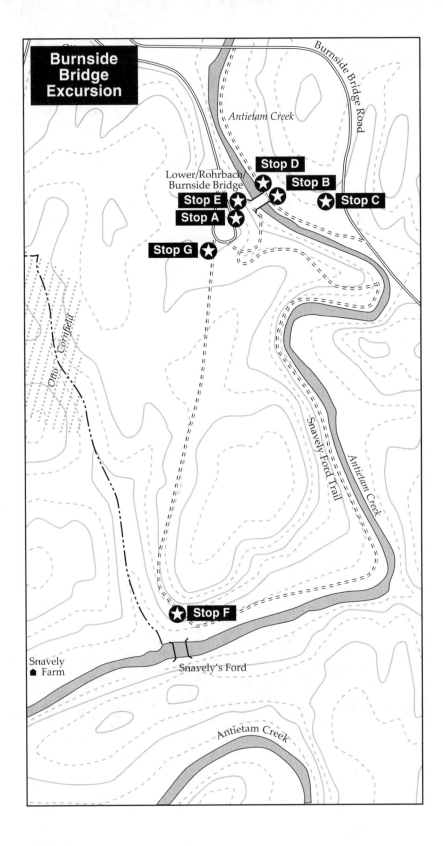

OPTIONAL EXCURSION 2: Burnside Bridge

Directions   Begin this excursion at the "Point Blank Range" overlook, which is stop 10a.

Take charge across the Burnside Bridge. From a sketch made at the time.
BLCW 2:652

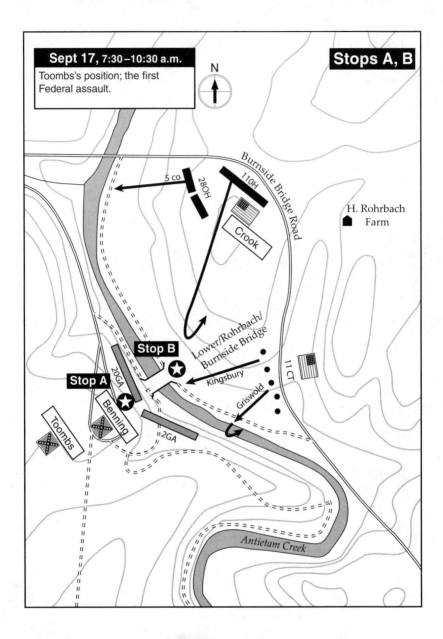

5 co

28OH

110H

Crook

Burnside Bridge Road

H. Rohrbach Farm

Lower/Rohrbach/ Burnside Bridge

Stop B

Kingsbury

11 CT

Griswold

Stop A

20GA

Benning

2GA

Toombs

Antietam Creek

STOP A   *Toombs's* Position, 7:30–10:00 A.M.

Orientation   Face the direction of Antietam Creek, which flows from left
                             to right in front of you. You are standing in a September
                             1862 Confederate defensive position in the contest for what
                             was then known as the Rohrbach (or Lower) Bridge and as a
                             consequence of the battle became better known as the Burn-
                             side Bridge.

What Happened

On the morning of September 17, Brig. Gen. Robert *Toombs's* brigade of Maj. Gen. David R. *Jones's* division was posted on the heights overlooking the Lower Bridge. His line, manned by a little over 500 men in all, started about 40 yards above the bridge with Col. John B. *Cummings's* 20th Georgia. To *Cummings's* right, located approximately where you are standing, was a quarry in which were posted about 25 to 30 men. These men were the left flank of Lt. Col. William R. *Holmes's* 2nd Georgia, which extended the line along the bluffs overlooking the Antietam. Col. Henry L. *Benning* exercised direct command over these two regiments. To the right of *Holmes's* command was a half company of South Carolinians; the other half of the company was posted at Snavely's Ford. In between these units was the 50th Georgia, which consisted of only 100 men. To support his position, *Toombs* had under his direct command batteries of artillery commanded by Capt. John L. *Eubank*, Capt. Benjamin F. *Eshleman*, and Capt. John B. *Richardson*. He also benefited from fire from Confederate guns on Cemetery Hill. Also nearby, although deployed in the vicinity of the Harpers Ferry Road to cover the far right of the entire Confederate position at Sharpsburg, was Col. Thomas T. *Munford's* cavalry brigade.

Robert Toombs, first secretary of state of the Confederacy; member of the Confederate Senate; Brigadier-General, C.S.A. From a photograph.
BLCW 1:102

STOP B   The First Federal Assault, 10:00–10:30 A.M.

Directions   *Turn right* and *follow* the paved path that leads to the bridge.
                      After crossing the bridge to the east bank of the Antietam,
                      stop and *turn right* to face south down the gravel path lead-
                      ing to the bridge.

Orientation   From this position, Snavely's Ford is about two miles down-
                      stream from where you are standing. The Middle Bridge is
                      approximately a mile and a half upstream.

What Happened   Shortly after 10:00 A.M., *Toombs's* men received their first test
                      when the 440 men of Col. Henry W. Kingsbury's 11th Con-
                      necticut finished deploying in open order south and east
                      of the bridge and began advancing toward the Antietam.
                      As soon as Kingsbury's men came into range, *Benning's* men
                      opened fire. Despite taking heavy casualties, the 11th Con-
                      necticut's left wing, which Kingsbury had placed under the
                      direction of Capt. John Griswold, was able to reach the creek
                      a few hundred yards downstream from the bridge where
                      they began exchanging fire at short range with the Confed-
                      erates across the creek. It did not take long for Griswold to
                      recognize that the terrain placed his command at a severe
                      disadvantage and that it would be suicide to continue the
                      battle where it was. He concluded that the only thing to do
                      was to try to push across the creek. Griswold raised his sword
                      and led his men into the Antietam, which proved to be a
                      formidable obstacle. Although relatively shallow, its banks
                      were slippery and the bottom was tangled with branches
                      and rocks in some places and composed of a clinging mud in
                      others. As Griswold's men floundered in the creek, the Geor-
                      gians fired at them from point-blank range. The slaughter
                      was terrific and it quickly became clear that the decision to
                      wade the creek was a bad one. Griswold managed to person-
                      ally reach the west bank of the Antietam, but he was mortal-
                      ly wounded while in the water and died shortly thereafter.
                      Those men that could make their way back to the east bank
                      found cover behind fences that bordered the creek on either
                      side of the entrance to the bridge. Meanwhile, Kingsbury
                      was in the open fields east of the bridge personally leading
                      the right wing of his regiment toward the bridge. His con-
                      spicuous leadership attracted the attention of the Georgians
                      on the opposite bank, who shot him four times. By the time
                      the mortally wounded Kingsbury was taken from the field,
                      the remnants of his command were spread out behind the
                      fence and stone walls bordering the creek. In less than half
                      an hour, a third of the regiment had fallen.

(At this point, *turn around* and face north.) The heroics of Kingsbury and his men were for naught, for the element of the Federal plan that called for Brig. Gen. George Crook's brigade to take advantage of covering fire by Kingsbury's men to rush the bridge in massed columns went horribly awry. Even though he had three regiments in his command, Crook decided to make his attack with only the 11th and 28th Ohio. To make matters worse, Crook lost his sense of direction in preparing his attack. As a consequence, when Crook personally led five companies of the 28th Ohio down the hill in front of the creek, he ended up about 350 yards upstream from the bridge. There, these companies would remain, skirmishing from behind the cover of a small sandy ridge and fence with scattered Confederates on the other side of the creek, until other units captured the bridge early in the afternoon. As the 28th Ohio's advance was coming to an ignominious fizzle, the 11th Ohio made a disjointed attack directly against the bridge that was greeted with severe Confederate infantry and artillery fire that prevented its men from even reaching the creek.

Vignette

Colonel Kingsbury was considered one of the most promising officers in the Union army when he led the 11th Connecticut into battle at Antietam. When his father, an officer in the antebellum army, died in 1856, two future Civil War generals, Simon Bolivar *Buckner* and Ambrose Burnside, became the teenaged Kingsbury's legal guardians. After graduating fourth in the West Point class of 1861, Kingsbury married a girl whose brother-in-law was David R. *Jones*, commander of the Confederate division defending the Lower Antietam on September 17, 1862. After being wounded, Kingsbury was taken to the Rohrbach house, where he recognized that his injuries were fatal and instructed surgeons to devote their attention to other soldiers. Before Kingsbury died on September 18, Burnside made his way to the Rohrbach house and spent a considerable amount of time with his former ward. When he learned of Kingsbury's death, *Jones* was grief stricken, and there is speculation that this event contributed to his fatal stroke only a few months after Antietam. As stipulated in the will he drew up in early 1862, the executor of Kingsbury's estate was none other than his former guardian and corps commander, Ambrose Burnside.

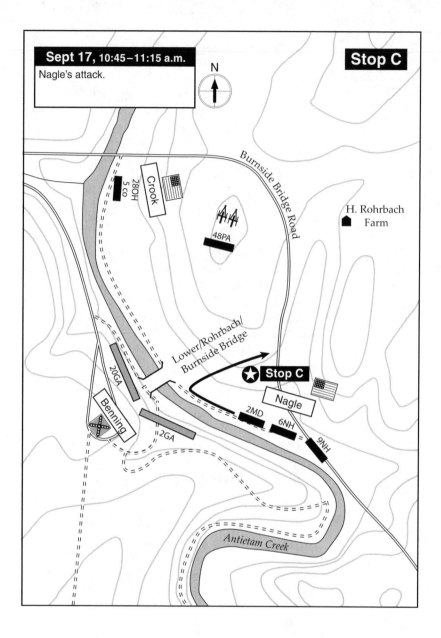

STOP C

Nagle's Attack, 10:45–11:15 A.M.

Directions

Turn around and *walk* south (downstream) following the gravel path that runs along Antietam Creek for about 150 yards to a break in the fence on your left. *Turn left* here, *proceeding* through the break in the fence about 75 yards across the field and up the ridge to where the monument to the 11th Connecticut and a marker describing its actions at Antietam are located. *Stop* at a point between the monument and marker, *turn around*, and face toward the creek with the bridge to your right front.

Of particular concern to Burnside and Cox as they watched Kingsbury and Crook come to grief was the failure of three brigades commanded by Brig. Gen. Isaac P. Rodman to carry out their part in their battle plan by crossing the creek downstream to turn the Confederate left. Rodman found the crossing one of McClellan's staff officers identified the day before but saw that the steep bluff on the west bank of the Antietam made a crossing at that point impractical in the face of small arms fire from Confederate troops scattered atop the bluffs. Rodman then decided to search for a ford that was reported to be further downstream.

After Kingsbury's and Crook's attack failed, Burnside and Cox turned to Sturgis's division. This time, Burnside instructed Sturgis to have his command approach the bridge from the south by following the Sharpsburg–Rohrersville road (which today is indicated by the path that runs along the creek) along the east bank of the creek. Sturgis selected Brig. Gen. James Nagle's brigade to make the attack. Advancing along the road toward the bridge in column of fours at the double-quick and with bayonets fixed, Lt. Col. Jacob E. Duryea's 2nd Maryland would spearhead the advance, followed by the other three regiments of Nagle's brigade. Brig. Gen. Edward Ferrero's brigade would follow Nagle and hopefully help him secure a bridgehead on the west bank of the Antietam.

After a brief artillery bombardment, Duryea's men pushed quickly down from the cover of the hill on the east side of the creek to the Rohrbach Farm Lane. Upon reaching the road ahead of the rest of the regiment, Duryea's officers knocked out one of the panels in the post and rail fence that lined the road, allowing their men to pass through it. At that point, a vicious fire from across the creek greeted the tightly packed ranks of Duryea's command as they passed through the opening into the road and led the Union line to recoil. But Duryea and his subordinates were able to restore order, reform their command, and resume the push toward the bridge. They followed the Rohrbach Farm Lane to its intersection with the Sharpsburg–Rohrersville road about 200 yards south of the bridge, then turned right and continued their advance toward the bridge. About midway between the intersection and the bridge, the Sharpsburg–Rohrersville road bent rightward, and at this point Duryea's front ranks came under fire from *Benning's* men in the quarry above the bridge. Duryea continued to push forward, but by the time he reached a point about 250 feet from the bridge, the severity of the fire in his front and flank was so great that he could go no further. His shattered ranks began falling back to take cover wherever they could find it and return fire across the creek. In only about ten minutes, Duryea's command lost over 40 percent of its strength. Although their losses did not match those of Duryea's command, the other regiments in Nagle's command could get no closer to the bridge than the Marylanders had and eventually joined them in taking whatever cover they could find from where they could exchange fire with the Confederates on the other side of the creek.

Confederate sharp-shooter.
BLCW 2:202

STOP D   The Federals Capture the Bridge, noon–1:00 P.M.

Directions   *Walk* back to the bridge, and after passing its eastern en-
                               trance, *stop* at the monument to the 51st Pennsylvania In-
                               fantry on your right. It is the one shaped like a drum. *Turn
                               around* and face south with the opening to the bridge on
                               your right.

What Happened   As Nagle's men recoiled from their failed attack, Sturgis pre-
                               pared for another try at the bridge. This time, he would use
                               two regiments from Brig. Gen. Edward Ferrero's brigade,
                               which were to cross over the hill overlooking the entrance
                               to the bridge and attack the bridge head on, as Crook had
                               intended to do earlier. Upon receiving his orders to attack,
                               Ferrero selected Col. Robert Potter's 51st New York and Col.
                               John F. Hartranft's 51st Pennsylvania to make the assault.
                               Unlike Crook's attack, this one would be properly prepared.
                               Ferrero's approximately 670 officers and men were careful-
                               ly led to the point on the hill overlooking the creek from
                               where they were to make their assault, while Cox made sure
                               that a powerful artillery bombardment and heavy skirmish
                               fire from the elements of Crook's and Nagle's commands
                               that were still near the bridge would cover the attack.

                               Around 12:30 P.M., Ferrero's men crossed the hill and
                               charged toward the bridge about 300 yards away, with Pot-
                               ter's men on the left and Hartranft's on the right, and were
                               immediately subjected to a storm of Confederate artillery
                               and infantry fire. As they pushed forward, some of the 51st
                               Pennsylvania's company commanders looked at the fence in
                               front of the narrow bridge and concluded that there was no
                               way the two regiments could charge over it and the bridge
                               together. Consequently, without directions from Hartranft,
                               they led their men to the right and took cover behind the
                               stone fence north of the bridge entrance. When Potter saw
                               this, he shifted his command to the left and took up a po-
                               sition behind the rail fence bordering the road. There, like
                               Hartranft's men, they began firing across the stream at *Ben-
                               ning's* men. Meanwhile, Col. William S. Clark of the 21st
                               Massachusetts led his regiment forward to the bridge on his
                               own initiative and took up a position to the left of Potter's
                               command.

                               Within a few minutes after Potter's and Hartranft's men
                               reached the bridge, they noticed a slackening in Confeder-
                               ate fire, as the Georgians' cartridge boxes were nearly emp-
                               ty and the fire of Federal batteries on the east side of the
                               creek made maintaining their positions increasingly diffi-
                               cult. From across the creek *Benning's* men could be seen pull-

ing out of their positions a few at a time. Potter noticed this and suggested to Hartranft that it was time to charge across the bridge. Hartranft did not think he could get his men to leave their cover, but told Potter that if he wished to lead his New Yorkers across the bridge, that it would be fine. Potter then ordered the company commander closest to him to bring up his command and follow their colonel across the bridge. As Potter pushed toward the bridge and waved his sword to urge his men forward, though, he saw men from Hartranft's command rushing toward the bridge.

Leading the way was Capt. William Allebaugh, who commanded the company responsible for the 51st Pennsylvania's colors and who had decided that he had had enough and that it was time to get across the bridge. Allebaugh led his command to the opening of the bridge and then rushed across the bridge accompanied by five other men—the three regimental color bearers, one member of the color guard, and Sgt. William F. Thomas. By the time Allebaugh's group reached the west side of the creek, the rest of the regiment was moving across the bridge side by side with Potter's New Yorkers. As Ferrero's men rushed across the bridge to secure Allebaugh's bridgehead, Hartranft exhausted his voice cheering his regiment on. "Come on boys," he called to them while on the bridge, "for I can't halloo any more." As Hartranft replaced the sound of his voice with waves of his hat to encourage his Pennsylvanians, *Benning* officially gave the order for his Georgians to withdraw. Meanwhile, about 350 yards above the bridge, five companies of the 28th Ohio were wading the creek under Crook's personal direction.

STOP E   The Union Bridgehead, 1:00–3:00 P.M.

Directions   *Recross* the bridge and *turn right* upon reaching the west
                              bank of the Antietam. *Walk* along the creek to a point about
                              25 yards north of the bridge, and *turn left* to face the bluff.

Orientation   You are standing in the trace of the old Sharpsburg–Rohrers-
                              ville road that connected the Rohrbach Bridge with Sharps-
                              burg. If you look to your right, you will see how the road
                              trace joins the modern park road, as the Sharpsburg–Rohrers-
                              ville road did in 1862. Willcox's division followed this road
                              and the ravine through which it ran during their advance to-
                              ward Sharpsburg on the afternoon of September 17.

What Happened   Upon reaching the west bank of the creek, Ferrero's men
                              pealed off to the right upon exiting the bridge and were
                              soon thereafter joined on the west side of the creek by
                              the 35th Massachusetts. As the Federals poured across the
                              bridge, on the heights overhead Lt. Col. William R. *Holmes*
                              of the 2nd Georgia decided to personally lead the less than
                              two dozen men of his command still on the field in a coun-
                              terattack. After issuing orders for the attack, *Holmes* impet-
                              uously rushed down the bluff with his men trailing well
                              behind him, shaking his sword in defiance. The Federals im-
                              mediately opened fire and riddled *Holmes's* body with bul-
                              lets, bringing an abrupt end to his counterattack. Shortly
                              thereafter, the 35th Massachusetts ascended the bluff where
                              it overlooked the bridge and the Sharpsburg–Rohrersville
                              road. In the meantime, Nagle, leaving behind the exhaust-
                              ed and battered 2nd Maryland, led his brigade across the
                              bridge and extended the line southward until they made
                              contact with the lead elements of Rodman's division, which
                              had just crossed downstream at Snavely's Ford. As Sturgis
                              consolidated the Federal bridgehead, Burnside notified Mc-
                              Clellan that the IX Corps was finally across the creek and
                              could hold the bridge. McClellan responded by sending back
                              staff officer Thomas Key with orders to Burnside to continue
                              his offensive. In McClellan's mind, the question of victory or
                              defeat at that moment rested on the IX Corps maintaining
                              its offensive momentum. By doing so, it would relieve the
                              pressure on the Federal right, which Sumner reported to be
                              in desperate straits, and possibly deliver a decisive stroke
                              against the Confederate right that would cut *Lee's* army off
                              from its only line of retreat across the Potomac. According
                              to a postwar account, if Burnside did not comply with the
                              order to continue his offensive, McClellan authorized Key to
                              relieve Burnside on the spot.

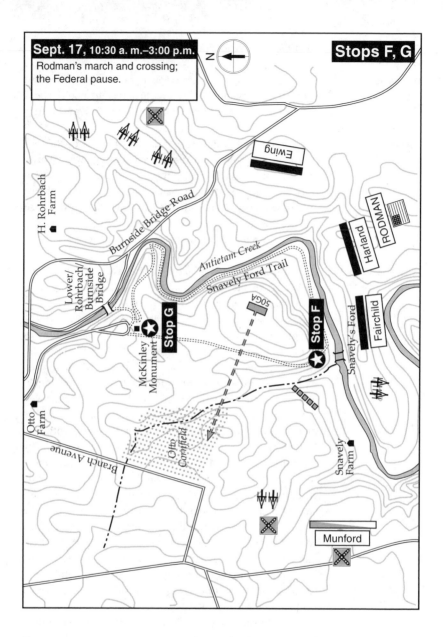

N

Ewing

H. Rohrbach Farm

Burnside Bridge Road

Lower/ Rohrbach/ Burnside Bridge

Antietam Creek

Snavely Ford Trail

RODMAN

Harland

McKinley Monument

Stop G

50GA

Stop F

Snavely's Ford

Fairchild

Otto Farm

Branch Avenue

Otto Cornfield

Snavely Farm

Munford

STOP F   Rodman's March and Crossing, 10:30 A.M.–1:15 P.M.

Directions   This next stop involves a rather lengthy, albeit easy and pleasant, walk along the Antietam. If you do not have the time or desire to do a 2.5 mile hike, you can do this stop and the next one at the McKinley Monument, which is located at the southern end of the parking area. To reach the McKinley Monument, *return* to the paved trail that takes you back to the parking lot. Instead of turning right to return to the

"Point Blank Range" overlook, *continue straight* for about 50 yards to the large monument on your right.

For those who wish to do this stop at Snavely's Ford, *return* to the paved trail that takes you back to the parking area. At the point where you turn right to retrace your steps back to the "Point Blank Range" overlook, you will notice a trail *on your left*. Get onto this trail and *follow* it (essentially you will do a 180-degree U-turn) in the direction of the Georgians' overlook. After about 200 yards, the trail *splits*, with the short paved trail to the left leading to the Georgians' overlook (which provides the perspective of the Confederates who overlooked the creek across from where Kingsbury's and Nagle's men made their attacks). Take the trail *on the right* and *follow* it to where it overlooks Snavely's Ford, which is indicated by a small sign on the left side of the trail. *Stop* here and face toward the creek.

En route. Note both the depth of the Antietam and the terrain on either side. Except for the area around the Rohrbach Bridge and Snavely's Ford, you will not find a usable crossing for a large body of infantry that is approachable from the Federal and Confederate sides of the stream. This is important, for the Federals needed not only a spot where the creek was shallow enough for men to get across without drenching their powder but also one that could be approached relatively easily and quickly as well as advanced from after crossing the creek. With the exception of the area around the bridge and Snavely's Ford, the bluffs on either side of the creek denied the Federals easy access to or easy exit from the creek.

Orientation

From Snavely's Ford, the Lower Bridge is about two miles upstream.

What Happened

As Burnside and Cox conceived it, the task of seizing the Lower Bridge would be facilitated by having Rodman's command cross at a ford that some of McClellan's engineer officers had discovered the day before less than a half mile downstream from the bridge. When Rodman went into bivouac on the night of September 16, he believed that he was opposite the ford. As it turned out, the next ford below the bridge turned out to be situated below a steep bluff and was inaccessible to a large body of troops. This fact was discovered shortly after the 3,200-man column, which consisted of the two brigades from Rodman's division commanded by Col. Harrison S. Fairchild and Col. Edward Harland and a brigade from the Kanawha Division commanded by Col. Hugh Ewing, began its march sometime between 10:00 and 10:30

A.M. Shortly thereafter, however, skirmishers reported that they had found a usable crossing downstream. With a local farmer as a guide, Rodman ordered his column to continue along the winding banks of the creek to Snavely's Ford.

When Fairchild's lead regiment, Lt. Col. Edgar A. Kimball's 9th New York, reached the hill overlooking the ford around 1:00 P.M., it could see smoke from the battle for the Lower Bridge and halted only briefly before pushing down an old road to the ford. The creek at that point was about 75 feet wide, with the water hip deep and flowing relatively swiftly. Kimball's men were in the creek, with Rodman personally accompanying them, when they came under fire from Confederate skirmishers posted behind a stone wall on the far side of the creek. Without pausing to return fire, the New Yorkers reached the opposite bank, moved to the right, and began deploying into line before commencing an advance up the high bluff. The rest of Fairchild's brigade followed Kimball's men across the creek and moved by the right flank along the creek until they linked up with skirmishers from Nagle's brigade. Harland's brigade followed Fairchild's across the creek, drove the Confederates from the stone fence, and despite taking some minor harassing fire from some Confederate infantry and artillery posted on the Snavely farm, were able to reach the top of the bluff where they formed to the left of Fairchild's brigade.

Major-General Jacob D. Cox. From a photograph. BLCW 4:305

STOP G

The Federal Pause, 1:00–3:00 P.M.

Directions

If you did not take the trail to Snavely's Ford, *remain in place*. If you did take the trail, *continue* following it from the stop at Snavely's Ford to the T intersection with a gravel road. *Turn left* here and *proceed* along the road toward the Burnside Bridge parking area. Just before you reach the parking area, you will see a large monument to Sgt. (and later President) William McKinley on your right. *Stop* here.

What Happened

By 1:30 P.M., Burnside and Cox had the bulk of three divisions across the Antietam. Rodman's division held the left, supported by Ewing's brigade, and extended the line to the bend of the Antietam below the bridge. Sturgis's division held the right, supported by Crook's brigade, and extended the line to a point on the Sharpsburg–Rohrersville road about 300 yards north of the bridge. There would be no immediate advance on Sharpsburg, however, despite a steady stream of messages from McClellan demanding one. Shortly after crossing the Antietam and learning of Rodman's successful effort at Snavely's Ford, Sturgis decided that continuing the offensive was impracticable, as his division was low on ammunition. Upon learning this, Cox endorsed Sturgis's decision to hold his command in place and urged Burnside to move Brig. Gen. Orlando Willcox's division forward to relieve Sturgis. Willcox's men marched forward promptly enough, but upon reaching the creek they were held up by a decision—made by whom is unclear—that the men and their equipment would all cross over the narrow bridge.

After crossing the Antietam, Willcox's men turned right and moved forward along the Sharpsburg–Rohrersville road. After passing the point where the road turned left to climb the ravine that led from Sharpsburg to the Antietam, Willcox deployed his two brigades on either side of the road facing north and west toward Sharpsburg. To his left Rodman's division was still in position, although it was subjected to an uncomfortable fire from Confederate artillery while it waited for Willcox to move into position. Not until after 3:00 P.M. would Burnside and Cox finally issue orders directing Willcox and Rodman to resume the advance toward Sharpsburg. Despite the vexing delay, a decisive victory for the Union army nonetheless seemed assured, as only a single Confederate division stood between the 8,500 soldiers of the IX Corps and the streets of Sharpsburg.

Vignette

As they awaited word to advance in the fields around where you are standing, Rodman's men endured Confederate artillery fire from the high ground in front of them. "The practice of the rebel artillerymen was something wonderful in its accuracy," Lt. M. J. Graham of the 9th New York later wrote. "They dropped shot and shell right into our line repeatedly. They kept the air fairly filled with missiles of every variety. . . . The shrapnel or canister was very much in evidence. . . . I watched solid shot–round shot–strike with what sounded like an innocent thud in front of the guns, bounding over battery and park, fly through the tree tops, cutting some of them off so suddenly that it seemed to me they lingered for an instant undecided which way to fall. These round shot did not appear to be in a hurry. They came along slowly and deliberately, apparently, and there appeared no horror in them until they hit something."

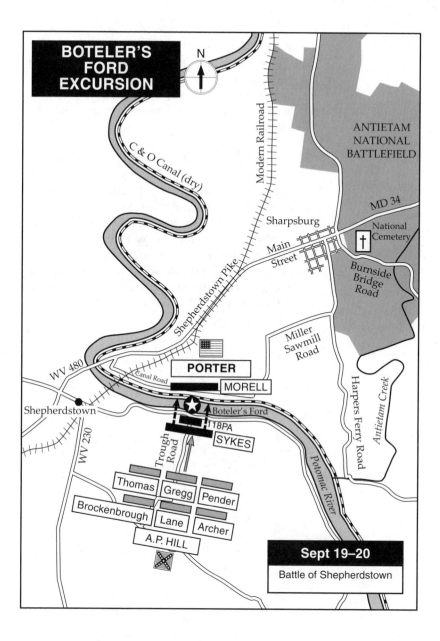

BOTELER'S
FORD
EXCURSION

N

C & O Canal (dry)

Modern Railroad

ANTIETAM
NATIONAL
BATTLEFIELD

MD 34

Sharpsburg

National
Cemetery

Main
Street

Shepherdstown Pike

Burnside
Bridge
Road

Miller
Sawmill
Road

WV 480

Canal Road

PORTER

MORELL

Harpers Ferry Road

Antietam Creek

Shepherdstown

WV 230

Boteler's Ford

Trough Road

118PA

SYKES

Potomac River

Thomas | Gregg | Pender

Brockenbrough | Lane | Archer

A.P. HILL

Sept 19–20

Battle of Shepherdstown

OPTIONAL EXCURSION 3: Boteler's Ford

Directions   From the Antietam National Battlefield Visitor Center parking lot, *turn left* onto DUNKER CHURCH ROAD and *proceed* to
MD 65. *Turn left* onto MD 65 and *proceed* 0.8 mile (along the
way MD 65 becomes N. CHURCH STREET) to the intersection
with E. MAIN STREET (MD 34). *Turn right* and *drive* 3.1 miles on
MD 34 (which becomes SHEPHERDSTOWN PIKE after you leave
Sharpsburg) to CANAL ROAD. *Turn left* onto CANAL ROAD and

proceed 1.4 miles to a small pull off on the right side of the road. Exit your vehicle. *Follow* the path that crosses the dry C and O Canal and its towpath until you reach a point near the shore of the Potomac River where you can see white water upstream (your right) and downstream (your left). *Stop here and face toward the river.*

Orientation

You are looking at the half-mile-wide crossing of the Potomac at Boteler's Ford (also called Pack Horse, Blackford's, or Shepherdstown Ford). Because the bridge over the Potomac between Sharpsburg and Shepherdstown was destroyed at the time, this was the only crossing over the river conveniently available to the Army of Northern Virginia during the battle of Antietam. Cemetery Hill is approximately five miles east of here; the Middle Bridge over Antietam Creek is a mile beyond that. Shepherdstown is just upstream from you on the other side of the river.

STOP A   Recrossing the Potomac, September 18–19, 1862

What Happened   Around 2:00 P.M. on September 18, Gen. Robert E. *Lee* met with Maj. Gen. James *Longstreet* to advise him he had decided to cross the Potomac that night and to discuss preparations for the move back across Boteler's Ford. Shortly thereafter, it began to rain. What began as a heavy thunderstorm had become merely a light drizzle by the time night fell. The army's wagons and wounded would be the first across the foggy, waist-deep river. Once they had cleared the road back to Boteler's Ford, *Longstreet's* command would follow, then *Jackson's*. A. P. *Hill's* division would be the last division of infantry to fall back, with Brig. Gen. Fitzhugh *Lee's* and Brig. Gen. Thomas *Munford's* cavalry brigades, supported by a single ten-pounder Parrott rifle commanded by Lt. John *Ramsey*, serving as the rear guard.

Around 9:00 P.M., *Longstreet* pulled his command back from their forward positions and began moving back toward Boteler's Ford. Upon reaching the Potomac, *Longstreet's* men found that bonfires had been lit on both sides of the river to mark the location of the ford and, at approximately 2:00 A.M., began crossing the river. By the time daylight came on September 19, *Jackson's* men were crossing. General *Lee* remained on the Maryland bank, while *Jackson* sat on horseback in the middle of the Potomac urging the men along. The last of *Lee's* infantry, *Hill's* division, began to cross over around 8:00 A.M. Two hours later, Fitz *Lee's* and *Munford's* cavalry linked up with two companies of South Carolina skirmishers that had been left behind and began crossing. About midway across the river, they came under fire from Federal skirmishers, the vanguard of McClellan's pursuit. However, Confederate artillery on the Virginia side then opened up a fire sufficient to dissuade the Federals from doing anything more. General *Lee* personally watched as the last man from his army safely reached the Virginia side of the Potomac.

Vignette   One of the last officers to cross the Potomac later recalled that as he "rode into the river I passed General *Lee*, sitting on his horse in the stream, watching the crossing of the wagons and artillery. Returning my greeting, he inquired as to what was still behind. There was nothing but the wagons containing my wounded, and a battery or artillery, all of which were near at hand, and I told him so. 'Thank God!' I heard him say as I rode on." After successfully crossing back into Virginia, one of the bands in Lafayette *McLaws's* division began playing "Maryland, My Maryland" but quickly learned the song was no longer popular with the men in the ranks, who shouted, "Stop that! Stop that! Give us no more of that." "The Band," *McLaws* later wrote, "realized that it had made an unfortunate selection, at once changed from 'Maryland, My Maryland' to 'Carry me back to Old Virginny' . . . the men saluted the change with shouts of welcome."

A straggler on the line of march.
BLCW 2:515

STOP B   The Battle of Shepherdstown, September 19–20, 1862

What Happened   At dawn on September 19, Maj. Gen. William B. Franklin's
VI Corps began to push forward to make an attack on Nico-
demus Heights. In accordance with McClellan's orders, the
Army of the Potomac's other corps commanders advanced
strong skirmish lines in support. They quickly learned the
Confederates were gone. When McClellan received news of
the Confederate retreat, he ordered Brig. Gen. Alfred Pleasonton's cavalry division forward in pursuit. Pleasonton's
men reached the heights overlooking Boteler's Ford just in
time to see the last of *Lee's* troops cross the river. After two
hours of exchanging artillery and rifle fire with the Confederates posted on the other side of the river, Pleasonton's cavalry was relieved by Maj. Gen. Fitz John Porter's corps. Porter
immediately posted his artillery and pushed a regiment of
sharpshooters forward to the banks of the C and O Canal.

Lee assigned the tasks of commanding the Confederate
rear guard and guarding the ford to Brig. Gen. William N.
Pendleton, his chief of artillery. *Pendleton* had under his command less than 600 infantry and forty-four pieces of artillery, which he posted on the high bluffs across the river
from where you are standing. As the afternoon passed, the
superiority of the Federal artillery combined with effective
fire from Porter's infantry began to take a serious toll on
Pendleton's command. Detecting a slackening in Confederate
resistance, Porter ordered a party of 500 men to cross the
river. Under the cover of the superior Union artillery, the
Federals rushed across the river and pushed up the heights
on the Virginia side of the Potomac. The Confederates were
surprised by the sudden appearance of the Federals. Exhausted from the battle of September 17, they were in no
condition to put up an effective resistance, and after firing
a few half-hearted volleys of musketry, they suddenly broke
and fled from the field. *Pendleton* rushed back to army headquarters, told *Lee* what had happened, and reported the
Army of Northern Virginia's entire artillery reserve may
have been lost. "All?" a stunned *Lee* asked. "Yes, General, I
fear all," *Pendleton* replied. Fortunately for the Confederates,
news of what happened had already reached *Jackson*, who responded by directing A. P. *Hill* to take his division and drive
the Federals back across the river the next morning.

Encouraged by his success the previous day, Porter sent
four brigades across the river at 7:00 A.M. on September 20
and ordered them to advance along the road that ran from
Boteler's Ford to Charlestown. Suddenly, just as they had
begun their advance, they ran into *Hill's* men. Porter then

authorized a withdrawal back to the Maryland shore, and covered by Union artillery on the Maryland side of the river, most of the men successfully made it back across the river. One regiment, however, Col. Charles M. Prevost's green 118th Pennsylvania Infantry, also known as the Corn Exchange Regiment, remained on the Virginia side. The orders to recross the river for some reason failed to reach Prevost and he refused to move without orders from his direct superior. Unfortunately, in addition to being completely new to the army, Prevost's command was also burdened with faulty Enfield rifles. Consequently, when *Hill's* Confederates charged their position, the Pennsylvanians were unable to fire back and were quickly overwhelmed. As they tumbled back down the bluff and across the river, Prevost's men suffered terrible casualties. Of the 700 men he had led into the battle, only 431 made it back to Maryland. In all, losses in Porter's command totaled 363: 71 killed, 161 wounded, and 131 missing. The Confederates lost 33 killed and 252 wounded in all during the two days' battle.

Vignette

Private Joe Meehan of the 118th Pennsylvania later recalled his experience at Shepherdstown: "There was considerable confusion among our men and much noise, from the suddenness with which we found ourselves called into a brisk fight. A cry reached me about this time to fix bayonets. . . . I shouted the order loudly to those about me. Captain O'Neil, who was near me, asked what I said. I replied: 'They are calling to fix bayonets.' He raised his voice and called out: 'Fix bayonets'; but there were few besides myself who did it. The rebels were now approaching quite close. I had broken the nipple of my gun and had picked up another gun lying near me, but as, with the first one, I had great trouble in getting it to go off. It made me very angry; I felt that I would give all the world to be able to shoot the advancing foe. I had fired but about a half-dozen shots, when as many again could have been got off had the guns been good for anything. I had . . . raised my rifle for a shot when I felt what seemed like a blow with a heavy fist on my left shoulder from behind. I did not realize at first that I was shot, feeling no particular pain, but my almost useless arm soon told me what it was. . . . I then took my first look back of me and found myself very nearly alone. Two wounded men, McElroy and Tibben, of Company A, were right behind me on the ground. I passed them both, and began to descend the hill with numerous others. There was great disorder. About halfway down, among the brush, an officer was trying to stem the tide of descent. I slid down the slope, with my one free arm to aid me, and reaching the bottom of the bluff ran a short distance till I came to three archways in the hill. Into the first of these I got for protection. . . . Our artillery at this time was shelling the heights to cover our retreat. The shells fell short, and one of them exploded in the archway next to me, tearing almost off the leg of Corporal James Wilson."

Further Reading   Carman, "Maryland Campaign," chap. 22, 6–10, chap. 25, 1–13; Carmichael, "'We Don't Know What To Do With Him,'" 259–88; Harsh, *Taken at the Flood*, 437–48, 454–67; Snell, "Baptism of Fire," 119–42.

To return to the Visitor Center: *Turn around* and *drive* 1.4 miles on CANAL ROAD to MD 34. *Turn right* and *proceed* 3.1 miles (en route, the SHEPHERDSTOWN PIKE becomes MAIN STREET) to the intersection with N. CHURCH STREET/S. CHURCH STREET. *Turn left* onto N. CHURCH STREET (MD 65) and *drive* 0.8 mile to DUNKER CHURCH ROAD. *Turn right* onto DUNKER CHURCH ROAD and *proceed* to the Visitor Center parking lot.

Union cavalry scouting in front of
the Confederate advance. BLCW 3:244

South Mountain

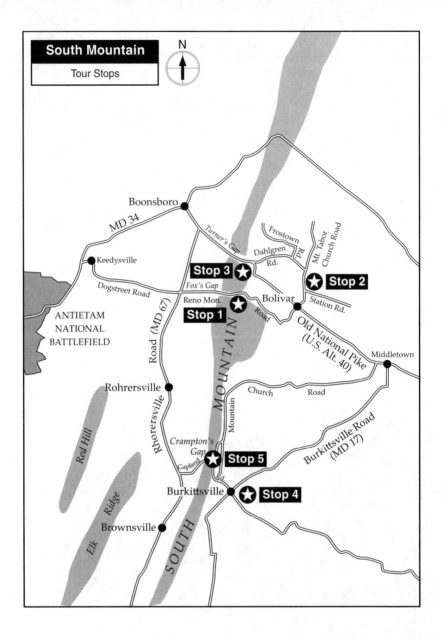

Overview of the Battle of South Mountain,
September 14, 1862

On September 10, the Army of Northern Virginia ended its four-day occupation of Frederick, Maryland. As five divisions made their way to Harpers Ferry and Martinsburg to deal with the Union garrisons there, the "main body" of the Confederate army—consisting of Maj. Gen. David R. *Jones's*, Brig. Gen. Nathan *Evans's*, and Brig. Gen. John Bell *Hood's* divisions, under the overall command of Maj. Gen. James *Longstreet* and accompanied by Gen. Robert E. *Lee* personally—passed through Turner's Gap where the National Pike crossed South Mountain to enter the Cumberland Valley. They were followed by a division commanded by Maj. Gen. Daniel H. *Hill*, which halted its march on September 11 at Boonsboro just west of Turner's Gap. There, *Hill* took up a position from which he could intercept any Federals attempting to flee Harpers Ferry up Pleasant Valley. Maj. Gen. James E. B. *Stuart's* cavalry remained west of South Mountain in order to keep an eye out in the direction of Washington.

On the afternoon of September 12, the vanguard of Maj. Gen. George B. McClellan's Army of the Potomac, Brig. Gen. Jacob Cox's division of the IX Corps, reached Frederick and received a tumultuous welcome from its residents. McClellan then ordered Maj. Gen. Ambrose Burnside's and Maj. Gen. Edwin Sumner's wings of the Army of the Potomac to converge on Frederick on September 13 and directed Cox and Brig. Gen. Alfred Pleasonton's cavalry to continue moving west along the National Pike. To the south, Maj. Gen. William Franklin's wing was to advance to Buckeystown. This would place his command in a position from which it could march to Harpers Ferry to rescue the garrison there or move to Frederick to support Burnside and Sumner, while not being out of position if *Lee* attempted to recross the Potomac and attack Washington from the Virginia side, as Union general in chief Henry W. Halleck repeatedly (and wrongly) warned McClellan they might.

On September 13 Pleasonton pressed forward along the National Pike to Hagan's Gap in Catoctin Mountain. There, he encountered the Jeff Davis Legion of *Stuart's* command and quickly drove the Confederates from the gap. *Stuart* reported this development to *Lee* and D. H. *Hill* and asked *Hill* to send a brigade to Turner's Gap to prepare a defense. *Stuart* then attempted to make a stand just west of Middletown behind Catoctin Creek, but was again driven off by Pleasonton. Around 5:00 P.M., *Stuart* was near Bolivar, a small village below Turner's Gap, when a civilian informed

him that McClellan had received a document of such importance that after reading it he shouted, "Now I know what to
do!" *Stuart* immediately concluded the Federal commander
must have learned the Confederate army was divided and
would move south from Frederick in an attempt to relieve
Harpers Ferry. This suspicion was reinforced by a report
from the lower Middletown Valley that Union cavalry had
reached Burkittsville at the base of Crampton's Gap.

Concluding the greatest danger would come from that
quarter, *Stuart* ordered the bulk of his force to Crampton's
Gap. *Stuart* then rode up to Turner's Gap and found Col.
Alfred *Colquitt's* brigade, which *Hill* had sent to the gap in response to *Stuart's* earlier message. After a brief conversation
with *Colquitt*, in which *Stuart* gave no hint of any danger,
Stuart proceeded to Boonsboro. There, he found a regiment
of cavalry and ordered it to Fox's Gap, where the Old Sharpsburg Road crossed South Mountain about one mile south
of Turner's Gap. Meanwhile, *Colquitt* looked east from Turner's Gap and saw the Federals were in much greater force
than Stuart had suggested. *Colquitt* immediately ordered his
men forward and deployed them on either side of the National Pike about halfway down the mountain, where they
skirmished with Pleasonton's cavalry. Realizing the morning would bring on a fight much bigger than he could han-
dle alone, *Colquitt* asked *Hill* for reinforcements. *Hill* ordered
Brig. Gen. Samuel *Garland's* brigade to *Colquitt's* support.
Upon reaching Turner's Gap, *Garland* encountered *Colquitt*
and they agreed *Garland's* best course of action would be to
move south to defend Fox's Gap.

As Pleasonton was pushing through the Middletown Valley on September 13, two Union soldiers found a copy of *Lee's*
Special Orders No. 191 (which laid out how the Confederate
commander had divided his forces three days earlier to deal
with Union garrisons at Martinsburg and Harpers Ferry) and
forwarded it to McClellan. Based on the information in the
"Lost Order" and reports from Pleasonton and other sources,
McClellan ordered Franklin to march to Burkittsville on September 14 and seize Crampton's Gap. Burnside's command,
supported by Sumner's, would advance along the National
Pike to South Mountain and force its way into the Cumberland Valley—or at least hold the Confederate "main body"
in place—by attacking Turner's Gap. This would facilitate
Franklin's efforts, which, if successful, would put his command in a position from which it could drive a wedge between the Confederates at Turner's Gap and Harpers Ferry.
Franklin would then rescue the garrison at Harpers Ferry
and, once that was accomplished, turn north to assist Burn-

side and Sumner or push west to cut the Confederate "main body" off from the Potomac.

After driving *Stuart's* cavalry from Middletown, Pleasonton continued to push west toward South Mountain. That afternoon, McClellan had forwarded him a copy of Special Orders No. 191, which suggested that *Lee* intended for D. H. *Hill's* division, plus the Confederate "main body" to be at or near Boonsboro in position to defend South Mountain. Consequently, Pleasonton approached Turner's Gap with considerable care. Pleasonton suspected the Confederates would be strongly positioned there, and his suspicions seemed to be confirmed when he made contact with *Colquitt's* infantry. Consequently, Pleasonton decided to search for another route through the mountain that would make it possible to turn the Confederate position. He quickly located Fox's Gap and began focusing his attention there.

For his part, *Lee* responded to reports of McClellan's approach by ordering *Longstreet's* two divisions to leave Hagerstown and march to Boonsboro to support *Hill's* defense of Turner's Gap. *Lee* also directed *Longstreet* to construct a fallback position behind Beaver Creek north and west of Boonsboro from where he might fall on the northern flank of any Union force that pushed through Turner's Gap. To defend Crampton's Gap, *Lee* only had a few brigades of cavalry and small regiments of infantry. To make matters worse, when *Stuart* arrived at Burkittsville at midmorning on September 14, he decided to reduce the strength of the force there further by taking one brigade south to guard the road that passed along the Potomac at Weverton. This left only about 1,000 men to defend Crampton's Gap. That morning, however, Maj. Gen. Lafayette *McLaws* ordered two brigades from his command to South Mountain to assist in defense of the passes at Brownsville and Burkittsville.

The battle of South Mountain began in earnest around 9:00 A.M. on September 14 with the arrival at Fox's Gap of *Cox's* division, which attacked and routed *Garland's* brigade, mortally wounding *Garland* in the process. Cox, however, decided not to exploit his victory but to await the arrival of the rest of the IX Corps. Burnside and IX Corps commander Maj. Gen. Jesse Reno endorsed Cox's decision and pushed the rest of their commands forward. Like Pleasonton, Burnside assumed the Confederate position at Turner's Gap would be strong. Consequently, he decided that while Reno's corps turned the Confederate position from the south using Fox's Gap, Hooker's would do the same from the north. Upon reaching Bolivar, Hooker turned north and, after a short march, halted at Mt. Tabor Church and deployed his command in the fields north and west of the church. At Burnside's direction, a brigade from Hooker's corps, Brig. Gen. John Gibbon's, remained on the National Pike to press directly against the Confederate defenses there. When McClellan arrived at the front, he endorsed Burnside's decisions.

As Burnside brought up his forces during the late morning and early afternoon, *Hill* ordered Brig. Gen. Robert *Rodes* to post his brigade north of Turner's Gap and sent reinforcements to Fox's Gap. When the lead elements of *Longstreet's* two divisions arrived, they were ordered into the battle as well. The defenders of Fox's Gap were far too few, however, to hold out when Reno's entire command arrived during the afternoon. The IX Corps quickly overwhelmed the Confederate defenders at Fox's Gap, although the mortal wounding of Reno and arrival of *Hood's* division put an end to the Federal drive along the ridgeline toward Turner's Gap. To the north, the badly outnumbered Confederates were routed by Hooker's command and only darkness prevented the Federals from gaining possession of Turner's Gap. Meanwhile, Gibbon's brigade pushed forward along the National Pike, but lacked the strength to drive *Colquitt* from Turner's Gap. For his part, Franklin reached Burkittsville around noon, but waited until late afternoon before attacking Crampton's Gap. The Federals then quickly overwhelmed a Confederate position at the base of the gap and pushed into the gap, where they encountered and routed one of *McLaws's* brigades.

Lee's initial instinct on the evening of September 14 was to continue the fight west of South Mountain. However, the battering that McClellan's legions inflicted on his command at Turner's Gap and Fox's Gap destroyed whatever hopes *Lee* had of continuing the fight north of the Potomac. Reluctantly, *Lee* directed *Hill* and *Longstreet* to fall back toward the Potomac crossing at Shepherdstown. Orders were also issued to *McLaws* and *Jackson* to abandon the operation at Harpers Ferry and hasten their commands to Shepherdstown. It appeared the Maryland campaign had come to a decisive and dismal end for the Army of Northern Virginia.

STOP 1   Fox's Gap

Directions   From the Antietam National Battlefield Visitor Center parking lot, *turn left* onto DUNKER CHURCH ROAD and *proceed* to MD 65. *Turn left* and *drive* 0.8 mile to the intersection with MAIN STREET (MD 34) and *turn left*. *Proceed* 6.1 miles on MD 34 to Boonsboro. *Turn right* (east) onto MAIN STREET (U.S. ALTERNATE ROUTE 40) in Boonsboro; after *driving* 0.6 mile, *turn right* onto MD 67 (ROHRERSVILLE ROAD). *Proceed* 1.6 miles on MD 67 to its intersection with MOUNT CARMEL CHURCH ROAD/RENO MONUMENT ROAD. *Turn left* onto RENO MONUMENT ROAD and *drive* 2.1 miles until you see the parking area for Reno Monument on your right. *Pull into* the parking area.

Major-General Jesse L. Reno, killed at Fox's Gap. From a photograph. BLCW 2:585

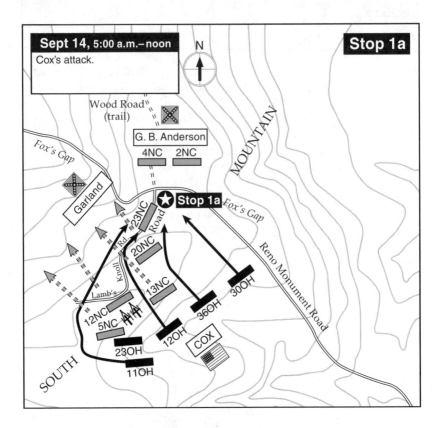

Stop 1a

Sept 14, 5:00 a.m.–noon

Cox's attack.

N

Wood Road
(trail)

G. B. Anderson

4NC   2NC

Fox's Gap

Garland

MOUNTAIN

Stop 1a   Fox's Gap

23NC

Ridge Rd.

20NC

Knoll

Reno Monument Road

Road

13NC

Lamb's

12NC

5NC

30OH

36OH

120H

COX

23OH

SOUTH

11OH

STOP 1A   Cox's Attack, 5:00 A.M.–noon

Directions   Exit your car, *cross* the road over to a point between the in-
                     terpretive markers and the intersection, and face east to-
                     ward the Reno Monument (the walled monument in front
                     of you).

Orientation   You are standing in Fox's Gap, where the Old Sharpsburg
                     Road (modern RENO MONUMENT ROAD) passes through South
                     Mountain. A few hundred yards to the south (your right), the
                     paved road you just crossed picks up the trace of the "ridge
                     road" that ran along the crest of South Mountain in 1862
                     and connected to the Old Sharpsburg Road in front of you
                     roughly at the western boundary of the Reno Monument. At
                     the time of the battle, this road was bounded on both sides
                     by stone fences for about 300 yards south of Old Sharpsburg
                     Road. Just east of the "ridge road," there was a four-acre clear-
                     ing in 1862 known as Wise field. If you look left across RENO
                     MONUMENT ROAD, you will see a path that roughly follows the
                     "wood road" that in 1862 connected Fox's Gap with Turner's
                     Gap, which is about a mile to the north. About three-quarters

of a mile south from where you are standing, the "ridge road" connected in 1862 with a "mountain road" that intersected with the Old Sharpsburg Road at the base of the gap.

To the east, about nine miles from where you are standing is Catoctin Mountain, a spur of South Mountain, from which you are separated by the Middletown Valley. Middletown is about five miles to the east; Frederick is approximately twelve miles to the east on the other side of Catoctin Mountain. There are three gaps that were of importance to the September 14, 1862, battle of South Mountain. From north to south, they are Turner's Gap, Fox's Gap, and Crampton's Gap, which is about five miles south from here. Behind you, to the west, is the Cumberland Valley. Just to the south and west from where you are standing is Elk Ridge, which for about six miles divides the Cumberland Valley. At the southern end of Elk Ridge are Maryland Heights and the Potomac River. The valley between Elk Ridge and South Mountain is known as Pleasant Valley. Sharpsburg and the Antietam battlefield are west of Elk Ridge.

What Happened   Early on September 14 Brig. Gen. Alfred Pleasonton's Union cavalry division began the battle for South Mountain by probing Fox's Gap. At the time, a determined push by Pleasonton could have probably carried the gap, as the only Confederates there were the 250 men of Col. Thomas *Rosser's* 5th Virginia Cavalry, supported by a section of two guns commanded by Capt. John *Pelham*. Upon reaching the base of the gap, however, Pleasonton's men began to receive artillery fire, and he responded by cautiously deploying his dismounted troopers into line south of the Old Sharpsburg Road and sending a request back to IX Corps headquarters for infantry support.

When Pleasonton issued his call for help, Col. Eliakim P. Scammon's brigade of Brig. Gen. Jacob D. Cox's Kanawha Division of Maj. Gen. Jesse L. Reno's IX Corps was already on the march from Middletown. As he crossed Catoctin Creek just west of Middletown, Cox encountered Col. Augustus Moor of the 28th Ohio, who had been captured during a skirmish two days earlier and subsequently paroled. When Cox informed Moor that he was headed toward South Mountain, Moor replied, "My God! Be careful!" Then, remembering that providing information about the situation in Cox's front violated the terms of his parole, Moor refused to say anything more. Deducing from Moor's statement that he would face heavy resistance at South Mountain, Cox ordered his entire division to hurry forward and sent a message to Reno advising him of the situation.

When Cox reached Fox's Gap, he instructed Scammon's men to avail themselves of the services of a civilian who offered to guide them along the "mountain road" that branched off the Old Sharpsburg Road to the south and west, hoping this would enable them to reach a point from which he could attack the right flank of the Confederates defending the gap. When Cox's men neared the crest around 9:00 A.M., they encountered Brig. Gen. Samuel *Garland's* North Carolina brigade and Capt. James W. *Bondurant's* artillery battery, which had just arrived from Boonsboro. Upon his arrival at Fox's Gap, *Garland* had deployed his command in front of and in the "ridge road" that ran along the crest of the mountain south from the Wise farm at the Old Sharpsburg Road.

With Lt. Col. Rutherford B. Hayes's 23rd Ohio leading the effort, Scammon attacked *Garland's* position and, after a tough fight in which *Garland* was mortally wounded, was able to drive the North Carolinians from their defensive positions. Cox's men then pivoted to the right and advanced northward astride the ridge road. They quickly reached the Wise farm and engaged in a bitter, half-hour struggle with the 13th North Carolina along with two regiments from Brig. Gen. George B. *Anderson's* brigade that had just arrived on the scene. The Federals managed to drive the Confederates from their positions, and afterward Cox pushed skirmishers some distance north of the Wise farm before deciding, due to the exhaustion of his command and uncertainty regarding the size of the enemy force confronting him, to break off the engagement. Consequently, around noon he pulled back south from the gap to await the arrival of the rest of the IX Corps.

Vignette

Before ordering his men forward, Lieutenant Colonel Hayes told them, "Now, boys, remember you are the 23rd and give them Hell. In these woods the rebels don't know but we are 10,000; and if we fight, and when we charge yell, we are as good as 10,000." Hayes was one of two members of the 23rd Ohio who participated in the Maryland Campaign and eventually became president of the United States. Although Hayes was wounded at Fox's Gap, the other future president in the ranks of the 23rd Ohio, Sgt. William McKinley, came out of the battle unscathed. Ironically, exactly thirty-nine years later on September 14, 1901, President McKinley would die after being mortally wounded by an assassin's bullet.

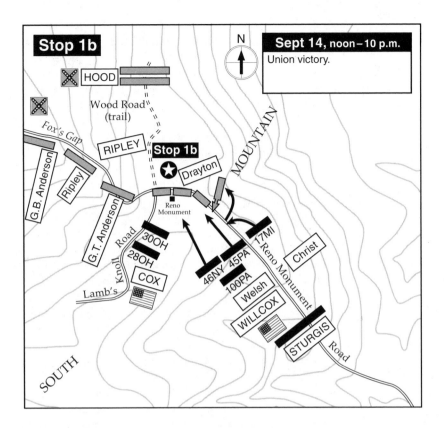

STOP 1B   Union Victory, noon–10:00 P.M.

Directions   Remain in place or *walk* about 25 yards toward the Reno
                           Monument, then *turn left* and *cross* RENO MONUMENT ROAD.
                           After crossing the road, *proceed* about 150 yards forward into
                           the open area, which is now known as 17th Michigan field.
                           Turn around and face toward the Reno Monument.

What Happened   During the lull in the fighting that followed Cox's morning
                           success, D. H. *Hill* dispatched reinforcements to Fox's Gap.
                           Shortly after 3:30 P.M., the Confederates had four brigades
                           under the overall command of Brig. Gen. Roswell *Ripley* on
                           the scene, with orders to secure the road intersection around
                           the Wise farm and launch a counterattack that would drive
                           the Federals from Fox's Gap. As they arrived at the gap dur-
                           ing the afternoon, *Ripley's* men went into position in the Old
                           Sharpsburg Road along the western slope of South Moun-
                           tain. The leftmost Confederate brigade, Brig. Gen. Thom-
                           as *Drayton's*, held the area around the Wise farm, with part
                           of the brigade deployed in the Old Sharpsburg Road facing
                           south and part facing east behind a stone wall to cover the

left flank. *Ripley's* plan was that the four brigades would swing south and east out of the Old Sharpsburg Road with Brig. Gen. George B. *Anderson's* on the right, *Ripley's* own brigade next to him, and Brig. Gen. George T. *Anderson's* between *Ripley* and *Drayton*. This attack, it was hoped, would overwhelm the Federals and sweep them from the mountain.

The Confederate counterattack never really got going. No sooner had *Ripley* ordered it to begin than the three brigades on the right and center got hopelessly tangled up in the thick vegetation, losing all momentum and coordination. Meanwhile, *Drayton's* men were left to deal with a series of attacks against their position by Brig. Gen. Orlando Willcox's division of the Union IX Corps, which began arriving on the field around 2:00 P.M. Col. William Withington's green, but tenacious, 17th Michigan Infantry especially distinguished itself. They pushed back skirmishers covering *Drayton's* left flank north of the Old Sharpsburg Road. Then, coming under fire from Confederate guns positioned to the north at Turner's Gap, as well as from *Bondurant's* and Capt. John *Lane's* batteries, Withington's men crossed to the south side of the Old Sharpsburg Road, where they briefly supported attacks against the Confederate position there.

After the 17th Michigan crossed the road, the bulk of the two Georgia regiments north of the Old Sharpsburg Road that had been facing east redeployed into a southward facing position in the road. Then, when Confederate artillery fire began to slacken, most of Withington's men recrossed the Old Sharpsburg Road and resumed their attack. Sweeping around to the north side of the road, Withington's men advanced to a position from where they could fire into the Confederates posted in the cut of the Old Sharpsburg Road. With Withington's men firing into their flank and rear, the 45th Pennsylvania attacking their front, the 46th New York and elements of Cox's command menacing their right, and their mobility hampered by the depth of the road cut, *Drayton's* brigade was in serious trouble. Men fell by the score, and their position quickly dissolved. Upon learning of *Drayton's* rout, *Ripley* ordered a general retreat from Fox's Gap.

Meanwhile, Brig. Gen. Samuel Sturgis's division arrived at Fox's Gap and began relieving Willcox's men. By the time this task was completed, it was late in the day. As his men regrouped at the crest of the mountain, Reno rode forward to the Wise farm to see what was going on and was mortally wounded. In the meantime, Brig. Gen. John Bell *Hood's* division was able to push forward to reclaim some of the ground that had been lost. The arrival of *Hood's* command, in combination with Reno's wounding and nightfall, ended whatever hopes the Federals might have had of continuing their attack along the ridge to Turner's Gap, although both sides continued to exchange small arms fire until at least 10 P.M. Recognizing their position had become untenable, the Confederates withdrew from Fox's Gap during the night of September 14–15. The losses of the IX Corps in the battle for Fox's Gap came to 157 killed, 691 wounded, and 41 missing. The Confederates suffered at least 850 casualties.

Analysis

It is tempting to attribute the Union success at Fox's Gap purely to numerical superiority. Yet it was not until the end of the battle that the Federals enjoyed an advantage in numbers sufficient to negate the considerable advantages the terrain gave the Confederate defenders. In addition to the physical challenge the Union attackers faced in having to attack uphill, the area around Fox's Gap was heavily vegetated, with stone walls and fences bordering the roads and open areas. These factors provided the Confederates with excellent positions from which they could have conducted a stubborn defense that should have enabled them to nullify the Union advantage in numbers for nearly an entire day. Rather than maximizing the advantages provided by the terrain, however, the Confederates compromised their effort by deciding to launch a counterattack against the Federals. This was clearly a mistake. Had *Ripley's* men been deployed defensively, there is no reason to believe they would not have been able to hold off the Federal advance much longer. Moreover, the terrain made sweeping movements, such as *Ripley's* attempted counterattack, incredibly difficult if not impossible. Consequently, *Drayton's* brigade was left to bear the brunt of the late afternoon Federal attack. In the end, it ultimately was a victory of superior numbers for the Union, but given the terrain, a more effective defense of Fox's Gap could have been made.

Vignette

As his men advanced to the battle, Capt. James B. Wren of the 48th Pennsylvania recorded in his diary, "Quite a scene. . . . Thear was a solid Ball fired at us from the enemy & it struck short & roaled along the field & [it] appeared to be almost stopped when one of our Soldiers ran afrunt of it and put his foot square on it & it tossed him head over heals. He done it in a Joke but it was serious to him as he was so severely Jarred that he had to be taken to the Hospital." Shortly after suffering his own mortal wound, Reno encountered Sturgis and called to him from a stretcher, "Hallo, Sam, I'm dead." From the tone of Reno's comment, Sturgis presumed his wound was not serious. "Oh no General," Sturgis laconically remarked, "not so bad as that, I hope." "Yes, yes," Reno replied a few minutes before he lost consciousness, "I'm dead – good-by!"

Further Reading   Carman "Maryland Campaign," chap. 8, 423–64; Cox, "Forcing Fox's Gap and Turner's Gap," 2:585–89; Harsh, *Taken at the Flood*, 257–65; Hill, "The Battle of South Mountain, or Boonsboro," 2:561–64, 566–67; Sears, *Landscape Turned Red*, 129–36, 140–41.

Confederate dead at the cross-roads by Wise's house at Fox's Gap. From a sketch made the day after the battle. BLCW 2:583

STOP 2 Mt. Tabor Cemetery

Directions Return to your vehicle. *Exit* the parking area and *turn right* onto RENO MONUMENT ROAD. *Drive* 1.0 mile to BOLIVAR ROAD. *Turn left* onto BOLIVAR ROAD and *proceed* 0.7 mile to its intersection with U.S. ALTERNATE ROUTE 40 (OLD NATIONAL PIKE). *Go through* the intersection onto MT. TABOR CHURCH ROAD. After driving 0.9 mile you will see STATION ROAD on the right-hand side of the road. (STATION ROAD comes up very suddenly, so be alert.) *Turn right* onto STATION ROAD and immediately *pull over* on the left side of the road. (You may find it more convenient to find a place to first turn around on STATION ROAD before pulling over to what will then be the right side of the road, with your car pointed toward the intersection when you park.) Exit your car, *walk* over to the brick sign for Mt. Tabor Lutheran Cemetery in the grassy field at the northeast corner of the intersection of STATION ROAD and MT. TABOR CHURCH ROAD, and face west toward South Mountain.

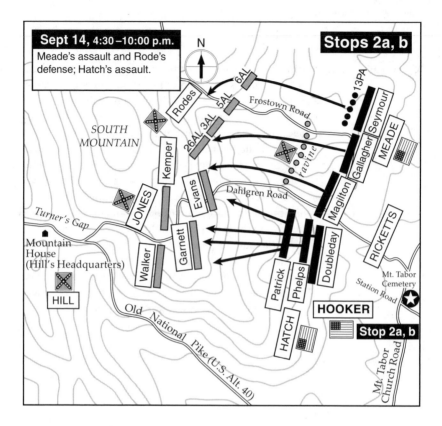

Sept 14, 4:30–10:00 p.m.
Meade's assault and Rode's defense; Hatch's assault.

N

Stops 2a, b

SOUTH MOUNTAIN

Rodes
6AL
5AL
3AL
26AL
Frostown Road
13PA
Seymour
Gallagher
MEADE
Kemper
ravine
Evans
Dahlgren Road
Magilton
Turner's Gap
JONES
Garnett
Mountain House
(Hill's Headquarters)
Walker
Patrick
Phelps
Doubleday
RICKETTS
Mt. Tabor Cemetery
Station Road
HILL
Old National Pike (U.S. Alt. 40)
HATCH
HOOKER
Stop 2a, b
Mt. Tabor Church Road

STOP 2A Meade's Assault and *Rodes's* Defense, 4:30–6:00 P.M.

Orientation Where you are now standing was the grounds of Mt. Tabor Church in 1862. If you look to your left (south) along the mountain you may be able to see the high point with modern structures on it known as Lamb's Knoll, which slopes down toward the north to Fox's Gap. If you follow the ridgeline to the north, the gap to the right of Fox's Gap is Turner's Gap. The large hill directly in front of you is a spur of the main ridge of South Mountain. The Old National Pike (modern U.S. ALTERNATE ROUTE 40) is located south of it and crosses the mountain at Turner's Gap. To your right, Mt. Tabor Road intersects with Frostown Road, which runs west toward a steep ravine separating the southern spur of South Mountain from the main ridge. After joining modern DAHLGREN ROAD, this road continues around the northern and western edges of the eastern spur of South Mountain to connect with the Old National Pike near Mountain House in Turner's Gap.

What Happened As the battle opened at Fox's Gap early on the morning of September 14, D. H. *Hill* ascended a lookout station at

Turner's Gap and saw Union marching columns "as far as the eye could see" moving toward him. "It was a grand and glorious spectacle," Hill later wrote, "and it was impossible to look at it without admiration." Hill responded by ordering forward the brigades he had left at Boonsboro to Turner's Gap and by sending messages to *Lee* requesting assistance. Around noon Brig. Gen. Robert *Rodes* reached Mountain House and was directed to take his Alabama brigade and four batteries of artillery north of the National Pike to occupy the eastern spur of South Mountain.

As *Hill* positioned his troops, Maj. Gen. Ambrose Burnside, commander of the wing of the Union army composed of the I and IX Corps, reached Middletown. Upon learning of Cox's success at Fox's Gap, Burnside ordered Reno to take the rest of the IX Corps to Fox's Gap and issued orders to I Corps commander Maj. Gen. Joseph Hooker to hurry his command forward. As Hooker's divisions began to arrive at Bolivar, the community near the base of Turner's Gap, around 2:00 P.M., Burnside directed them to turn north and follow the road to Frostown (modern MT. TABOR CHURCH ROAD). Upon reaching Mt. Tabor Church, Hooker deployed his men in the fields to the west with an eye on advancing astride the road (modern DAHLGREN ROAD) that ran around the eastern spur of South Mountain and into the gap between it and the main ridge to turn Turner's Gap from the north. At Burnside's direction, one of Hooker's brigades, Brig. Gen. John Gibbon's, remained back at Bolivar.

Shortly before 5:00 P.M., Hooker had about 9,000 men in position and ordered them to attack with Brig. Gen. George Meade's division on the right, Brig. Gen. John P. Hatch's on the left, and Brig. Gen. James B. Ricketts's in reserve. He assigned Hatch the task of taking the eastern spur of South Mountain, while the brigades of Meade's division, commanded by Col. Albert Magilton and Col. Thomas Gallagher, would advance into and up the steep ravine in their front. To Gallagher's right Brig. Gen. Truman Seymour's brigade would attack along the high ground just north of the ravine. As Hooker deployed, *Rodes* moved four regiments from the southern spur of South Mountain to the main ridge to cover the terrain over which Meade was to advance. As Hooker's men began their attack, *Longstreet* reached Turner's Gap and assumed command on the field. He then pushed Brig. Gen. Nathan *Evans's* one-brigade division forward to support the artillery on the eastern spur of South Mountain. Soon after arriving on the scene, however, *Evans* moved over to the saddle between the eastern spur and main ridge of South Mountain in order to better support *Rodes*. *Rodes* and *Evans* only had about 1,750 men, but the Federals would have to make a steep climb just to reach their positions.

On the Union right, a wave of skirmishers from the 13th Pennsylvania spearheaded Seymour's advance and their forward movement led *Rodes* to shift Col. John B. *Gordon's* 6th Alabama over to the high ground north of the ravine in an effort to prevent Seymour from turning his left flank. Seymour, recognizing the importance of the ground *Gordon* was moving to occupy, rushed forward to seize it and maneuvered his brigade into a position from which it could envelop *Gordon's* flanks. Recognizing the danger, *Gordon* pulled back and conceded the high ground north of the ravine to the Pennsylvanians. Seymour then continued his advance and encountered a new Confederate position behind a stone wall on the far side of a cornfield. This too was quickly overwhelmed.

Meanwhile, Gallagher's and Magilton's brigades attacked into the ravine. Although the Confederates put up a tenacious defense, the collapse of *Rodes's* left rendered their position overlooking the gorge untenable in the face of an assault by overwhelming numbers. *Rodes* coolly directed his men to fall back up the mountain, following the ravine through which Dahlgren Road passed, and managed to cobble another defensive line, this one facing northward. But the Federal advance was simply too strong to be stopped. Meade drove *Rodes* from his final position and by nightfall had possession of the high ground on the main ridge of South Mountain overlooking Turner's Gap. This rendered Confederate possession of the gap untenable. The cost to Meade's command was 95 killed, 296 wounded, and one missing, out of about 4,000 men. Of the approximately 1,200 men *Rodes* brought into the battle, 61 were killed, 157 were wounded, and 304 were missing at the end of the day. Evans lost 216 of his 550 men, with 23 killed, 148 wounded, and 45 missing.

Vignette

Confederate artillerist Edward Porter Alexander arrived on the field north of Turner's Gap shortly before Meade opened his attack and later wrote, "Rodes's Ala. Brigade was a short distance in front of me down the slope & stretched a couple of hundred yards or so to the left. From some point about 300 yards I judged to my right, but hidden by trees was a battery. . . . But there was not enough artillery to stop so large a body of men, & it appeared that their line overlapped ours so far that their advance would envelope our flank and turn it. . . . [t]hey sent out in front a long line of skirmishers from the Pa. Bucktails, for with my glasses I could see the tail each man wore on his hat. These fellows came ahead sometimes running, sometimes crouching behind bushes, or fences, & Rodes's skirmishers in front began to pop at them, & they returned it & their bullets began to whistle & hit all about, though they were over 600 yards off. I was always an excellent rifle shot & I entered into the game with delight. I put all eight men behind a big rock to loading & handing me their guns & began to fire at the rate of about 8 shots a minute. I don't think I hit many, for distances varied rapidly, & all had to be guessed, but I did distinctly see one fellow drop at my shot. . . . And after awhile I saw away up at my level & only about 400 yards away a heavy line of battle which had passed clear around Rodes's left flank & were now swinging around to take him in reverse. I reopened my little fire at them but only for a few minutes, for Rodes's men were soon falling back & changing front to meet them, & I saw that the enemy's force was so superior that the utmost we would be able to do would be to delay them until night, which was now fast coming on."

Major-General R. E. Rodes,
c.s.a. From a photograph.
blcw 2:580

STOP 2B   Hatch's Assault, 4:30–10:00 P.M.

What Happened   For the task of storming the eastern spur of South Mountain, Hatch placed Brig. Gen. Marsena Patrick's brigade in the lead, with Col. Walter Phelps Jr.'s brigade behind him and Brig. Gen. Abner Doubleday's bringing up the rear. When Hatch's men moved forward to begin their attack, the ground between them and Turner's Gap was practically devoid of Confederate infantry. Confederate artillerists on top of the eastern spur of South Mountain did their best to slow the Union advance, but their fire was as ineffective, *Hill* later proclaimed, "as blank cartridge salutes in honor of a militia general."

Fortunately for *Hill*, at this point three brigades from Maj. Gen. David R. *Jones's* division arrived at Mountain House. As *Evans* shifted over to assist *Rodes* in his fight with Meade, two of *Jones's* brigades, Brig. Gen. James *Kemper's* and Brig. Gen. Richard *Garnett's*, less than 850 men in all, turned left off the National Pike onto the old Hagerstown Road (modern Dahlgren Road) and went into position well to the rear of *Evans's* command. *Kemper* deployed astride the road, while about 200 yards to his right *Garnett* took up a position defending the summit of the eastern spur of South Mountain. The final brigade from *Jones's* division to reach the field, Col. Joseph *Walker's*, formed to the right and rear of *Garnett's* position.

As Patrick's men moved up the hill, a gap opened between his two lead regiments, which led him to halt the advance to fill the gap and reorganize his lines. While Patrick was halted, however, Phelps's brigade came up and began to push through their position. At that point, Hatch arrived on the scene, sorted out the two brigades, and soon had them moving forward again. Shortly thereafter, the Federals made contact with enemy skirmishers. After briefly halting to deploy into line, Phelps's brigade drove the Confederate skirmishers back up the steep and heavily wooded hill toward a position *Garnett* had established behind a stone fence near the summit that separated the woods from a cornfield. Phelps's men of iron then rushed toward the fence with a cheer and drove the Confederates from their position. In an intense fight at the fence line, Col. J. B. *Strange* of the 19th Virginia was killed and Hatch fell wounded, with Doubleday taking his place as division commander.

As *Garnett's* position at the stone fence disintegrated, Patrick's command joined the fight by moving two regiments into position on Phelps's right and having two others extend the line to Phelps's left. In response to the menace to his flanks posed by the extension of the Federal line, *Garnett* refused both his flanks and continued the contest as darkness engulfed South Mountain. The Federals were content to maintain their position behind the stone fence from which Phelps had driven *Garnett*. Low level skirmishing continued until well after dark, when the Confederates pulled back to Turner's Gap.

Vignette

Although legend holds that it was during the fight at South Mountain that John Gibbon's brigade of Hatch's division received the nickname the Iron Brigade, in fact on September 14, 1862, there was already another command in the division that had that title—Phelps's. One of the regiments in this Iron Brigade derived some of its motivation on September 14 from a desire for vengeance. Just before they went into the fight, Col. William M. Searing told the men of the 30th New York, "Boys, the men who killed your Colonel at Manassas are now in front of you, let us charge and avenge his death." "The yell that the boys gave as they sprang forward to the charge," wrote one man after the war, "could have been heard a mile away. The revenge was complete as Lt. Andrews, who was detailed to bury the dead says—'The line of battle of the rebels was perfectly defined by their dead lying on the mountainside, and upon the feet of a Virginia Colonel were found the military top boots worn by Col. Frisby when he was killed at Bull Run, for the name 'Col. Edward Frisby 30th nyv' was written on both of them. The boots were sent home to Mrs. Frisby."

Further Reading

Carman, "Maryland Campaign," chap. 8, 465–88; Clemens, "'Black Hats' off to the Original 'Iron Brigade,'" 47–58; Harsh, *Taken at the Flood*, 260, 262–64, 265–67; Hartwig, "It Looked Like a Task to Storm," 36–49; Sears, *Landscape Turned Red*, 136–40; U.S. War Department, *War of the Rebellion*, vol. 19, ser. 1, pt. 1:213–15.

STOP 3   Mountain House

Directions   Return to your car and *turn left* from STATION ROAD onto MT.
TABOR CHURCH ROAD. *Take* that road for 0.9 mile to the Boli-
var intersection. At Bolivar *turn right* onto OLD NATIONAL PIKE
(U.S. ALTERNATE ROUTE 40) and *drive* 1.9 miles to the parking
area for the Old South Mountain Inn on the left-hand side of
the road. *Turn* into the parking lot and exit your vehicle. After exiting your vehicle *walk* over to the edge of the road and
face east (the direction from which you just came), or *cross*
the road (*very* carefully; this is a major highway) and *walk* up
to a point on the high ground behind the stone chapel that
will give you a good view into the Middletown Valley.

Further Exploration   Note: This takes you along a very steep and rugged unpaved
road that is only recommended for cars and drivers capable
of handling such a road. It does, however, give you a good
sense of the terrain over which Meade's division attacked
the Confederate left. Begin at the Mt. Tabor Lutheran Cemetery by returning to your car and *turning right* from STATION
ROAD onto MT. TABOR CHURCH ROAD. After traveling 0.1 mile,
turn left onto FROSTOWN ROAD and *proceed* 0.4 mile along that
road to its intersection with DAHLGREN ROAD. It was at approximately this point that Hooker deployed his corps, with
Hatch's division on the left side of the road and Meade's on
the right side of the road and Brig. Gen. James B. Ricketts's
in support. Reset your odometer, *continue* straight onto DAHL-
GREN ROAD, and *proceed* 1.4 miles to its intersection with the
OLD NATIONAL PIKE (U.S. ALTERNATE ROUTE 40). In the attack
of the I Corps toward Turner's Gap on the afternoon of September 14, Meade's division advanced through the ravine to
the right of the road and Hatch's command advanced on the
left. Upon reaching OLD NATIONAL PIKE, *turn right* and *proceed*
to the parking area for the Old South Mountain Inn on the
left side of the road.

Orientation   You are standing in Turner's Gap in South Mountain. Middletown is about five miles east of you as the crow flies. Catoctin Mountain is approximately three miles beyond Middletown. About 100 yards in front of you is the point where
the road from Mt. Tabor Church, along which Hooker's command advanced, and the road from Fox's Gap met at the National Pike in 1862. In 1862 the Old South Mountain Inn was
known as Mountain House and served as D. H. *Hill's* headquarters during the battle of South Mountain.

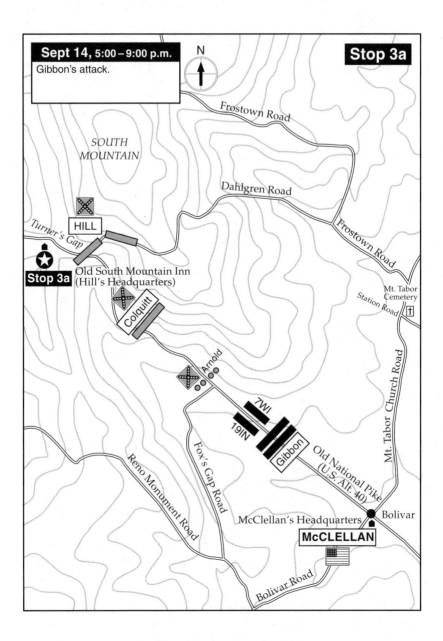

Sept 14, 5:00 – 9:00 p.m.
Gibbon's attack.

N

SOUTH MOUNTAIN

Frostown Road

Dahlgren Road

Frostown Road

Turner's Gap

HILL

Stop 3a

Old South Mountain Inn
(Hill's Headquarters)

Colquitt

Mt. Tabor
Cemetery

Station Road

Arnold

7WI

19IN

Gibbon

Old National Pike
(U.S. Alt. 40)

Mt. Tabor Church Road

Reno Monument Road

Fox's Gap Road

McClellan's Headquarters

Bolivar

McCLELLAN

Bolivar Road

STOP 3A   Gibbon's Attack, 5:00–9:00 P.M.

What Happened   While Hooker's men went into position to attack the Confed-
                    erate left and Reno's men were battling the Confederates at
                    Fox's Gap, Burnside held one brigade from Hatch's division
                    of Hooker's corps back at Bolivar. This brigade was distinc-
                    tive within the Army of the Potomac for two reasons. First, it
                    was the only brigade in the Army of the Potomac composed
                    entirely of men from west of the Appalachian Mountains;

second, at the direction of its commander, Brig. Gen. John Gibbon, the men of this brigade were clad in black slouch hats instead of the blue kepi worn by the rest of the army. As the sun began to set on September 14, with the sounds of gunfire from both north and south of Turner's Gap indicating the progress of the attacks on D. H. *Hill's* flanks, Burnside decided to order Gibbon's command forward to attack Turner's Gap directly.

Gibbon had deployed his men in column on either side of the National Pike, with Capt. John B. Callis's 7th Wisconsin on the right (north) and Col. Solomon Meredith's 19th Indiana on the left (south) sides of the road. They were supported by Col. Lucius Fairchild's 2nd and Lt. Col. Edward S. Bragg's 6th Wisconsin, which also provided two companies of skirmishers to cover the brigade's front. Upon beginning their advance, Gibbon's men immediately came under fire from four companies of skirmishers posted in a heavy stand of woods south of the road commanded by Capt. W. M. *Arnold.* These belonged to Col. Alfred *Colquitt's* Georgia brigade, to which *Hill* had assigned responsibility for defending the approach to Turner's Gap along the National Pike. *Colquitt* posted his main battle line about 400 yards up the mountain from *Arnold's* position where the road that connected Frostown and Fox's Gap crossed the National Pike.

Gibbon's men pushed back the rebel skirmish line and made steady progress until they encountered *Colquitt's* main battle line. Concerned that *Colquitt's* command might be able to overlap his right, Gibbon directed Bragg to extend the brigade front in that direction by deploying to the right of Callis. He then ordered Meredith, supported by Fairchild, to deploy his regiment in line and swing around to a position parallel to the road in an attempt to envelop *Colquitt's* position from the south. *Colquitt,* however, held a position that was too strong to be overcome by a single brigade. Gibbon quickly realized this and soon became satisfied merely to exert pressure on *Colquitt's* position by maintaining an active firefight. This would last until it became too dark to continue the fight. When it was over, Gibbon and *Colquitt* held their men in position with bayonets fixed. For his determined defense of Turner's Gap, *Colquitt* would receive the sobriquet the "Rock of South Mountain."

Vignette

"Thus we went down into the valley and began to climb the slope of the mountain," wrote Maj. Rufus Dawes of the 6th Wisconsin. "For about a half a mile of advance, our skirmishers played a deadly game of 'Bo-peep,' hiding behind logs, fences, rocks and bushes. . . . General Gibbon mounted upon his horse and riding upon high ground where he could see his whole line, shouted orders in a voice loud and clear as a bell and distinctly heard throughout the brigade. It was always, 'Forward! Forward!' . . . The rebels behind the stone wall and in the timber would shout: 'O, you d——d Yanks, we gave you h——ll again at Bull Run!' Our men would shout back: 'Never mind Johnny, its no McDowell after you now. "Little Mac" and "Johnny Gibbon" are after you now.' . . . [T]he fire was deadly. It was dark and our only aim was by the flashes of the enemy's guns. Many of our men were falling, and we could not long endure it. Colonel Bragg took the left wing, directing me to keep up the fire with the right wing, and crept up into the woods on our right, advancing a considerable distance up the mountain. . . . Owing to the thick brush and the darkness of night, it was a difficult matter to scramble up the stony side of the mountain. . . . Gradually by direction of Colonel Bragg we ceased firing and lay still on the ground. A man in company 'A' exclaimed: 'Captain Noyes, I am out of cartridges!' It is likely that the enemy in the woods above us heard him, for they immediately opened upon us a heavy fire. We returned the fire, and for a short time the contest was very sharp. This was the last of the battle."

Further Exploration   If you look across OLD NATIONAL PIKE from the parking area, you will see a sign indicating the entrance to Washington Monument State Park. On July 4, 1827, construction began on South Mountain of what would be the first monument to George Washington. Upon completion, the monument stood thirty feet tall and would see service as a signal station during the Civil War. By the 1920s, however, neglect and the elements had left the monument in ruins. In 1934 it was deeded to the state of Maryland and completely rebuilt by the Civilian Conservation Corps. Shortly thereafter, a forty-acre park was developed that eventually expanded to over a hundred acres. In addition to the monument, the modern park has a Visitor Center with exhibits on the human and natural history of the area, picnic shelters, hiking trails (the Appalachian Trail, which runs along South Mountain, passes through the park), and a playground. There is a small entrance fee for the park.

Further Reading   Carman, "Maryland Campaign," chap. 8, 488–94, 505; Sears, *Landscape Turned Red*, 141–42; U.S. War Department, *War of the Rebellion*, vol. 19, ser. 1, pt. 1:247–48, 249–50, 1052–53.

STOP 4   Burkittsville

Directions   *Exit* the parking lot of the South Mountain Inn and *turn right* onto the OLD NATIONAL PIKE (U.S. ALTERNATE ROUTE 40). (If you did the Washington Monument excursion, *turn left* onto U.S. ALTERNATE ROUTE 40). *Proceed* 4.9 miles on U.S. AL-TERNATE ROUTE 40 to Middletown, and *turn right* onto MD 17 (BURKITTSVILLE ROAD). *Drive* 5.9 miles on MD 17 to E. MAIN STREET/W. MAIN STREET in Burkittsville. *Turn left* onto E. MAIN STREET, then *turn left* into the parking area for the St. Paul Lutheran Church and Union Cemetery. After parking your car, *walk* up the paved entrance to the cemetery and *turn left* where it forks. *Walk* about 75 yards to where another path enters from the right. *Stop* here and turn left to face South Mountain.

Major-General William B. Franklin. From a photograph. BLCW 2:377

STOP 4A   Franklin's Assignment, 5:00 A.M.–noon

Orientation   From where you are standing, South Mountain dominates
your line of sight. If you follow the ridgeline northward (to
the right), you may be able to see the high point with a tower on it known as Lamb's Knoll, which then slopes down to
Fox's Gap. Fox's Gap is approximately five miles north of
Crampton's Gap, which is in front of you. Approximately
a mile and a half south of Crampton's Gap is Brownsville
Pass. If you look just below and to the right of where you are
standing, you will see Burkitt's Run. The town of Burkittsville was here at the time of the battle and has not changed
much since 1862. If you turn around, you may be able to see
Catoctin Mountain behind you in the distance.

What Happened   After a copy of *Lee's* Special Orders No. 191 reached him on
September 13, which confirmed reports that *Lee* had divided
his forces between Harpers Ferry and the Boonsboro-Hager-
stown area, it took McClellan until approximately 6:00 P.M.
to develop his plan of operations for September 14. While
Burnside's two corps held the Confederate "main body" at
Boonsboro in place by attacking at Turner's Gap, McClellan intended for Maj. Gen. William B. Franklin's wing of the
army–composed of the two divisions of Franklin's VI Corps
plus Maj. Gen. Darius Couch's independent division–to attack Burkittsville and carry Crampton's Gap. This would
place Franklin's command in a position from which it could
drive a wedge between the Confederate forces at Harpers
Ferry and those at Boonsboro and Hagerstown.

In his orders, McClellan directed Franklin to put his command on the march at dawn. By daylight, Franklin had
roused the VI Corps from its bivouac at Buckeystown and
had them on the march toward Mountville Pass in Catoctin Mountain. Couch's division, however, began their march
six miles behind Franklin's corps at Licksville. After passing
through Mountville Pass, Franklin halted his march with
the intention of giving Couch a chance to catch up, even
though McClellan had explicitly directed Franklin not to let
Couch's movements delay his own. After waiting about an
hour at Jefferson in vain (Couch would not catch up until
after the fight for Crampton's Gap was over), Franklin ordered the VI Corps to resume the march to Burkittsville with
Col. Richard Rush's 6th Pennsylvania Cavalry–better known
as "Rush's Lancers" for the conspicuous red lances they carried–screening its advance.

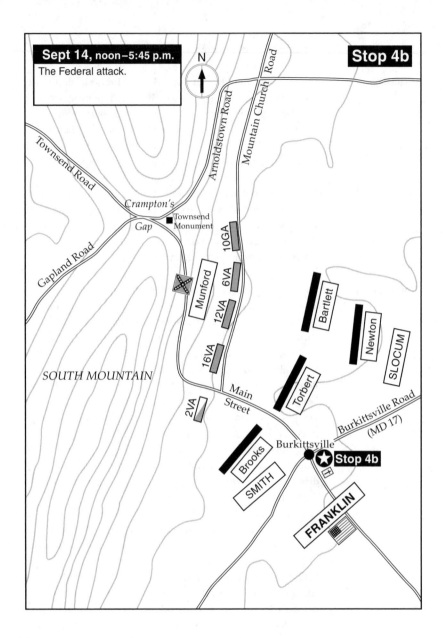

Sept 14, noon–5:45 p.m.
The Federal attack.

N

Stop 4b

Townsend Road

Arnoldstown Road

Mountain Church Road

Crampton's
Gap

Townsend
Monument

Gapland Road

10GA

6VA

Munford

12VA

Bartlett

Newton

SLOCUM

16VA

Torbert

SOUTH MOUNTAIN

Main
Street

2VA

Burkittsville Road
(MD 17)

Brooks

Burkittsville

Stop 4b

SMITH

FRANKLIN

STOP 4B   The Federal Attack, noon–5:45 P.M.

What Happened   Shortly after noon, Franklin reached Burkittsville and began
                     deploying his two divisions. Franklin had two passes through
                     South Mountain to concern himself with: Crampton's Gap
                     west of Burkittsville and Brownsville Pass about a mile and
                     a half south of Crampton's Gap. Col. Thomas *Munford* had
                     about 1,000 Confederates with which to defend Crampton's
                     Gap, of which 800 were infantry from Col. William *Parham's*

brigade from Maj. Gen. Richard H. *Anderson's* division. *Parham's* men were posted behind a stone fence that ran along the eastern edge of Mountain Church Road at the base of the gap, while about 200 dismounted cavalry defended their flanks and three pieces of artillery in Crampton's Gap supported the position. At Brownsville Pass, three regiments from Brig. Gen. Paul *Semmes's* brigade were posted, backed by four pieces of artillery. Back in Pleasant Valley on the other side of South Mountain, Brig. Gen. Howell *Cobb's* brigade of four regiments rested at Brownsville.

Franklin focused his attention on Crampton's Gap. After carrying out a careful reconnaissance that led him to conclude that he would face formidable resistance, Franklin deployed his command around Burkittsville. He posted Maj. Gen. Henry W. Slocum's division of three brigades north of the road that ran from Burkittsville to the gap (modern Main Street). Slocum then deployed his command astride Burkitt's Run, with Col. Alfred Torbert's brigade on the left, Col. Joseph J. Bartlett's on the right, and Brig. Gen. John Newton's in support. When Brig. Gen. William F. "Baldy" Smith's division reached the field, Franklin posted it to the left of Slocum. While Brig. Gen. Winfield Scott Hancock's brigade demonstrated against *Semmes's* position at Brownsville Pass, Brig. Gen. William T. Brooks's would support Slocum's left as he advanced against *Munford's* position.

Finally, at approximately 5:30 P.M., Franklin's assault began. Despite having overwhelming superiority in numbers, Franklin's men were briefly stymied by stiff resistance from *Munford's* well-positioned command. But then Franklin directed his commanders to extend their flanks to envelop the Confederate position, and the strength of the Union attack became too much for *Munford* to resist. Within fifteen minutes, Slocum's men had overwhelmed the Confederate defensive line at the base of the mountain and begun pushing forward into Crampton's Gap.

Analysis

Franklin made a commendable march to reach Burkittsville on the morning of September 14. However, his great caution in positioning his troops and reconnoitering the position in front of him cost him much of the benefit of his impressive effort that morning. The delay in launching and carrying out the attack on Crampton's Gap meant the Confederates would be able to get enough forces into the gap to put up a respectable fight. It also ensured Franklin would not be able to get through the gap until September 15, ruining McClellan's hopes that he could get a strong force into Pleasant Valley in time to rescue the garrison at Harpers Ferry.

Vignette
As the Federals advanced toward Mountain Church Road, Sgt. George *Barnard* of the 12th Virginia was shot in the leg. He later wrote, "I then lay as flat as possible and wondered how long the fight would last, thinking I would give the wealth of the Indies, if I had it, to be on the other side of the mountain. . . . The firing now seemed to have entirely ceased, when one of our men exclaimed, 'Look yonder, Boys! They are coming across the field!' immediately upon which the command ran down our line, 'Fix bayonets, men! Fix bayonets!!' followed in a few seconds by another, 'Fall back, men! Fall back!!' when there was a general grabbing up of guns, blankets, knapsacks, canteens & c., and a backward movement. My own condition just now can be better imagined than described. I could not get away, and just as our men were leaving, I heard someone say, 'See yonder, boys! Cavalry!!' I would be trampled to death by cavalry, or the enemy, coming up, would bayonet me! . . . In less than a minute, looking up I discovered the enemy's line—the veritable Yankees—the men all excitement, just over the fence, yelling and firing at our men, who were retreating up the hill. I now thought of danger from a new source. Our men up the hill would return the enemy's fire, and it would be a miracle if we escaped. The enemy now began to put their guns through the lower rails of the fence, the muzzles of which were only a foot or two from our heads. None, who ever experienced such an ordeal, can appreciate the desperation of our condition. If the enemy did not kill me, I thought our men would, whose bullets I expected every minute to pierce me, one of which I am satisfied did graze my hip."

Further Reading
Carman, "Maryland Campaign," chap. 7, 384–87, 398–412; Harsh, *Taken at the Flood*, 231–32, 275–81; Reese, *Sealed with Their Lives*, 13–21, 40–60, 66–108, 128–59.

STOP 5   Gathland State Park

Directions   Return to your car. *Turn right* onto E. MAIN STREET. *Proceed* 0.3
mile to MOUNTAIN CHURCH ROAD and *turn right*. *Drive* 1.0 mile
to ARNOLDSTOWN ROAD and *turn left*. *Proceed* 0.5 mile to the
parking area on the right for Gathland State Park–be alert,
for it comes up very suddenly. Exit your car, *cross* ARNOLD-
STOWN ROAD, and *walk* over to the War Correspondents Arch.
Pass under it to a point overlooking the cleared slope. Face
down the hill.

    En route. If you look to your right as you drive along
MOUNTAIN CHURCH ROAD, you will see remnants of the stone
wall behind which many of *Munford's* and *Parham's* men
were posted at the base of Crampton's Gap. The most conspicuous landmark in the gap itself is the War Correspondents Arch. George Alfred Townsend, better known by his
pen name "Gath," was one of the nation's leading war correspondents during the Civil War. His fascination with the
war combined with his interest in architecture and the natural beauty of the area to inspire him to purchase land and
erect a complex of buildings in Crampton's Gap. The most
conspicuous of his creations was the memorial he built to
his fellow war correspondents. Dedicated in October 1896,
it has tablets upon which the names of 157 correspondents
and artists are inscribed. In 1949 "Gathland" was deeded to
the state of Maryland for use as a state park. A small museum is open to the public from April through September.

Orientation   You are standing in Crampton's Gap facing in the direction
of Burkittsville and the Middletown Valley. Catoctin Moun-
tain, on the other side of the Middletown Valley, is about
ten miles from where you are standing. The road to the left
and rear that you just crossed over from the parking lot
is the ARNOLDSTOWN ROAD. To your right is GAPLAND ROAD,
which continues down the mountain to Burkittsville. Directly below you is what was known in 1862 as Whipp's Ravine.
Brownsville Pass is approximately a mile and a half to the
south (your right) from where you are now standing. Fox's
Gap is about five miles to the north (your left) and Turner's
Gap is a mile beyond that.

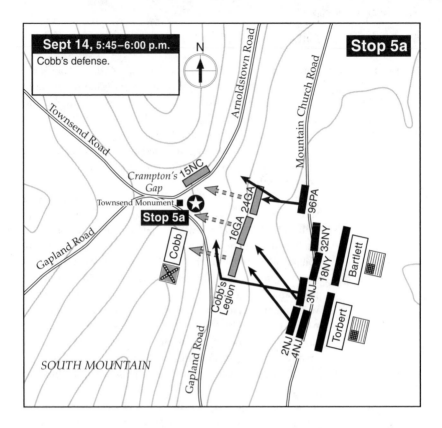

STOP 5A   *Cobb's* Defense, 5:45–6:00 P.M.

What Happened   As *Munford's* and *Parham's* position at the eastern base of Crampton's Gap began to give way, a brigade of Georgia and North Carolina troops commanded by Brig. Gen. Howell *Cobb* arrived in the gap. Although senior in rank, *Cobb* delegated the placement of his troops to *Munford* upon arriving on the scene. *Munford* directed the lead regiment of *Cobb's* command, the 15th North Carolina, to take up a position behind a stone wall that lined the Arnoldstown Road. *Munford* then ordered two Georgia regiments, along with a battalion of infantry commanded by Lt. Col. Jefferson *Lamar* known as *Cobb's* Legion to cross the Arnoldstown and Gapland roads and form a line about halfway down the eastern slope of the mountain astride Whipp's Ravine.

After driving the last of *Munford's* men from their position at the base of the gap, Col. Torbert's and Col. Bartlett's brigades continued their advance up the slope of South Mountain just as *Cobb's* men had formed into line. On the Union right, Bartlett's brigade, with Col. Henry L. Cake's 96th Pennsylvania spearheading the assault, quickly overwhelmed the Confederate defenders and pushed up Whipp's Ravine into Crampton's Gap. Meanwhile, Col. Henry W. Brown's 3rd New Jersey from Torbert's command passed around the open Confederate right flank to reach Gapland Road, which ran behind *Lamar's* position. While Brown attacked *Lamar's* position from the rear, the rest of the New Jersey brigade attacked its front and flank. *Cobb's* Legion was decimated and, after *Lamar* was killed, began retreating through Crampton's Gap toward Pleasant Valley.

Vignette

As his command surged toward *Cobb's* line in Whipp's Ravine, Colonel Bartlett later wrote "The 18th N.Y. and the 32nd N.Y. were nearly out of ammunition, but they, together with the 96th Pa., on their right, were directed in front of this newly-developed strength of the enemy, and if they now faltered the victory would be lost. Maj. [John C.] Meginnis, of the 18th, said to me: 'Colonel, my men are out of cartridges.' I replied: 'Never mind, Major; push on; we have got 'em on the run. The regiments [on] each side of you have got ammunition, and are using it.' The gallan[t] Major, smilingly, encouraged his men and pushed vigorously onward. The 32nd N.Y. was being cheered on by the brave Col. [Roderick N.] Matheson, as my horse struggled along the steep side in rear of his regiment. A moment after I had spoken an encouraging word of praise to him, he fell, wounded; but smiling still, he waved on his gallant men, and shouted: 'You've got 'em boys; push on.' The enemy no longer had a stone wall in front of them, and our fire was telling well upon their ranks, as we could see by the numbers of killed and wounded which we passed over. . . . The rout was complete; they did not stop to return our fire but fled to the summit. There but a slight and unorganized resistance was offered, which ceased entirely when our regiments emerged from the woods."

STOP 5B   Last Stand at Crampton's Gap, 6:00–7:00 P.M.

Directions   *Turn around* and *walk* back under the arch to the stone monument to the New Jersey Brigade. Face toward the picnic
shelter. In 1862 the section of Gathland State Park in front
of you was an open field belonging to a farmer by the name
of George W. Padgett and was bordered to the west (the direction in which you are now facing) by a stone wall.

What Happened   After overwhelming *Cobb's* position, Torbert's and Bartlett's
men converged on the intersection of the Arnoldstown and
Gapland roads directly in front of you. *Cobb* responded by
rallying what troops he could behind the stone wall on the
western edge of the gap. To bolster his defense, *Cobb* posted
in the intersection the two guns from the Troup Light Artillery, commanded by Lt. Henry *Jennings*, that had just arrived from Pleasant Valley. The twelve pounder, "Jennie,"
was pointed down the Arnoldstown Road, while the six
pounder, "Sallie Craig," was aimed to fire down Gapland
Road. When the Union lines reached a point about 50 yards
from the intersection, *Jennings's* guns opened fire with canister. The shock of the Confederate fire brought the Union advance to a halt long enough for each of *Jennings's* guns to fire
five rounds. *Jennings* was unable, however, to do anything
about the 4th New Jersey, which left Gapland Road and
moved to the high ground to your left to take the Confederate artillery in flank. Thus, as the Federals in his front recovered from the initial shock of his fire and began to renew
their advance, *Jennings* gave the order to withdraw. Without
artillery, *Cobb* recognized his fall-back position behind the
stone wall could not be held and ordered a general retreat
to Pleasant Valley. The gunners of the Troup Light Artillery
managed to carry away the "Sallie Craig" but were compelled to leave the "Jennie" behind when its carriage broke.
Franklin's victory came at a cost of 113 killed, 418 wounded,
and 2 missing, for a total of 533 casualties. The 602 prisoners captured by Franklin's men made up the bulk of Confederate losses at Crampton's Gap, which totaled 962, including 70 killed and 289 wounded.

STOP 5C   Franklin Moves into Pleasant Valley, September 15, 1862

What Happened   By the time Franklin learned his men had driven the Confederates from their defensive positions and seized control
of Crampton's Gap, it was already dark. Consequently, he
waited until the next morning to carry out the second part
of his instructions from McClellan, to move into Pleasant
Valley and relieve Harpers Ferry. Around 7:00 A.M. on September 15, Franklin personally rode up to Crampton's Gap
and reached a point from where he could look into Pleasant
Valley. To the south, he saw that Maj. Gen. Lafayette *McLaws*
had managed to patch together a Confederate battle line
across the valley floor. As Franklin contemplated the situation, the sound of artillery fire from Harpers Ferry was audible from his position, indicating that the window of opportunity for saving the garrison was closing. *McLaws* had
at most 5,000 men, and not all of them deployed, but they
were in a strong position that concealed his true strength.
Franklin, who with the arrival of Couch's division during
the night had over 15,000 men, deduced that he faced a superior force that barred his way to Harpers Ferry. Nonetheless, he ordered Smith's and Couch's divisions to move into
the valley and began to carefully reconnoiter *McLaws's* position. As he was doing this, the sound of gunfire from Harpers Ferry suddenly stopped and was replaced by cheering on
the Confederate side of the field, indicating that Franklin
had failed in his assignment. Harpers Ferry had fallen. Later
in the day, *McLaws* withdrew down Pleasant Valley in line
with *Lee's* orders to join the rest of the Army of Northern
Virginia at Sharpsburg. Franklin remained in Pleasant Valley until the morning of September 17, when, in line with
orders McClellan issued the previous evening, he directed
Slocum's and Smith's divisions to march to Keedysville to
join the rest of the army for the battle of Antietam.

Vignette   Despite his anxiety over the size of *McLaws's* force, Franklin decided at midmorning to advance skirmishers toward
the Confederate position. They were, one Confederate later
recalled, "within two hundred yards of our lines when the
roar of Jackson's guns suddenly ceased. There followed a few
moments of painful suspense. The enemy halted, evidently
arrested by the significant quiet. Then from away down the
valley came rolling nearer and nearer, as the news reached
the troops, ringing cheers and we knew the Ferry had surrendered. . . . A skirmisher of the enemy, as our cheers rang
out in response, sprang up on a stone wall and called over to
us, 'What the hell are you fellows cheering for?' We shouted

back, 'Because Harpers Ferry is gone up, G— d— you.' 'I thought that was it,' shouted the fellow as he got down off the wall."

Further Reading   Carman, "Maryland Campaign," chap. 7, 412–22, 567–80; Franklin, "Notes on Crampton's Gap and Antietam," 2:596; Harsh, *Taken at the Flood*, 281–82; Reese, *Sealed with Their Lives*, 126–28, 140–42, 159–66; Sears, *Landscape Turned Red*, 148–49, 154–56.

To return to the Antietam National Battlefield Visitor Center: Return to your car. *Turn right* out of the parking area and *drive* to the intersection of ARNOLDSTOWN ROAD and GAPLAND ROAD. *Turn right* and *proceed* 0.9 mile down GAPLAND ROAD to MD 67 (ROHRERSVILLE ROAD). *Turn right* onto MD 67 and *drive* 5.0 miles to the intersection with MT. CARMEL CHURCH ROAD/ RENO MONUMENT ROAD. *Turn left* onto MT. CARMEL CHURCH ROAD and *proceed* to the intersection with DOGSTREET ROAD. *Turn right* onto DOGSTREET ROAD and *drive* 2.5 miles to S. MAIN STREET (MD 845) in Keedysville. *Turn left* and *proceed* 0.3 mile to the intersection with MD 34. *Turn left* onto MD 34 and *drive* 2.7 miles to the intersection with S. CHURCH/N. CHURCH STREET (MD 65). *Turn right* onto N. CHURCH STREET and *travel* 0.8 mile to DUNKER CHURCH ROAD. *Turn right* onto DUNKER CHURCH ROAD and *enter* the parking area.

To reach the first stop for the Harpers Ferry tour from Gathland State Park: *Turn right* out of the parking lot and *drive* to the intersection of the ARNOLDSTOWN ROAD and GAPLAND ROAD. *Turn right* and *proceed* 0.9 mile down GAPLAND ROAD to MD 67 (ROHRERSVILLE ROAD). *Turn left* onto MD 67 and *proceed* 4.8 miles to U.S. 340 WEST. *Drive* 4.2 miles on U.S. 340 WEST to the traffic light. At the light, *turn left* and *proceed* to the parking area for the Visitor Center for Harpers Ferry National Historical Park on Cavalier Heights.

Harpers Ferry, from the
Maryland side. BLCW 1:120

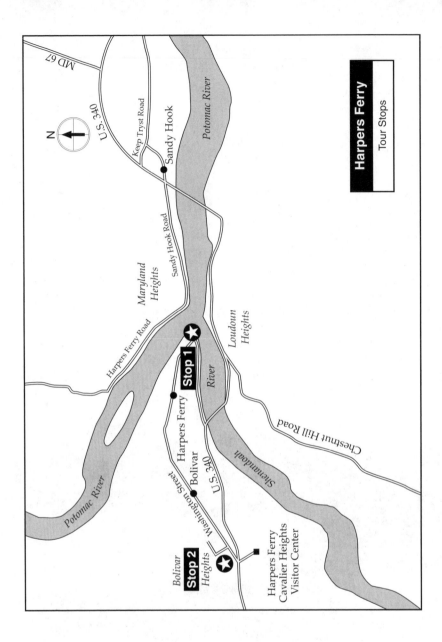

Harpers Ferry

Tour Stops

Overview of the Siege of Harpers Ferry, September 13–15, 1862

After four relatively uneventful days in the vicinity of Frederick, Maryland, Gen. Robert E. *Lee* once again had his Army of Northern Virginia on the march on September 10, 1862. The inability of Confederate quartermasters to procure sufficient supplies from the Unionist population of western Maryland and the insecurity of the line running from Frederick to Richmond via Manassas Junction led *Lee* to the conclusion that he had to depend principally on a line of communications through the Shenandoah Valley. Yet the presence of Union garrisons in Virginia (now West Virginia) at Martinsburg and Harpers Ferry made the security of such a supply line uncertain. To eliminate this problem, on September 9 *Lee* developed a plan for the elimination of these garrisons that was spelled out in Special Orders No. 191.

Lee directed six divisions to eliminate the menace posed by the Martinsburg and Harpers Ferry garrisons. Maj. Gen. Thomas J. "Stonewall" *Jackson* would lead Brig. Gen. Alexander *Lawton's*, Maj. Gen. Ambrose P. *Hill's*, and Brig. Gen. John R. *Jones's* divisions across the Potomac near Sharpsburg, put the garrison at Martinsburg to flight, and approach Harpers Ferry from the north and west. Maj. Gen. Lafayette *McLaws* was to take his and Maj. Gen. Richard H. *Anderson's* divisions, ascend Elk Ridge, and take possession of Maryland Heights at its southern end. Brig. Gen. John *Walker's* division would cross the Potomac below Harpers Ferry and seize Loudoun Heights. With *Jackson* to the west, *McLaws* on Maryland Heights, and *Walker* on Loudoun Heights, the Union garrison at Harpers Ferry would be doomed. In part because he expected the Union garrisons would flee rather than risk certain capture, *Lee* anticipated the entire operation would be over in only three days—well before any serious threat could materialize from the direction of Washington.

Responsibility for holding Martinsburg and Harpers Ferry rested upon the shoulders of Brig. Gen. Julius White and Col. Dixon Miles, respectively. In all, White and Miles had about 14,000 men, who became the subject of a bitter dispute between Army of the Potomac commander Maj. Gen. George B. McClellan and Union general in chief, Henry W. Halleck. McClellan suggested that White and Miles abandon their positions, reasoning that Harpers Ferry and Martinsburg could not be defended, but Halleck rejected his advice. The garrisons, he directed, would remain where they were until McClellan could save them.

Meanwhile, problems developed in the implementation

of *Lee's* plan. After narrowly escaping capture by a Federal cavalry patrol at Boonsboro on September 10, *Jackson* decided to add several miles to his march by crossing the Potomac at Williamsport instead of near Sharpsburg. This enabled the Federals at Martinsburg to successfully escape to Harpers Ferry, and when White arrived at Harpers Ferry, he deferred command to Miles, who resolved to obey orders from Washington to hold their position. Making matters worse for the Confederates, not until September 13, one day after the deadline for completion of the operation laid out in Special Orders No. 191, would *Jackson's*, *McLaws's*, and *Walker's* commands complete the task of surrounding Harpers Ferry and gaining control of the high ground on Maryland Heights and Loudoun Heights.

During the afternoon of September 14, Confederate artillery on Schoolhouse Ridge, Maryland Heights, and Loudoun Heights opened fire on Harpers Ferry. When this failed to bring about Miles's surrender, *Jackson* directed *Hill's* division to work around the left of the main Federal position on Bolivar Heights. Jackson then shifted ten guns over to a position on Loudoun Heights, from which they could enfilade Bolivar Heights. Both moves were successfully executed, and when the morning mist lifted over Harpers Ferry on September 15, *Jackson* ordered his artillery to resume their bombardment. With no sign that McClellan would soon be arriving to relieve him, Miles concluded his situation was hopeless. Around 8:00 A.M., white flags began to appear on the Federal side of the lines. After a Confederate shell mortally wounded Miles in the leg, command of the garrison passed to White, who surrendered it unconditionally.

Harpers Ferry National Historical Park Visitor Center

Directions

From the Antietam National Battlefield Visitor Center parking lot, *turn left* onto DUNKER CHURCH ROAD and *proceed* to MD 65. *Turn left* onto MD 65 and *proceed* 0.8 mile (along the way MD 65 becomes N. CHURCH STREET) to the intersection with E. MAIN STREET (MD 34). *Turn right* at the intersection onto E. MAIN STREET (MD 34), which turns into W. MAIN STREET and becomes SHEPHERDSTOWN PIKE as you *proceed* through and beyond Sharpsburg. *Drive* 3.8 miles on MD 34, which becomes WV 480 when you cross the Potomac, to E. GERMAN STREET and *turn left*. *Drive* 0.2 mile through downtown Shepherdstown on E. GERMAN STREET and *turn right* onto PRINCESS STREET. After *driving* 0.1 mile, *turn left* onto E. WASHINGTON STREET (WV 230) and *proceed* 1.9 miles to where WV 230 forks (en route, WV 230 becomes SHEPHERDSTOWN PIKE). Take the *left fork* to stay on SHEPHERDSTOWN PIKE and *drive* 6.5 miles to U.S. 340. *Turn left* onto U.S. 340 and *proceed* 1.6 miles to the traffic light. At the light *turn right* and *proceed* to the parking area for the Harpers Ferry National Historical Park Visitor Center on Cavalier Heights.

Orientation

The Visitor Center on Cavalier Heights is the place to begin your visit to Harpers Ferry. It contains a small bookstore (a larger one is in the town itself) as well as exhibits on the town and its history. It is also the place to pay your entrance fee and to be picked up by the shuttle bus that will take you to the historic town. It is possible to drive into Harpers Ferry, but it is highly recommended that you take the shuttle, as parking in the town is very limited in order to preserve its historic flavor. There is much to see and do in Harpers Ferry, and a visit to the town can easily consume an entire day. In addition to its significant role in the Civil War in general, and in the 1862 Maryland campaign in particular—not to mention its natural beauty—Harpers Ferry contains sites of significance in the history of the John Brown Raid, the Lewis and Clark Expedition, early American industrialization, the nineteenth-century "transportation revolution," and the African American experience of the nineteenth and twentieth centuries.

STOP 1   Harpers Ferry

Directions   *Board* the shuttle that takes you from the Visitor Center on
Cavalier Heights to the Lower Town section of Harpers Fer-
ry. Upon disembarking from the shuttle, *walk* east along
SHENANDOAH STREET through the town until it terminates
at its intersection with POTOMAC STREET. *Turn right* and *walk*
along the gravel path, passing under a railroad bridge, to a
point overlooking the confluence of the Shenandoah and
Potomac rivers. *Turn around* and face toward the town.

En route. You will pass a brick structure known as John
Brown's Fort, located to your right as you step off the pavement onto the gravel path. It was in this building that
Brown and his raiders made their last stand in October
1859, before surrendering to a force of soldiers and marines
commanded by then Lt. Col. Robert E. *Lee*. In 1859 this building was actually located about 70 yards west of its current
location on the high ground on the other side of the gravel
path. The original location is indicated by a stone obelisk.

Orientation   As you face the town, you are standing at "The Point" where
the Shenandoah River on your left flows into the Potomac
River on your right. If you look to your right across the Potomac River, you will see Maryland Heights, the southern
end of Elk Ridge. Pleasant Valley is east of Elk Ridge, while
Sharpsburg and the Antietam battlefield are west of it. To
your left, on the other side of the Shenandoah River, is Loudoun Heights. As you look toward Harpers Ferry, you will
see Camp Hill overlooking the town. Further beyond Camp
Hill is another high ridge known as Bolivar Heights that is
not visible to you from this point.

STOP 1A Strategic Point and Deathtrap

What Happened From this vantage point, it is easy to understand why Thomas Jefferson once proclaimed the area around Harpers Ferry offered "one of the most stupendous scenes in nature . . . worth a voyage across the Atlantic." It was also on the banks of the river on the Virginia (West Virginia after June 1863) side of the Potomac River that one of the first armories established by the United States government for the production of firearms was built. (It was located on the other side of the railway bridge, under which you just passed.) The 1859 raid on the armory by abolitionist John Brown was a major catalyst in the growth of sectional tensions that produced the Civil War.

In addition to being at the confluence of the Potomac and Shenandoah rivers, Harpers Ferry was in 1862 the location of the junction connecting the Winchester and Potomac Railroad with the Baltimore and Ohio Railroad. The Baltimore and Ohio linked Baltimore and Washington with the Ohio River valley. It crossed the Potomac from Maryland to Harpers Ferry, and then ran along the Potomac north and west toward Martinsburg—as does the modern railroad. From its junction with the Baltimore and Ohio, the Winchester and Potomac ran south into the Shenandoah Valley between the Blue Ridge and the Allegheny Mountains, of which Harpers Ferry is the northeastern point. Also running along the Maryland side of the Potomac River in 1862 was the Chesapeake and Ohio Canal, which connected Washington with western Maryland. The fact that Harpers Ferry was an important transportation hub, located at the head of a rich agricultural area that was vital to the Confederate war effort, made it a critical strategic point for both the Union and Confederacy. The topography, however, made Harpers Ferry a potential deathtrap. Without possession of the heights dominating the town—Maryland Heights especially—any force attempting to hold the low-lying town would find its position untenable. Indeed, Stonewall *Jackson* is said to have once remarked that he would rather attempt to capture the town forty times than try to defend it once.

Harpers Ferry had already experienced more than its fair share of wartime hardship by September 1862. In April 1861 the town was evacuated by U.S. forces and seized by Virginia militia, but not before Federal authorities set fire to the armory. The Confederates evacuated the town a few months later but not before shipping the equipment in the armory south, burning most of the rest of the town's factories, and destroying the Baltimore and Ohio railroad bridge.

The Federals then reoccupied the town and used it as a base for forces operating in the Shenandoah Valley and guarding the Baltimore and Ohio. Of the approximately 3,000 people who lived in Harpers Ferry at the beginning of the war, only about 100 families remained in September 1862.

Feeling the enemy. From a war-time sketch. BLCW 3:224

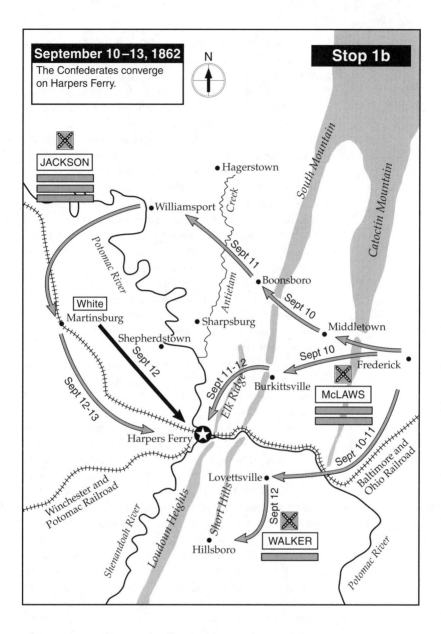

September 10–13, 1862
The Confederates converge on Harpers Ferry.

N

Stop 1b

JACKSON

Hagerstown

South Mountain

Catoctin Mountain

Williamsport

Creek

Potomac River

Sept 11

Boonsboro

Antietam

Sept 10

White
Martinsburg

Sharpsburg

Middletown

Shepherdstown

Sept 10

Frederick

Sept 12

Sept 11-12

Elk Ridge

Burkittsville

McLAWS

Sept 12-13

Harpers Ferry

Sept 10-11

Baltimore and Ohio Railroad

Winchester and Potomac Railroad

Lovettsville

Sept 12

Shenandoah River

Loudoun Heights

Short Hills

Hillsboro

WALKER

Potomac River

STOP 1B   The Confederates Converge on Harpers Ferry,
                 September 10–13, 1862

What Happened   On September 9 General *Lee* issued orders for the operation
                 to clear the Union garrisons at Martinsburg and Harpers
                 Ferry from the Shenandoah Valley; early the next morning
                 the three columns that were to execute it were in motion.
                 The first of these, Brig. Gen. John *Walker's* division, was to
                 cross the Potomac at Point of Rocks and advance from there

to Loudoun Heights. The second, which consisted of Maj. Gen. Lafayette *McLaws's* and Maj. Gen. Richard H. *Anderson's* divisions and which were to be commanded by the former, was to push through Catoctin Mountain and South Mountain into Pleasant Valley, ascend Elk Ridge, and seize Maryland Heights. The final column, three divisions commanded by *Jackson*, was to march through the mountains into the Cumberland Valley and cross the Potomac near Sharpsburg. This would interpose *Jackson's* forces between Martinsburg and Harpers Ferry. *Lee* presumed that the Union garrisons in both towns—the former due to a dramatic disadvantage in numbers, the latter due to the nature of the terrain—would flee rather than let themselves be trapped in untenable positions. Thus, he anticipated his three columns would secure their objectives by the morning of September 12.

As he passed through Frederick, *Jackson* loudly asked one of his engineers to make a map of the region around Chambersburg, Pennsylvania, in an attempt to mislead the citizens of Frederick regarding his intentions. Moving west along the National Pike, *Jackson* then led his three divisions over Catoctin Mountain and through the Middletown Valley to South Mountain at Turner's Gap. By noon his approximately 14,000 men had gone into bivouac on either side of South Mountain, with one division near Boonsboro and the rest just east of Turner's Gap. Shortly thereafter, a Union cavalry force suddenly appeared south of Boonsboro and charged into the town. At the time, *Jackson* was approaching the town on foot, and only the timely warning of two staff officers enabled him to escape capture. As *Jackson* rode off to safety, the Black Horse Troop compelled the Yankee cavalry to retreat back toward Sharpsburg. *Jackson's* men, however, would march no further on September 10, and the incident at Boonsboro undoubtedly contributed to *Jackson's* decision to march to Williamsport the next day and cross the Potomac there, a decision that added eleven miles to his march and left the road open for the garrison at Martinsburg to escape to Harpers Ferry.

After following *Jackson's* men over Catoctin Mountain, *McLaws's* 8,000-man force turned south at Middletown and by the end of the day its lead elements had reached Burkittsville. For his part, *Walker* marched his 4,000 men to Point of Rocks on September 10 and crossed the Potomac at that point that night. The following day, however, neither *McLaws's* nor *Walker's* commands made much progress, as signs that the enemy was still at Harpers Ferry and uncertainty about what lay between them and the town inspired caution in both commanders. On September 11 *Jackson's* command crossed the Potomac at Williamsport and reached a position from which it could block any attempt by the Martinsburg garrison to escape to the west. Despite an impressive march of over twenty miles by *Jackson's* men, the prospects for completing the operation to clear the Federals from Martinsburg and Harpers Ferry in line with the timetable laid out in *Lee's* orders were rapidly declining. By the morning of September 12, Martinsburg at least was free of Federal troops, as Brig. Gen. Julius White decided to abandon the town upon learning of *Jackson's* approach and marched his command to Harpers Ferry.

McLaws's command was also closing on Harpers Ferry. He pushed brigades commanded by Brig. Gen. Joseph *Kershaw* and Brig. Gen. William *Barksdale* to Solomon's Gap in Elk Ridge, which was four miles north of where the ridge terminated at the Potomac River. The rest of his command extended to the east across Pleasant Valley to South Mountain to cover the Federal escape route in that direction. From Solomon's Gap, *Kershaw* and *Barksdale* pushed south along Elk Ridge and, after a late afternoon skirmish with Federal troops posted about a mile north of Maryland Heights, *Kershaw* reorganized his lines in preparation for an attack on the morning of the thirteenth. For his part, *Walker* made a fairly easy thirteen-mile march on September 12 to Hillsboro. It was not a bad march performance; however, *Walker*, like the rest of the forces detached for the Harpers Ferry operation, had fallen behind the timetable laid out in Special Orders No. 191.

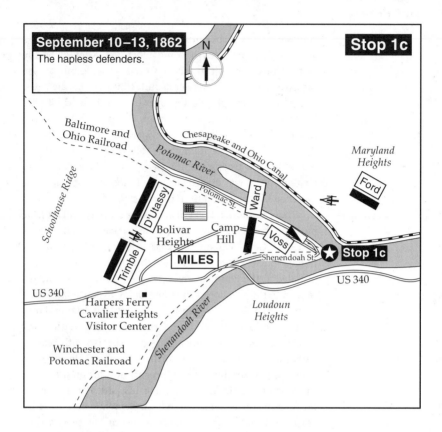

Baltimore and Ohio Railroad

Chesapeake and Ohio Canal

Potomac River

Maryland Heights

Schoolhouse Ridge

Potomac St.

D'Utassy

Bolivar Heights

Camp Hill

Ward

Voss

Ford

MILES

Shenendoah St.

Stop 1c

Trimble

US 340

US 340

Harpers Ferry Cavalier Heights Visitor Center

Shenandoah River

Loudoun Heights

Winchester and Potomac Railroad

STOP 1C   The Hapless Defenders, September 10–13, 1862

What Happened   When *Lee* crossed the Potomac, Union general in chief Henry Halleck mandated that Harpers Ferry be held at all costs. Unfortunately, the town was not in good hands. The commander of the garrison, Col. Dixon Miles, was under a cloud due to accusations that he had been drunk at First Manassas. Despite possessing forty years' experience in the regular army, Miles had been relegated to command the forces defending the Baltimore and Ohio in March 1862 while younger men received more prestigious commands. Harpers Ferry's backwater status was further impressed upon its commander in the late summer of 1862 when the War Department decided to send thousands of new recruits, raised under a July call for 300,000 troops, there on the assumption it was far from any danger. Consequently, the bulk of Miles's regiments in September 1862 had been in the service less than a year, many barely a month. Thus, Miles saw to it that each of his four brigades had at least one veteran regiment. Miles had made no effort, though, to fortify either Bolivar Heights or Maryland Heights during the six months he had been at Harpers Ferry, despite directions from his superiors to do so.

In all, Miles had approximately 14,000 men after the arrival of White's command on the afternoon of September 12. Although he outranked Miles, White—an Illinois lawyer friend of President Lincoln and a political appointee—immediately placed himself and his troops under Miles's command. When the Confederates arrived, Miles had over half of his command on Bolivar Heights with Col. Frederick D'Utassy's 1st Brigade holding the Union right and Col. William Trimble's 2nd Brigade extending the line to the left across Charlestown Road, but not all the way to the Shenandoah River. Miles placed Col. William Ward's 4th Brigade, along with his heavy artillery on Camp Hill, a towering eminence between Bolivar Heights and Harpers Ferry. Miles posted his 3rd Brigade, commanded by Col. Thomas H. Ford, on Maryland Heights, supported by the Naval Battery with three powerful guns located one-third of the way up the slope. Believing that artillery on Maryland Heights and Camp Hill would be sufficient to cover Loudoun Heights and that the terrain was too rugged for the Confederates to place artillery up there anyway, Miles left that piece of terrain unoccupied.

Further Reading   Carman, "Maryland Campaign," chap. 6, 285–324; Frye, "Drama Between the Rivers," 14–34; Harsh, *Taken at the Flood*, 145–49, 154–66, 168–80, 182–83, 186–87, 198–205; Sears, *Landscape Turned Red*, 89–95, 121–24, 143–45, 151–54; U.S. War Department, *War of the Rebellion*, vol. 19, ser. 1, pt. 1:951–55.

Saving a gun. BLCW 4:293

STOP 2   Bolivar Heights

Directions   *Return* to the Visitor Center on Cavalier Heights. Then, return to your car, *exit* the parking lot, and *proceed* to the traffic light. *Drive* through the intersection onto WASHINGTON STREET. *Follow* WASHINGTON STREET as it bends to the right. Immediately *on your left*, you will see the entrance to Bolivar Heights battlefield. *Turn left* here and *proceed* to the parking area at the top of the hill. Exit your car and *enter* the trail, where you will see a National Park Service marker labeled "Historic Heights." Note the break in the woods to your right where the cannon is located just as you leave the parking lot. Schoolhouse Ridge is the cleared ridge on the other side of the valley about a mile from your position on Bolivar Heights. From the "Historic Heights" marker, *follow* the trail through the point where it intersects with another trail and *continue* about 100 yards beyond the intersection to the National Park Service marker "The First Year of the War." Face east toward the town and Maryland Heights.

A Confederate of 1862. BLCW 2:282

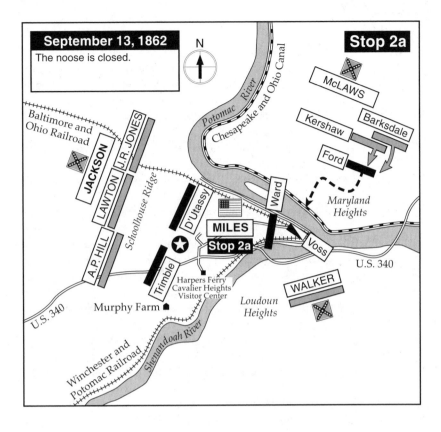

N

STOP 2A

The Noose Is Closed, September 13, 1862

Orientation

From this point, the water gap where the Potomac and Shenandoah rivers converge at Harpers Ferry should be clear in the distance. The high ground to your left front is Maryland Heights on the other side of the Potomac; to your right front on the other side of the Shenandoah River is Loudoun Heights. The high ground between you and the water gap with the large brick building on it is Camp Hill. If you look to your right you will see a cleared area on the other side of the highway. That is the Murphy farm.

What Happened

Jackson's three divisions began their march from Martinsburg early on September 13 and reached the Harpers Ferry–Charlestown Pike at midmorning. They then turned east and marched to Schoolhouse Ridge, located just west of Miles's main line on Bolivar Heights. *Walker's* command began its march that day around 6:30 A.M. Shortly after reaching the base of Loudoun Heights around 10:00 A.M., *Walker* learned *Jackson* wanted him to direct his command to ascend Loudoun Heights and participate in a siege of Harpers Ferry.

Walker and two of his regiments then made a tough climb to reach the top of Loudoun Heights by nightfall.

Miles entrusted the defense of Maryland Heights to Ford's brigade, which threw up two lines of abatis (an obstacle formed by tree branches laid on the ground, pointed in the direction from which an enemy advance was expected) and a line of breastworks on the crest of Elk Ridge about one mile north of its southern end at Maryland Heights. About the same time *Walker* and *Jackson* began their march on September 13, *Kershaw's* brigade advanced south along the crest of Elk Ridge toward the Federal breastworks. There, the Federals put up a tough fight, and around 11:00 A.M., *Kershaw* asked *Barksdale* to attempt to reach a position from which he could attack the Union right flank. Before *Barksdale* could do this, however, the Federals suddenly began retreating. The regiment at the center of Ford's line, the newly organized 126th New York, had fallen apart after a Confederate bullet ripped through the cheek of their commander, and their panic had quickly infected the rest of the Union line.

At that moment, Miles was en route to Ford's headquarters near the Naval Battery. Together, the two officers managed to stabilize the situation, but Ford informed Miles he did not believe he could maintain his position on Maryland Heights. Miles insisted, "You *can* and you *must*." But before returning to Harpers Ferry, Miles also advised Ford that he could exercise discretion on this and that if a retreat from Maryland Heights proved necessary, he must spike the guns to deny them to the enemy. Around 3:00 P.M., Ford decided that he had in fact had enough, and a half hour later, Miles was on Bolivar Heights when a staff officer called his attention to Maryland Heights. To his shock and amazement, Miles saw Ford's men retreating to Harpers Ferry. "God Almighty!" he cried out. "They are coming down! Hell and damnation!"

McLaws immediately pushed forward to claim possession of Maryland Heights, closing the noose around Harpers Ferry. Just how much effort and time it would take to bring about the surrender of the garrison was unclear when darkness fell on September 13, however. And time had become a precious commodity. *Jackson* was well aware that the Harpers Ferry operation was over a day behind the deadline set in Special Orders No. 191. More importantly, although *Jackson* did not know it, at nightfall on September 13 elements from McClellan's army of 75,000 were in the Middletown Valley and pressing against South Mountain.

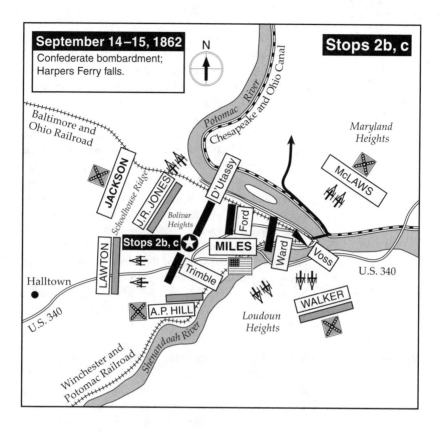

STOP 2B   Confederate Bombardment, September 14–15, 1862

What Happened   As night fell on September 13, Miles instructed Capt. Charles
H. Russell to make an effort to pass through the enemy lines
and reach McClellan, whom he was to advise that Harpers Ferry could hold out for forty-eight more hours, "but if he was
not relieved in that time he would have to surrender." Russell managed to reach McClellan's headquarters near Frederick around 9:00 A.M. on September 14 and was informed that
an entire corps was at that moment under orders to march to
and push through Crampton's Gap to relieve Harpers Ferry.
Unfortunately, the messengers McClellan dispatched to Harpers Ferry with this information never reached Miles.

Meanwhile, the Confederates prepared to bombard Harpers Ferry. By early afternoon on September 14, *McLaws* and
Walker had dragged artillery to the top of Maryland and Loudoun Heights, while *Jackson* finished posting his artillery on
Schoolhouse Ridge. Then, around 2:00 P.M., *Walker* opened
fire. *Jackson's* guns, then *McLaws's*, joined in, and for about
four and a half hours until dark, a storm of shot and shell
pounded the garrison at Harpers Ferry.

Although a horrible experience for the Federals, the bombardment was not sufficient to persuade Miles that it was time to surrender. Something more needed to be done—and fast, as Union forces had seized Crampton's Gap, creating the possibility that Maryland Heights might become a trap for *McLaws's* command. A frontal assault on Bolivar Heights was out of the question, for it would involve crossing the open, mile-wide valley that separated Schoolhouse Ridge from Bolivar Heights. Consequently, *Jackson* ordered Maj. Gen. Ambrose P. *Hill* to maneuver his division around the southern end of Bolivar Heights. Encountering minimal resistance, *Hill* managed to successfully negotiate the steep ravines along the banks of the Shenandoah River and reach a position with its left at the Murphy farm, which was behind the left flank and rear of the Union position on Bolivar Heights. *Jackson* also shifted ten pieces of artillery from Schoolhouse Ridge to a position on Loudoun Heights, where they could enfilade Bolivar Heights. With these two maneuvers, Harpers Ferry was doomed.

Vignette

When the Confederate bombardment opened, an officer in the 125th New York later wrote, "Our regiment was napping and lounging around . . . when suddenly . . . a shell came whizzing into our midst—we saw our helplessness; we were at their mercy; to remain was to be slaughtered, so we ran like hounds to get under the cover of a hillside. . . . I tell you, it is dreadful to be a mark for artillery, bad enough for any but especially for raw troops; it demoralizes them—it rouses one's courage to be able to fight in return, but to sit still and calmly be cut in two is too much to ask."

Confederate types of
1862. BLCW 1:548

STOP 2C   Harpers Ferry Falls, September 14–15, 1862

What Happened   The Confederates were not the only ones on the move late on September 14. Around 7:00 P.M., Col. Benjamin F. "Grimes" Davis presented a plan to Miles for a breakout by the cavalry. Miles reluctantly consented to Davis's proposal to cross the Potomac River on a pontoon bridge and then ride north and west in the direction of Sharpsburg and Hagerstown. The expedition was placed under the command of Col. Arno Voss. Under cover of darkness, Voss's 1,400 men successfully crossed the Potomac and rode along the base of Maryland Heights to the road to Sharpsburg. Just before dawn on September 15, they reached the road between Williamsport and Hagerstown just as a Confederate wagon train was moving toward them. They quickly seized the train, which happened to be carrying *Longstreet's* reserve ordnance, and led it north until they reached Greencastle, Pennsylvania.

Unaware of the Confederate maneuvers of the previous evening and Voss's expedition (word of the cavalry's activities was deliberately withheld from the other troops in Harpers Ferry to avoid creating "a stampede"), the Union defenders were stunned when the morning fog lifted and revealed the location of *Hill's* command. Then, the Confederates opened fire. Union morale, already fragile from the previous day's bombardment, collapsed. By 8:00 A.M. Union battery officers had exhausted their long-range ammunition in a futile attempt to counter the Confederate guns. On Bolivar Heights, Miles called together his subordinates, and they quickly decided they had no choice but to surrender. A rebel shell then exploded behind Miles and mortally wounded him in the leg. White assumed command and then rode forward to Schoolhouse Ridge to arrange the garrison's surrender. In the course of the siege, the Union garrison had lost 44 killed and 173 wounded. In all, 12,737 men, plus 73 pieces of artillery, 13,000 small arms, and 200 wagons were surrendered unconditionally. It was the largest surrender of United States troops in history and would hold that dubious distinction until 1942.

Analysis   In November 1862 a military commission investigating the events at Harpers Ferry concluded Ford "conducted the defense [of Maryland Heights] without ability, and abandoned his position with out sufficient cause, and has shown such a lack of incapacity as to disqualify him . . . for a command in the service." Then, although proclaiming that "an officer who cannot appear before any earthly tribunal . . . is entitled to the tenderest care," the commission declared that

"Miles' incapacity, amounting to almost imbecility led to the shameful surrender" of Harpers Ferry. Clearly, Miles was in a tough situation in September 1862, given the task of holding a difficult position with troops who were inadequate in numbers and grossly deficient in training and experience. Nonetheless, his failure to fortify his position during the months prior to the Maryland campaign, delegation of discretion to Ford on Maryland Heights when he knew that officer wanted to retreat, and refusal to let any but his cavalry attempt a break-out, all clearly mark him as the most important of the many contributors to the Harpers Ferry fiasco.

The commission also concluded McClellan could and should have marched quickly enough to relieve Harpers Ferry. To be sure, McClellan's march from Washington to South Mountain was hardly made with breathtaking speed. However, given the poor intelligence about the enemy's intentions and capabilities the general was receiving, it was more than respectable—certainly the fact that *Lee* was surprised when he learned McClellan was at Frederick suggests this was the case. Moreover, it was fast enough that the loss of over 12,000 men need not have occurred, had Miles competently conducted the defense of Harpers Ferry or been allowed to abandon the place. It should also be noted that as he moved into Maryland, McClellan was chastised by Halleck for moving with too much rapidity.

The commission's criticism of McClellan also served the purpose of precluding critical consideration of Halleck's insistence that Harpers Ferry be held at all. To be sure, by keeping the garrison at Harpers Ferry, Halleck complicated *Lee's* operational situation. However, the garrisons could have performed this function and threatened *Lee's* line of communications just about anywhere else in the lower Shenandoah Valley without the risk of being trapped in an indefensible position that Halleck's insistence on maintaining Harpers Ferry entailed. Although he rarely had a kind word for McClellan, the head of the postwar Antietam Battlefield Board could not refrain from criticizing the commission's findings and proclaiming, "Had Halleck given a candid reply to McClellan's request [that Miles abandon Harpers Ferry] it would read: 'In defiance of all sound military principles we have kept Colonel Miles so long at Harper's Ferry to hold an indefensible position, that he is now surrounded and cannot escape, and is peremptorily ordered not to escape if he could, but if you can relieve him from the trap in which we have placed him you are welcome to his services.' Halleck could not have been of more service to the Confederates had he been Lee's chief of staff, with authority to issue orders from the head of the Union army."

Shortly after the Union surrender, *Jackson* and his staff rode into Harpers Ferry to claim possession of the town. Wearing a worn uniform and weary expression, *Jackson* hardly cast a dashing image; however, one observer later wrote, "The curiosity in the Union army to see him was so great that the soldiers lined the sides of the road. Many of them uncovered as he passed, and he invariably returned the salute. One man had the echo of response all about him when he said aloud, 'Boys, he isn't much for looks, but if we'd had him we wouldn't have been caught in this trap.'"

Carman, "Maryland Campaign," chap. 6, 324–72; Frye, "Drama Between the Rivers," 14–34; Harsh, *Taken at the Flood*, 223–28, 267–75, 315–19; Sears, *Landscape Turned Red*, 143–45, 151–54.

To return to the Antietam National Battlefield Visitor Center: *Exit* the parking area and *drive* back to WASHINGTON STREET. *Turn right* onto WASHINGTON STREET and *proceed* to the traffic light. *Turn right* onto U.S. 340 and *drive* 1.6 miles to WV 230 (SHEPHERDSTOWN PIKE). *Turn right* onto WV 230 and *proceed* 8.6 miles to PRINCESS STREET. *Turn right* onto PRINCESS STREET, *proceed* 0.1 mile to E. GERMAN STREET, and *turn left*. *Drive* 0.2 mile on E. GERMAN STREET through downtown Shepherdstown to WV 480. *Turn right* onto WV 480 and *proceed* 3.8 miles to N. CHURCH STREET/S. CHURCH STREET (MD 65) in Sharpsburg (en route WV 480 becomes MD 34). *Turn left* onto N. CHURCH STREET and *drive* 0.8 mile to DUNKER CHURCH ROAD. *Turn right* onto DUNKER CHURCH ROAD and *proceed* to the parking lot for the Visitor Center.

To reach the first stop for the South Mountain tour from Bolivar Heights: *Exit* the parking area and *drive* back to WASHINGTON STREET. *Turn right* onto WASHINGTON STREET and *proceed* to the traffic light. *Turn left* onto U.S. 340 and *drive* 3.9 miles to the ramp onto MD 67 (ROHRERSVILLE ROAD) toward Boonsboro. *Proceed* north on MD 67 for 10.5 miles to MOUNT CARMEL CHURCH ROAD/RENO MONUMENT ROAD. *Turn right* onto RENO MONUMENT ROAD and *drive* 2.1 miles until you see the parking area for Reno Monument on your right. *Pull into* the parking area.

In the wake of battle. BLCW 2:686

After Antietam

The failure of the Confederate offensive into Maryland had profound consequences for the course of the Civil War. McClellan and the Army of the Potomac did more than simply turn back a Confederate offensive in September 1862. During the late summer and fall of 1862, a number of European leaders were coming to the conclusion that perhaps the time had come for them to take action to prevent the American experiment in fratricide and the domestic turmoil they were sure would follow President Lincoln's emancipation proclamation from destroying the stability in the Western Hemisphere on which their own interests depended. The outcome of the Maryland campaign, however, along with the turning back of a Confederate offensive into Kentucky in October, provided a vivid demonstration of the North's determination to preserve the Union. Upon sober reflection, the European powers—above all Great Britain—prudently concluded that they did not have the means necessary to force the North to accept anything less than restoration of the Union. And it was made clear by the heavy casualties the North accepted and the ferocity with which its soldiers fought in Maryland that the cost of antagonizing the North by intervening on behalf of the South would be infinitely higher than any benefits any country might hope to gain from intervention. More than anything else, it was the clear unwillingness of the North to give up the struggle, and the recognition of the high cost the North would impose on anyone who intervened on behalf of the South that led the European powers to conclude that prudence dictated leaving settlement of the "American question" to the Americans.

McClellan's victory also set the stage for a revolutionary event in American history. In July Lincoln had presented to his cabinet the draft of a proclamation freeing the slaves in the rebel states but had been persuaded to hold off issuing it until after the Union army had won a significant battlefield victory. When he learned of the outcome of the Maryland campaign, Lincoln took it as a divine sign that the time had come to issue the Preliminary Emancipation Proclamation. This proclamation, issued on September 22, gave the people of the rebellious states until January 1, 1863, to return to the Union; if they did not, their slaves would be emancipated by Federal armies as they moved into the South. This was the signal moment in the evolution of Union war policy from a conciliatory approach to the South that sought to preserve the "Union as it was and the Constitution as it is" to a "hard war" that would produce what some historians have labeled the "Second American Revolution."

Lincoln issued the proclamation even though McClellan had advised him on numerous occasions that he thought such a move unwise. Wherever Union armies had gone, they had been agents of liberation, delivering fatal blows to the South's "peculiar institution," something McClellan not only accepted but endorsed. McClellan feared, however, that an open proclamation of war against slavery would make the task of restoring the Union much more difficult. It would, he believed, validate the arguments of secessionists regarding the irreconcilability of Southern institutions with the authority of the Union and kill Unionist sentiment in the South. Nonetheless, McClellan's only public response to Lincoln's action was an order to his soldiers on October 7 reminding them of their obligation to submit to the decisions of the civil authorities and advising them the only proper way to bring about change in government policy was through action at the polls. The latter observation could not have been well received in Washington, as the 1862 congressional elections were only weeks away and Lincoln was extremely nervous about his party's prospects. Lincoln was right to be nervous, as the elections would see significant Democratic gains.

Lincoln's mood was sour during the weeks before the election because he anticipated the people of the North were going to blame his party for the slow progress of the war, when he was convinced the problem was McClellan. Initially, Lincoln expressed satisfaction with what McClellan had accomplished in Maryland. By the end of September, however, Lincoln's opinion of the general had dramatically declined in part because McClellan made it clear by his words and actions that he was not going to resume active operations for some time to come. Lincoln could not understand why this was the case, given the Confederate retreat from Maryland and the exceptionally fine weather that fall. In fact, McClellan's army was exhausted and experiencing the inevitable logistical and organizational problems that developed in armies after weeks of active campaigning, which were exacerbated in the Army of the Potomac's case by the rapid evacuation of the Peninsula, hasty slapping together of it and the Army of Virginia, and the large number of new troops that had to be incorporated into various subordinate commands. The soldiers understood these problems and many welcomed what they believed to be a necessary respite from active operations, but they were incomprehensible to McClellan's superiors in Washington.

Lee's superiors were much more understanding. Although there was disappointment over the outcome of the Maryland campaign, none of *Lee's* political superiors were disposed to find fault with his conduct of the campaign or his decision to rest his army in the vicinity of Winchester afterward. Indeed, among Confederate leaders, no one itched to resume active operations more than *Lee*, who yearned to take the war north across the Potomac again. But the Army of Northern Virginia badly needed time to refill its ranks, build up its supplies, and recuperate from the mauling it had received in Maryland. Needing to do the same with his own army, McClellan, to Lincoln's immense frustration, gave *Lee* that time.

Finally, on October 1, Lincoln paid a personal visit to the Army of the Potomac. McClellan and his subordinates greeted Lincoln cordially, motivated in part by a hope that if the president actually saw the army and its problems first-hand, he might better understand its inactivity and be a bit more patient regarding future operations. They were to be disappointed. Lincoln spent several days with the army, reviewing troops and talking with McClellan. His meetings with McClellan were quite pleasant; however, Lincoln also privately sneered during his visit that the army had become no more than McClellan's bodyguard and made a point of expressing concern to the general over his "overcautiousness." Within a few days after returning to Washington, Lincoln had a message sent to McClellan ordering him to cross the Potomac and begin active operations without delay.

As McClellan and his superiors debated when and how to resume operations, Confederate cavalry under *Stuart* crossed the Potomac near Williamsport on October 10 and rode north to raid Chambersburg, Pennsylvania. McClellan responded by putting his cavalry in motion and having his infantry move to block the crossings of the Potomac. *Stuart*, however, was able to stay one step ahead of his pursuers and recross the river safely. The fact that *Stuart* had ridden a complete circuit around the Army of the Potomac for the second time in less than five months further exacerbated Lincoln's frustration with McClellan and the army's inactivity. By mid-October, the tone of the messages he was receiving from Washington led McClellan to confide to one of his subordinates during a reconnaissance in force in the Shenandoah Valley that he did not expect to have command of the Army of the Potomac much longer.

In late October, Washington finally began meeting the army's needs for supplies, which enabled McClellan to resume operations. On October 26 his army began crossing the Potomac at Harpers Ferry and Berlin, Maryland. Acting on a plan that was all but imposed on him by Lincoln, Mc-

Clellan intended to make a rapid march south through the Loudoun Valley and act according to circumstances once he reached the Manassas Gap Railroad and the Orange and Alexandria Railroad. *Lee* quickly figured out what the Federals were doing and responded by ordering *Jackson's* wing of the army to remain in the Shenandoah Valley to threaten the Union right and rear, while *Longstreet's* wing marched south and east to Culpeper Court House.

In a series of respectable marches, McClellan's army pushed through the Loudoun Valley to the Rappahannock River and Warrenton, Virginia. McClellan was not quick enough, however, to win the race for the Orange and Alexandria Railroad, as *Longstreet* managed to reach Culpeper on November 3. For Lincoln, this was the last straw. When the results of the midterm elections were in on November 5, he personally drafted orders relieving McClellan of command. Two days later, they were delivered, and McClellan turned command of the Army of the Potomac over to Ambrose Burnside. McClellan then spent an emotional few days saying good-bye to his officers and men, making a point of urging them to give full cooperation to his successor.

Never again would a military victory that could lead to Southern independence seem more tantalizingly within reach for *Lee* than it did when the Army of Northern Virginia entered Maryland in September 1862. For the second time in a little over a year, the Union army had been forced to take sanctuary in the defenses surrounding their capital; the tipping point where the northern advantage in resources would become decisive—when the troops raised under the July 1862 call had received sufficient training, equipage, and organization to be effective soldiers—had not come yet. McClellan, however, in a triumph of personal leadership, took a beaten, disorganized army and used it to conduct a campaign that, if it did not accomplish all that it could have, effectively destroyed whatever hope *Lee* had of winning a decisive victory north of the Potomac in 1862. *Lee's* resolve to make the most of what he believed to be his greatest strategic opportunity and McClellan's determination to destroy that opportunity combined with the fighting spirit of their two great armies at Antietam to produce a day of valor, drama, and momentous consequences that has few, if any, equals in the history of the republic—and of carnage that will, hopefully, never be matched on American soil.

Appendix A: Orders of Battle

Union Forces

ARMY OF THE POTOMAC (McClellan)

I Army Corps (Hooker, Meade)

ESCORT: 2nd NY Cavalry (4 companies)

1st Division (Hatch, Doubleday)

1ST BDE	2ND BDE
(Hatch, Phelps)	(Doubleday, Wainwright, Hofmann)
22nd NY	
24th NY	7th IN
30th NY	76th NY
84th NY (14th Brooklyn Militia)	95th NY
2nd U.S. S.S.	56th PA

3RD BDE	4TH BDE
(Patrick)	(Gibbon)
21st NY	19th IN
23rd NY	2nd WI
35th NY	6th WI
80th NY (20th Militia)	7th WI

ARTILLERY (Monroe): 1st NH Light, 1st Battery; 1st NY Light, Battery L; 1st RI Light, Battery D; 4th U.S., Battery B

2nd Division (Ricketts)

1ST BDE	2ND BDE	3RD BDE
(Duryea)	(Christian, Lyle)	(Hartsuff, Coulter)
97th NY	26th NY	12th MA
104th NY	94th NY	13th MA
105th NY	88th PA	83rd NY (9th Militia)
107th NY	90th PA	11th PA

ARTILLERY: 1st PA Light, Battery F; PA Light, Battery C

3rd Division (Meade, Seymour)

1ST BDE	2ND BDE	3RD BDE
(Seymour, Roberts)	(Bolinger, Magilton)	(Gallagher, Anderson)
1st PA	3rd PA	9th PA
2nd PA	4th PA	10th PA
5th PA	7th PA	11th PA
6th PA	8th PA	12th PA
13th PA (1st Rifles)		

ARTILLERY: 1st PA Light, Battery A; 1st PA Light, Battery B; 5th U.S., Battery C

II Army Corps (Sumner)

ESCORT: Company D, 6th NY Cavalry; Company K, 6th NY Cavalry

1st Division (Richardson, Caldwell, Hancock)

1ST BDE	2ND BDE	3RD BDE
(Caldwell)	(Meagher, Burke)	(Brooke)
5th NH	29th MA	2nd DE
7th NY	63rd NY	52nd NY
61st NY	69th NY	57th NY
64th NY	88th NY	66th NY
81st PA		53rd PA

ARTILLERY: 1st NY Light, Battery B; 4th U.S., Batteries A & C

2nd Division (Sedgwick, Howard)

1ST BDE	2ND BDE	3RD BDE
(Gorman)	(Howard, Owen, Baxter)	(Dana, Hall)
15th MA		19th MA
1st MN	69th PA	20th MA
34th NY	71st PA	7th MI
82nd NY	72nd PA	42nd NY
1st CO, MA S.S.	106th PA	59th NY
2nd CO, MN S.S.		

ARTILLERY: 1st RI Light, Battery A; 1st U.S., Battery I

3rd Division (French)

1ST BDE	2ND BDE	3RD BDE
(Kimball)	(Morris)	(Weber, Andrews)
14th IN	14th CT	1st DE
8th OH	108th NY	5th MD
132nd PA	130th PA	4th NY
7th WV		

UNATTACHED ARTILLERY: 1st NY Light, Battery G; 1st RI Light, Battery B; 1st RI Light, Battery G

IV Army Corps

1st Division (Couch)

1ST BDE (Devens)	2ND BDE (Howe)	3RD BDE (Cochrane)
7th MA	62nd NY	65th NY
10th MA	93rd PA	67th NY
36th NY	98th PA	122nd NY
2nd RI	102nd PA	23rd PA
	139th PA	61st PA
		82nd PA

ARTILLERY: NY Light, 3rd Battery; 1st PA Light, Battery C; 1st PA Light, Battery D; 2nd U.S., Battery G

V Army Corps (Porter)
ESCORT: Detachment, 1st ME Cavalry

1st Division (Morell)

1ST BDE (Barnes)	2ND BDE (Griffin)	3RD BDE (Stockton)
18th MA	2nd DC	20th ME
22nd MA	9th MA	16th MI
2nd ME	32nd MA	12th NY
1st MI	4th MI	17th NY
13th NY	14th NY	44th NY
25th NY	62nd PA	83rd PA
118th PA		Brady's CO, MI S.S.
2nd CO, MA S.S.		

ARTILLERY: MA Light, Battery C; 1st RI Light, Battery C; 5th U.S., Battery D

2nd Division (Sykes)

1ST BDE (Buchanan)	2ND BDE (Lovell)	3RD BDE (Warren)
3rd U.S.	1st U.S.	5th NY
4th U.S.	2nd U.S.	10th NY
1/12th U.S.	6th U.S.	
2/12th U.S.	10th U.S.	
1/14th U.S.	11th U.S.	
2/14th U.S.	17th U.S.	

ARTILLERY: 1st U.S., Battery E; 1st U.S., Battery G; 5th U.S., Battery I; 5th U.S., Battery K

3rd Division (Humphreys)

1ST BDE (Tyler)	2ND BDE (Allabach)
91st PA	123rd PA
126th PA	131st PA
129th PA	133rd PA
134th PA	155th PA

ARTILLERY: 1st NY Light, Battery C; 1st OH Light, Battery L

ARTILLERY RESERVE (Hays): 1/NY Light, Battery A; 1/NY Light, Battery B; 1/NY Light, Battery C; 1/NY Light, Battery D; NY Light, 5th Battery; 1st U.S., Battery K; 4th U.S., Battery G

VI Army Corps (Franklin)
ESCORT: Company B, 6th PA Cavalry;
Company G, 6th PA Cavalry

1st Division (Slocum)

1ST BDE (Torbert)	2ND BDE (Bartlett)	3RD BDE (Newton)
1st NJ	5th ME	18th NJ
2nd NJ	16th NJ	31st NJ
3rd NJ	27th NJ	32nd NJ
4th NJ	96th NJ	95th PA

ARTILLERY: MD Light, Battery A; NJ Light, Battery A; MA Light, Battery A; 2nd U.S., Battery D

2nd Division (Smith)

1ST BDE	2ND BDE	3RD BDE
(Hancock, Cobb)	(Brooks)	(Irwin)
6th ME	2nd VT	7th ME
43rd NY	3rd VT	20th NY
49th PA	4th VT	33rd NY
137th PA	5th VT	49th NY
5th WI	6th VT	77th NY

ARTILLERY (Ayres): MD Light, Battery B; NY Light, 1st Battery; 5th U.S., Battery F

IX Army Corps (Burnside, Reno, Cox)
ESCORT: Company G, 1st ME Cavalry

1st Division (Willcox)

1ST BDE (Christ)	2ND BDE (Welsh)
28th MA	8th MI
17th MI	46th NY
79th NY	45th PA
50th PA	100th PA

ARTILLERY: MA Light, 8th Battery; 2nd U.S., Battery E

2nd Division (Sturgis)

1st BDE (Nagle)	2ND BDE (Ferrero)
2nd MD	21st MA
6th NH	35th MA
9th NH	51st NY
48th PA	51st PA

ARTILLERY: PA Light, Battery D; 4th U.S., Battery E

3rd Division (Rodman, Harland)

1ST BDE (Fairchild)	2ND BDE (Harland)
9th NY	8th CT
89th NY	11th CT
103rd NY	16th CT
	4th RI

ARTILLERY: 5th U.S., Battery A

Kanawha Division (Cox, Scammon)

1ST BDE (Scammon, Ewing)	2ND BDE (Moor, Crook)
12th OH	11th OH
23rd OH	28th OH
30th OH	36th OH
Gilmore's OH, VA (WV) CAV	Chicago IL Dragoons,
Harrison's CO, VA (WV) CAV	Schambeck's CO
OH Light ART, 1st Battery	KY Light ART, Simmonds's Battery

UNATTACHED TROOPS: 3rd Independent CO, OH CAV; 6th NY CAV (8 COS); 3rd NY ART, Battery L; 3rd U.S. ART, Batteries L & M

XII Army Corps (Mansfield, Williams)
ESCORT: Company L, 1st MI Cavalry

1st Division (Williams, Crawford, Gordon)

1ST BDE (Crawford, Knipe)	3RD BDE (Gordon, Ruger)
10th ME	27th IN
28th NY	2nd MA
46th PA	13th NJ
124th PA	107th NJ
125th PA	Pennsylvania Zouaves
128th PA	d'Afrique
	3rd WI

2nd Division (Greene)

1ST BDE	2ND BDE	3RD BDE
(Tyndale, Crane)	(Stainrook)	(Goodrich, Austin)
5th OH	3rd MD	3rd DE
7th OH	102nd NY	60th NY
66th OH	111th PA	78th NY
28th PA		Purnell (MD) Legion

ARTILLERY (Best): 4th ME Light Battery; 6th ME Light Battery; 1st NY Light, Battery M; 10th NY Light Battery; PA Light, Battery E; PA Light, Battery F; 4th U.S., Battery F

Cavalry (Pleasonton)

1ST BDE	2ND BDE	3RD BDE	4TH BDE	5TH BDE
(Whiting)	(Farnsworth)	(Rush)	(McReynolds)	(Davis)
5th U.S	8th IL	4th PA	1st NY	8th NY
6th U.S	3rd IN	6th PA	12th PA	3rd PA
	1st MA			
	8th PA			

ARTILLERY: 2nd U.S, Battery A; 2nd U.S, Batteries B & L; 2nd U.S, Battery M; 3rd U.S, Batteries C & G

UNATTACHED: 1st ME CAV; Detachment, 15th PA CAV

Confederate Forces   ARMY OF NORTHERN VIRGINIA (Lee)

Longstreet's Command
ESCORT: Independent Company, SC Cavalry

D. R. Jones's Division

TOOMBS BDE	G. T. ANDERSON'S BDE	DRAYTON'S BDE
(Toombs, Benning)	1st GA (Regulars)	50th GA
2nd GA	7th GA	51st GA
15th GA	8th GA	15th SC
17th GA	9th GA	Phillips's GA Legion
20th GA	11th GA	3rd SC BN

KEMPER'S BDE	JENKINS'S BDE	PICKETT'S BDE
1st VA	(Walker)	(Hunton, Garnett)
7th VA	1st SC	8th VA
11th VA	2nd SC Rifles	18th VA
17th VA	5th SC	19th VA
24th VA	6th SC	28th VA
	4th SC BN (5 COS)	56th VA
	Palmetto (SC) S.S	

ARTILLERY: Wise (VA) ART

Hood's Division

HOOD'S BDE (Wofford)	LAW'S BDE
18th GA	4th AL
1st TX	2nd MS
4th TX	11th MS
5th TX	6th NC

Hampton (SC) Legion

ARTILLERY (Frobel): German (SC) ART; Palmetto (SC) ART; Rowan (NC) ART

Evans's Division

EVANS'S BDE (Stevens)

17th SC

18th SC

22nd SC

23rd SC

Holcombe (SC) Legion

Macbeth (SC) ART

Artillery Reserve (Walton)

WASHINGTON (LA) BN

1st CO

2nd CO

3rd CO

4th CO

Jackson's Command
ESCORT: Company H, 4th VA Cavalry;
White's VA Cavalry (3 Companies)

Stonewall Division (Jones, Starke, Grigsby)

WINDER'S (STONEWALL) BDE
(Grigsby, Gardner, Williams)

2nd VA

4th VA

5th VA

27th VA

33rd VA

J. R. JONES'S BDE
(Jones, Johnson,
Penn, Page, Withers)

21st VA

42nd VA

48th VA

1st (Irish) VA BN

TALIAFERRO'S BDE
(Warren, Jackson, Sheffield)

47th AL

48th AL

10th VA

23rd VA

37th VA

STARKE'S BDE
(Starke, Williams,
Stafford, Pendleton)

1st LA

2nd LA

9th LA

10th LA

15th LA

Coppens's (1st LA Zouaves) BN

ARTILLERY (Shumaker): Alleghany VA Battery; Baltimore MD
Battery; Danville VA Battery; Eighth Star (VA) ART; Hampden VA Battery; Lee VA Battery; Rockbridge VA Battery; Winchester (VA) ART

Ewell's Division (Lawton, Early)

EARLY'S BDE	LAWTON'S BDE	HAY'S BDE	TRIMBLE'S BDE
(Early, Smith)	(Douglass, Lowe, Lamar)	5th LA	(Brown, Walker)
13th VA		6th LA	15th AL
25th VA	13th GA	7th LA	12th GA
31st VA	26th GA	8th LA	21st GA
44th VA	31st GA	14th LA	21st NC
49th VA	38th GA		1st NC BN
52nd VA	60th GA		
58th VA			

ARTILLERY (Courtney): Charlottesville VA ART; Chesapeake MD ART; Courtney VA ART; Johnson's (VA) Battery; LA Guard ART; 1st MD (Dement's) Battery; Staunton VA (Balthis's) ART

A. P. Hill's Light Division (Branch, Hill)

BRANCH'S BDE	ARCHER'S BDE	GREGG'S BDE
(Branch, Lane)	(Archer, Turney)	1st SC
7th NC	19th GA	(Provisional Army)
18th NC	1st TN	1st SC Rifles
28th NC	7th TN	12th SC
33rd NC	14th TN	13th SC
37th NC	5th AL BN	14th SC
FIELD'S BDE	PENDER'S BDE	THOMAS'S BDE
(Brockenbrough)	16th NC	14th GA
40th VA	22nd NC	35th GA
47th VA	34th NC	45th GA
55th VA	38th NC	49th GA
22nd VA BN		

ARTILLERY (Walker): Crenshaw's (VA) Battery; Fredericksburg (VA) ART (Braxton's battery); Letcher (VA) ART (Davidson's battery); Pee Dee (SC) ART (McIntosh's battery); Purcell (VA) ART (Pegram's battery)

Unattached Divisions

R. H. Anderson's Division (Anderson, Pryor)

ARMISTEAD'S BDE	MAHONE'S BDE	WRIGHT'S BDE
(Armistead, Hodges)	(Parham)	(Wright, Robert Jones, Gibson)
9th VA	6th VA	44th AL
14th VA	12th VA	3rd GA
38th VA	16th VA	22nd GA
53rd VA	41st VA	48th GA
57th VA	61st VA	

WILCOX'S BDE	PRYOR'S BDE	FEATHERSTON'S BDE
(Wilcox, Cumming, Herbert, Crow)	(Pryor, Hately)	(Featherston, Posey)
	14th AL	12th MS
8th AL	2nd FL	16th MS
9th AL	5th FL	19th MS
10th AL	8th FL	2nd MS BN
11th AL	3rd VA	

ARTILLERY (Saunders): Dixie (VA) ART; Donaldsonville (LA) ART; Moorman's (VA) Battery; Norfolk (VA) Huger's Battery; Portsmouth (VA) Grimes's Battery

D. H. Hill's Division

RODES'S BDE	G. B. ANDERSON'S BDE	GARLAND'S BDE
3rd AL	(Anderson, Tew, Bennett)	(Garland, McRae)
5th AL		5th NC
6th AL	2nd NC	12th NC
12th AL	4th NC	13th NC
26th AL	14th NC	20th NC
	30th NC	23rd NC

RAINS'S BDE	RIPLEY'S BDE
(Colquitt)	(Ripley, Doles)
13th AL	4th GA
6th GA	44th GA
23rd GA	1st NC
27th GA	3rd NC
28th GA	

ARTILLERY (Pierson): Hardaway's (AL) Battery; Jefferson Davis (AL) ART; Jones's (VA) Battery; King William (VA) ART

McLaws's Division

SEMMES'S BDE	COBB'S BDE	BARKSDALE'S BDE	KERSHAW'S BDE
10th GA	(Cobb, Sanders, McRae)	13th MS	2nd SC
53rd GA		17th MS	3rd SC
15th VA	16th GA	18th MS	7th SC
32nd VA	24th GA	21st MS	8th SC
	15th NC		
	Cobb's GA Legion		

ARTILLERY (Hamilton, Cabell): Magruder (VA) ART; 1st NC, Battery A (Manly's); Pulaski GA ART; Richmond (Fayette) ART; 1st CO, Richmond Howitzers; Troup (GA) ART

Walker's Division

WALKER'S BDE	RANSOM'S BDE
(Manning, Hall)	24th NC
3rd AR	25th NC
27th NC	35th NC
46th NC	49th NC
48th NC	Branch's Petersburg (VA) ART
30th VA	
French's Stafford (VA) ART	

Reserve Artillery (Pendleton)

BROWN'S BN	NELSON'S BN
Powhatan (VA) ART	Amherst (VA) ART
2nd CO, Richmond (VA) Howitzers	Fluvanna (VA) ART
3rd CO, Richmond (VA) Howitzers	Huckstep's (VA) Battery
Salem (VA) ART	Johnson's (VA) Battery
Williamsburg (VA) ART	Milledge (GA) ART
CUTTS'S BN	S. D. LEE'S BN
Blackshears's (GA) Battery	Ashland (VA) ART
Irwin (GA) ART	Bedford (VA) ART
Patterson's (GA) Battery	Brooks (SC) ART
Ross's (GA) Battery	Eubank's (VA) Battery
JONES'S BN	Madison (LA) ART
Long Island (VA) Battery	Parker's (VA) Battery
Morris Louisa (VA) ART	OTHER BATTERIES
Orange (VA) ART	Cutshaw's (VA) Battery
Turner's (VA) Battery	Rice's (VA) Battery

Cavalry Division (Stuart)

F. LEE'S BDE	ROBERTSON'S BDE	HAMPTON'S BDE
1st VA	(Robertson, Munford)	1st NC
3rd VA	2nd VA	2nd SC
4th VA	7th VA	10th VA
5th VA	12th VA	Cobb's (GA) Legion
9th VA	17th VA BN	Jeff Davis (MS) Legion

ARTILLERY (Pelham): Chew's (VA) Battery; Hart's (SC) Battery; Pelham's (VA) Battery; Stuart's (VA) Horse ART

You will get much more from your battlefield tour if you take a few minutes to become familiar with the following information and then refer to it as necessary.

The Organization of Civil War Armies

Following is a diagram of the typical organization and range of strength of a Civil War army:

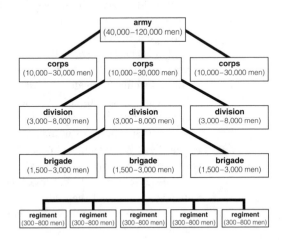

The Basic Battlefield Functions of Civil War Leaders

In combat environments the duties of Civil War leaders were divided into two main parts: decision making and moral suasion. Although the scope of the decisions varied according to rank and responsibilities, they generally dealt with the movement and deployment of troops, artillery, and logistical support (signal detachments, wagon trains, and so on). Most of the decisions were made by the leaders themselves. Their staffs helped with administrative paperwork but in combat functioned essentially as glorified clerks; they did almost no sifting of intelligence or planning of operations. Once made, the decisions were transmitted to subordinates either by direct exchange or by courier, with the courier either carrying a written order or conveying the order verbally. More rarely, signal flags were used to send instructions. Except in siege operations, when the battle lines were fairly static, the telegraph was almost never used in tactical situations.

Moral suasion was the art of persuading troops to perform their duties and dissuading them from failing to perform them. Civil War commanders often accomplished this by personal example, and conspicuous bravery was a vital attribute of any good leader. It is therefore not surprising that 8 percent of Union generals—and 18 percent of their Confederate counterparts—were killed or mortally wounded in action. (By contrast, only about 3 percent of Union enlisted men were killed or mortally wounded in action.)

Although any commander might be called upon to intervene directly on the firing line, army, corps, and division commanders tended to lead from behind the battle line, and their duties were mainly supervisory. In all three cases their main ability to influence the fighting, once it was underway, was by the husbanding and judicious commitment of troops held in reserve.

Army commanders principally decided the broad questions—whether to attack or defend, where the army's main effort(s) would be made, and when to retreat (or pursue). They made most of their key choices before and after an engagement rather than during it. Once battle was actually joined, their ability to influence the outcome diminished considerably. They might choose to wait it out or they might choose, temporarily and informally, to exercise the function of a lesser leader. In the battles of the Civil War, army commanders conducted themselves in a variety of ways: as detached observers, "super" corps commanders, division commanders, and so on, all the way down to de facto colonels trying to lead through personal example.

Corps commanders chiefly directed main attacks or supervised the defense of large, usually well-defined sectors. It was their function to carry out the broad (or occasionally quite specific) wishes of the army commander. They coordinated all the elements of their corps (typically infantry divisions and artillery battalions) in order to maximize its offensive or defensive strength. Once battle was actually joined, they influenced the outcome by "feeding" additional troops into the fight—sometimes by preserving a reserve force (usually a division) and committing it at the appropriate moment, sometimes by requesting additional support from adjacent corps or from the army commander.

Division commanders essentially had the same functions as corps commanders, though on a smaller scale. When attacking, however, their emphasis was less on "feeding" a fight than on keeping the striking power of their divisions as compact as possible. The idea was to strike one hard blow rather than a series of weaker ones.

The following commanders were expected to control the actual combat—to close with and destroy the enemy:

Brigade commanders principally conducted the actual business of attacking or defending. They accompanied the attacking force in person or stayed on the firing line with the defenders. Typically, they placed about three of their regiments abreast of one another, with about two in immediate support. Their job was basically to maximize the fighting power of their brigades by ensuring that these regiments had an unobstructed field of fire and did not overlap. During an attack it often became necessary to expand, contract, or otherwise modify the brigade frontage to adapt to the vagaries of terrain, the movements of adjacent friendly brigades, or the behavior of enemy forces. It was the brigade commander's responsibility to shift his regiments as needed while preserving, if possible, the unified striking power of the brigade.

Regiment commanders were chiefly responsible for making their men do as the brigade commanders wished, and their independent authority on the battlefield was limited. For example, if defending they might order a limited counterattack, but they usually could not order a retreat without approval from higher authority. Assisted by *company commanders*, they directly supervised the soldiers, giving specific, highly concrete commands: move this way or that, hold your ground, fire by volley, forward, and so on. Commanders at this level were expected to lead by personal example and to display as well as demand strict adherence to duty.

Civil War Tactics

Civil War armies basically had three kinds of combat troops: infantry, cavalry, and artillery. Infantrymen fought on foot, each with his own weapon. Cavalrymen were trained to fight on horseback or dismounted, also with their own individual weapons. Artillerymen fought with cannon.

INFANTRY

Infantry were by far the most numerous part of a Civil War army and were chiefly responsible for seizing and holding ground.

The basic Civil War tactic was to put a lot of men next to one another in a line and have them move and shoot together. By present-day standards the notion of placing troops shoulder to shoulder seems insane, but it still made good sense in the mid-nineteenth century. There were two reasons for this: first, it allowed soldiers to concentrate the fire of their rather limited weapons; second, it was almost the only way to move troops effectively under fire.

Most Civil War infantrymen used muzzle-loading muskets capable of being loaded and fired a maximum of about three times a minute. Individually, therefore, a soldier was nothing. He could affect the battlefield only by combining his fire with that of other infantrymen. Although spreading out made them less vulnerable, infantrymen very quickly lost the ability to combine their fire effectively if they did so. Even more critically, their officers rapidly lost the ability to control them.

For most purposes, the smallest tactical unit on a Civil War battlefield was the regiment. Theoretically composed of about 1,000 officers and men, in reality the average Civil War regiment went into battle with about 300 to 600 men. Whatever its size, however, all members of the regiment had to be able to understand and carry out the orders of their colonel and subordinate officers, who generally could communicate only through voice command. Since in the din and confusion of battle only a few soldiers could actually hear any given command, most got the message chiefly by conforming to the movements of the men immediately around them. Maintaining "touch of elbows"–the prescribed close interval–was indispensable for this crude but vital system to work. In addition, infantrymen were trained to "follow the flag"–the unit and national colors were always conspicuously placed in the front and center of each regiment. Thus, when in doubt as to what maneuver the regiment was trying to carry out, soldiers could look to see the direction in which the colors were moving. That is one major reason why the post of color-bearer was habitually given to the bravest men in the unit. It was not just an honor; it was insurance that the colors would always move in the direction desired by the colonel.

En route to a battle area, regiments typically moved in a column formation, four men abreast. There was a simple maneuver whereby regiments could very rapidly change from column to line once in the battle area, that is, from a formation designed for ease of movement to one designed to maximize firepower. Regiments normally moved and fought in line of battle–a close-order formation actually composed of two lines, front and rear. Attacking units rarely "charged" in the sense of running full tilt toward the enemy; such a maneuver would promptly destroy the formation as faster men outstripped slower ones and everyone spread out. Instead, a regiment using orthodox tactics would typically step off on an attack moving at a "quick time" rate of 110 steps per minute (at which it would cover about 85 yards per minute). Once the force came under serious fire, the rate of advance might be increased to a so-called double-quick time of 165 steps per minute (about 150 yards per minute). Only when the regiment was within a few dozen yards of the defending line would the regiment be ordered to advance at a "run" (a very rapid pace but still not a sprint). Thus, a regiment might easily take about ten minutes to "charge" 1,000 yards, even if it did not pause for realignment or execute any further maneuvers en route.

In theory, an attacking unit would not stop until it reached the enemy line, if then. The idea was to force back the defenders through the size, momentum, and shock effect of the attacking column. (Fixed bayonets were considered indispensable for maximizing the desired shock effect.) In reality, however, the firepower of the defense eventually led most Civil War regiments to stop and return the fire—often at ranges of less than 100 yards. And very often the "charge" would turn into a stand-up firefight at murderously short range until one side or the other gave way.

It is important to bear in mind that the preceding description represents a simplified idea of Civil War infantry combat. As you will see as you visit specific stops, the reality could vary significantly.

ARTILLERY

Second in importance to infantry on most Civil War battlefields was the artillery. Not yet the "killing arm" it would become during World War I, when 70 percent of all casualties would be inflicted by shellfire, artillery nevertheless played an important role, particularly on the defense. Cannon fire could break up an infantry attack or dissuade enemy infantry from attacking in the first place. Its mere presence could also reassure friendly infantry and so exert a moral effect that might be as important as its physical effect on the enemy.

The basic artillery unit was the *battery*, a group of between four and six fieldpieces commanded by a captain. Early in the war, batteries tended to be attached to infantry brigades. But over time it was found that they worked best when massed together, and both the Union and Confederate armies quickly reorganized their artillery to facilitate this. Eventually, both sides maintained extensive concentrations of artillery at corps level or higher. Coordinating the fire of 20 or 30 guns on a single target was not unusual, and occasionally (as in the bombardment that preceded Pickett's Charge at Gettysburg) concentrations of well over 100 guns might be achieved.

Practically all Civil War fieldpieces were muzzle-loaded and superficially appeared little changed from their counterparts of the seventeenth and eighteenth centuries. In fact, however, Civil War artillery was quite modern in two respects. First, advances in metallurgy had resulted in cannon barrels that were much lighter than their predecessors but strong enough to contain more powerful charges. Thus, whereas the typical fieldpiece of the Napoleonic era fired a 6-pound round, the typical Civil War–era fieldpiece fired a round double that size, with no loss in ease of handling. Second, recent improvements had resulted in the development of practical rifled fieldpieces that had significantly greater range and accuracy than their smoothbore counterparts.

Civil War fieldpieces could fire a variety of shell types, each with its own preferred usage. *Solid shot* was considered best for battering down structures and for use against massed troops (a single round could sometimes knock down several men like ten pins). *Shell*—hollow rounds that contained an explosive charge and burst into fragments when touched off by a time fuse—were used to set buildings afire or to attack troops behind earthworks or under cover. *Spherical case* was similar to shell except that each round contained musket balls (78 in a 12-pound shot, 38 in a 6-pound shot); it was used against bodies of troops moving in the open at ranges of from 500 to 1,500 yards. At ranges of below 500 yards, the round of choice was *canister*, essentially a metal can containing about 27 cast-iron balls, each 1.5 inches in diameter. As soon as a canister round was fired, the sides of the can would rip away and the cast-iron balls would fly directly into the attacking infantry or ricochet into them off the ground, making the cannon essentially a large-scale shotgun. In desperate situations, double and sometimes even triple charges of canister were used.

As recently as the Mexican War, artillery had been used effectively on the offensive, with fieldpieces rolling forward to advanced positions from which they could blast a hole in the enemy line. The advent of the rifled musket, however, made this tactic dangerous—defending infantry could now pick off artillerists who dared to come so close—and so the artillery had to remain farther back. In theory, the greater range and accuracy of rifled cannon might have offset this a bit, but rifled cannon fired comparatively small shells of limited effectiveness against infantry at a distance. The preferred use of artillery on the offensive was therefore not against infantry but against other artillery—what was termed "counterbattery work." The idea was to mass one's own cannon against a few of the enemy's cannon and systematically fire so as to kill the enemy's artillerists and dismount his fieldpieces.

CAVALRY

"Whoever saw a dead cavalryman?" was a byword among Civil War soldiers, a pointed allusion to the fact that the

battlefield role played by the mounted arm was often neg-
ligible. For example, at the battle of Antietam–the single
bloodiest day of the entire war–the Union cavalry suffered
exactly 5 men killed and 23 wounded. This was in sharp contrast to the role played by horsemen during the Napoleonic
era, when a well-timed cavalry charge could exploit an infantry breakthrough, overrun the enemy's retreating foot
soldiers, and convert a temporary advantage into a complete battlefield triumph.

Why the failure to use cavalry to better tactical advantage?
The best single explanation might be that for much of the war
there was simply not enough of it to achieve significant results. Whereas cavalry had comprised 20 to 25 percent of Napoleonic armies, in Civil War armies it generally averaged 8
to 10 percent or less. The paucity of cavalry may be explained
in turn by its much greater expense compared with infantry.
A single horse might easily cost ten times the monthly pay of
a Civil War private and necessitated the purchase of saddles,
bridles, stirrups, and other gear as well as specialized clothing
and equipment for the rider. Moreover, horses required about
26 pounds of feed and forage per day, many times the require-
ment of an infantryman. One might add to this the continu-
al need for remounts to replace worn-out animals and that it
took far more training to make an effective cavalryman than
an effective infantryman. There was also the widespread be-
lief that the heavily wooded terrain of North America would
limit opportunities to use cavalry on the battlefield. All in all,
it is perhaps no wonder that Civil War armies were late in creating really powerful mounted arms.

Instead, cavalry tended to be used mainly for scouting
and raiding, duties that took place away from the main battlefields. During major engagements their mission was principally to screen the flanks or to control the rear areas. By
1863, however, the North was beginning to create cavalry
forces sufficiently numerous and well armed to play a significant role on the battlefield. At Gettysburg, for example,
Union cavalrymen armed with rapid-fire, breech-loading
carbines were able to hold a Confederate infantry division
at bay for several hours. At Cedar Creek in 1864, a massed
cavalry charge late in the day completed the ruin of the
Confederate army, and during the Appomattox campaign in
1865, Federal cavalry played a decisive role in bringing Lee's
retreating army to bay and forcing its surrender.

Appreciation of the Terrain

The whole point of a battlefield tour is to see the ground
over which men actually fought. Understanding the terrain

is basic to understanding almost every aspect of a battle. Terrain helps to explain why commanders deployed their troops where they did, why attacks occurred in certain areas and not in others, and why some attacks succeeded and others did not.

When defending, Civil War leaders often looked for positions that had as many of the following characteristics as possible:

First, it obviously had to be ground from which they could protect whatever it was they were ordered to defend.

Second, it should be elevated enough so as to provide good observation and good fields of fire—they wanted to see as far as possible and sometimes (though not always) to shoot as far as possible. The highest ground was not necessarily the best, however, for it often afforded an attacker defilade—areas of lower ground that the defenders' weapons could not reach. For that reason, leaders seldom placed their troops at the very top of a ridge or hill (the "geographical crest"). Instead, they placed them a bit forward of the geographical crest at a point from which they had the best field of fire (the "military crest"). Alternatively, they might choose to place their troops behind the crest so as to conceal their size and exact deployment from the enemy and gain protection from long-range fire. It also meant that an attacker, upon reaching the crest, would be silhouetted against the sky and susceptible to a sudden, potentially destructive fire at close range.

Third, the ground adjacent to the chosen position should present a potential attacker with obstacles. Streams and ravines made good obstructions because they required an attacker to halt temporarily while trying to cross them. Fences and boulder fields could also slow an attacker. Dense woodlands could do the same but offered concealment for potential attackers and were therefore less desirable. In addition to its other virtues, elevated ground was also prized because attackers moving uphill had to exert themselves more and got tired faster. Obstacles were especially critical at the ends of a unit's position—the flanks—if there were no other units beyond to protect it. That is why commanders "anchored" their flanks, whenever possible, on hills or the banks of large streams.

Fourth, the terrain must offer ease of access for reinforcements to arrive and, if necessary, for the defenders to retreat.

Fifth, a source of drinkable water—the more the better—should be immediately behind the position if possible. This was especially important for cavalry and artillery units, which had horses to think about as well as men.

When attacking, Civil War commanders looked for different things:

First, they looked for weaknesses in the enemy's position, especially "unanchored" flanks. If there were no obvious weaknesses, they looked for a key point in the enemy's position—often a piece of elevated ground whose loss would undermine the rest of the enemy's defensive line.

Second, they searched for ways to get close to the enemy position without being observed. Using woodlands and ridge lines to screen their movements was a common tactic.

Third, they looked for open, elevated ground on which they could deploy artillery to "soften up" the point to be attacked.

Fourth, once the attack was underway they tried, when possible, to find areas of defilade in which their troops could gain relief from exposure to enemy fire. Obviously, it was almost never possible to find defilade that offered protection all the way to the enemy line, but leaders could often find some point en route where they could pause briefly to "dress" their lines.

Making the best use of terrain was an art that almost always involved trade-offs among these various factors—and also required consideration of the number of troops available. Even a very strong position was vulnerable if there were not enough men to defend it. A common error among Civil War generals, for example, was to stretch their line too thin in order to hold an otherwise desirable piece of ground.

Estimating Distance

When touring Civil War battlefields, it is often helpful to have a general sense of distance. For example, estimating distance can help you estimate how long it took troops to get from point A to point B or to visualize the points at which they would have become vulnerable to different kinds of artillery fire. There are several easy tricks to bear in mind:

Use reference points for which the exact distance is known. Many battlefield stops give you the exact distance to one or more key points in the area. Locate such a reference point, and then try to divide the intervening terrain into equal parts. For instance, say the reference point is 800 yards away. The ground about halfway in between will be 400 yards; the ground halfway between yourself and the midway point will be 200 yards, and so on.

Use the football field method. Visualize the length of a football field, which of course is about 100 yards. Then estimate the number of football fields you could put between yourself and the distant point of interest.

Use cars, houses, and other common objects that tend to be roughly the same size. Most cars are about the same size, and so are many houses. *Become familiar with how large or small such objects appear at various distances—300 yards, 1,000 yards, 2,000 yards, and such. This is a less accurate way of estimating distance, but it can be helpful if the lay of the land makes it otherwise hard to tell whether a point is near or far. Look for such objects that seem a bit in front of the point of interest. Their relative size can provide a useful clue.*

Maximum Effective Ranges of Common Civil War Weapons

Rifled musket	400 yds.
Smoothbore musket	150 yds.
Breech-loading carbine	300 yds.
Napoleon 12-pounder smoothbore cannon	
Solid shot	1,700 yds.
Shell	1,300 yds.
Spherical case	500–1,500 yds.
Canister	400 yds.
Parrott 10-pounder rifled cannon	
Solid shot	6,000 yds.
3-inch ordnance rifle (cannon)	
Solid shot	4,000 yds.

Further Reading

Coggins, Jack. *Arms and Equipment of the Civil War.* 1962; reprint, Wilmington NC: Broadfoot, 1990. The best introduction to the subject: engagingly written, profusely illustrated, and packed with information.

Griffith, Paddy. *Battle Tactics of the Civil War.* New Haven CT: Yale University Press, 1989. Argues that in a tactical sense, the Civil War was more nearly the last great Napoleonic war than the first modern war. In Griffith's view the influence of the rifled musket on Civil War battlefields has been exaggerated; the carnage and inconclusiveness of many Civil War battles owed less to the inadequacy of Napoleonic tactics than to a failure to properly understand and apply them.

Jamieson, Perry D. *Crossing the Deadly Ground: United States Army Tactics, 1865–1899.* Tuscaloosa: University of Alabama Press, 1994. The early chapters offer a good analysis of the tactical lessons learned by U.S. Army officers from their Civil War experiences.

Linderman, Gerald F. *Embattled Courage: The Experience of Combat in the American Civil War.* New York: Free Press, 1987. This thoughtful, well-written study examines how Civil War soldiers understood and coped with the challenges of the battlefield.

McWhiney, Grady, and Perry D. Jamieson. *Attack and Die: Civil*

War Military Tactics and the Southern Heritage. Tuscaloosa: University of Alabama Press, 1982. Although unconvincing in its assertion that their Celtic heritage led Southerners to take the offensive to an inordinate degree, this is an excellent tactical study that emphasizes the revolutionary effect of the rifled musket. Best read in combination with Griffith's *Battle Tactics.*

After the battle—Position of
the Confederate batteries
in front of Dunker Church.
From a photograph.
BLCW 2:671

Sources	In general, the works cited in the "Further Reading" sections of each stop provide information, interpretation, and insight. The citations of those works in those sections should in every case be taken as an attribution of credit for the material presented there. The sources for specific items in each stop are provided in this appendix.

ANTIETAM

The Road to Antietam

The quotations "foreign yoke" and "main body" are from U.S. War Department, *The War of the Rebellion: A Compilation of the Official Records of the Union and Confederate Armies*, vol. 19, ser. 1, pt. 2 (Washington DC: Government Printing Office, 1887), 602, 604. The quotation "sheer necessity" is from George B. McClellan, *McClellan's Own Story: The War for the Union, the Soldiers Who Fought It, the Civilians Who Directed It, and His Relations to It and to Them*, ed. William C. Prime (New York: Charles L. Webster, 1887), 552. The quotation beginning "God bless" is from U.S. War Department, *War of the Rebellion*, vol. 19, ser. 1, pt. 1:53.

Stop 1

The quotation "complete success" and the one beginning "Through God's blessing" are from U.S. War Department, *War of the Rebellion*, vol. 19, ser. 1, pt. 1:951. The quotation beginning "We will make our stand" is from Joseph L. Harsh, *Taken at the Flood: Robert E. Lee and Confederate Strategy in the Maryland Campaign of 1862* (Kent OH: Kent State University Press, 1999), 305. The quotation in the vignette is from James Longstreet, "The Invasion of Maryland," in *Battles and Leaders of the Civil War*, ed. Robert U. Johnson and Clarence C. Buel (New York: Century, 1885–87), 2:667. The quotation beginning "We have" is from Ezra Ayers Carman, "The Maryland Campaign of 1862," typescript with annotations by Thomas G. Clemens, chap. 17, 195, Antietam National Battlefield Library.

Stop 2

The quotation in the first vignette is from Jacob Cox, "The Battle of Antietam," in *Battles and Leaders of the Civil War*, ed. Robert U. Johnson and Clarence C. Buel (New York: Century, 1885–87), 2:630–31. The quotations "eat me up" and "destroy the rebel army" are from U.S. War Department, *War of the Rebellion*, vol. 19. ser. 1, pt. 1:53, 215. The quotation in the second vignette is from David H. Strother, "Personal Recollections of the War by a Virginian," *Harper's New Monthly Magazine*, February 1868, 281–82.

Stop 3	The quotation in the vignette is from U.S. War Department, *War of the Rebellion*, vol. 19, ser. 1, pt. 1:218.

Stop 4   The quotation in the vignette is from Annette Suarez Mc-Donald, *Source Book on the Early History of Cuthbert and Randolph County, GA* (Atlanta GA: Cherokee Publishing Company, 1982), 183–84.

Stop 5   The quotations in the two vignettes are from Rufus R. Dawes, *A Full Blown Yankee of the Iron Brigade: Service with the Sixth Wisconsin Volunteers* (1890; repr., Lincoln: University of Nebraska Press, 1999), 87–91.

Stop 6   The quotation "slipped the bridle" is from Carman, "Maryland Campaign," chap. 15, 107. The quotation "Dead on the field" is from J. S. Johnston, "A Reminiscence of Sharpsburg," *Southern Historical Society Papers* 8 (1880): 527–28. The quotation in the first vignette is from Russell Duncan, ed., *Blue-Eyed Child of Fortune: The Civil War Letters of Colonel Robert Gould Shaw* (Athens: University of Georgia Press, 1992), 240. The quotation "They are flanking us!" is from U.S. War Department, *War of the Rebellion*, vol. 19, ser. 1, pt. 1:1044. The quotations in the second vignette are from Milo M. Quaife, ed., *From the Cannon's Mouth: The Civil War Letters of General Alpheus S. Williams* (1959; repr., Lincoln: University of Nebraska Press, 1995), 127; and U.S. War Department, *War of the Rebellion*, vol. 19, ser. 1, pt. 1:218–19.

Stop 7   The quotation in the first vignette is from Francis A. Walker, *History of the Second Army Corps in the Army of the Potomac* (New York: Charles Scribner's, 1886), 102, 106. The quotation beginning "My God" is from Carman, "Maryland Campaign," chap. 17, 221. The quotation in the second vignette is from Gregory A. Coco, ed., *From Ball's Bluff to Gettysburg . . . And Beyond: The Civil War Letters of Private Roland E. Bowen, 15th Massachusetts Infantry, 1861–1864* (Gettysburg: Thomas Publications, 1994), 127, 135. The quotation in the third vignette is from Duncan, *Blue-Eyed Child of Fortune*, 245.

Stop 8   The quotation in the vignette is from U.S. War Department, *War of the Rebellion*, vol. 19, ser. 1, pt. 1:506.

Stop 9   The quotation "push up on" is from Marion V. Armstrong Jr., *Unfurl Those Colors! McClellan, Sumner, and the Second Army Corps in the Antietam Campaign* (Tuscaloosa: University of Alabama Press, 2008), 171. The quotation in the vignette is from John B. Gordon, *Reminiscences of the Civil War* (New York: Scribner's, 1903), 85–87.

Stop 10   The quotation beginning "Why the bridge?" is from Henry Kyd Douglas, *I Rode with Stonewall* (Chapel Hill: University of North Carolina Press, 1945), 172. The quotation "a difficult task" is from U.S. War Department, *War of the Rebellion*, vol. 19. ser. 1, pt. 1:31. The quotation beginning "McClellan appears" is from McClellan, *McClellan's Own Story*, 609. The quotations in the vignette are from Thomas H. Parker, *History of the 51st Regiment of Pennsylvania Volunteers* (1869; repr., Baltimore: Butternut and Blue, 1998), 231–32.

Stop 11   The quotation in the vignette is from David L. Thompson, "With Burnside at Antietam," in *Battles and Leaders of the Civil War*, ed. Robert U. Johnson and Clarence C. Buel (New York: Century, 1885–87), 2:661–62.

Stop 12   The quotation beginning "General Hill" is from Carman, "Maryland Campaign," chap. 21, 59. The quotations in the vignette are from Harsh, *Taken at the Flood*, 419. The quotation beginning "Look out" is from U.S. War Department, *War of the Rebellion*, vol. 19, ser. 1, pt. 1:138.

Stop 13   The quotations beginning "General Lee," "Longstreet," and "Gentlemen" are from Carman, "Maryland Campaign," chap. 22, 4–5. The quotation beginning "My delay" is from Longstreet, "Invasion of Maryland," 2:671–72. The quotation "seemed completely unmanned" is from J. B. Polley, *Hood's Texas Brigade: Its Marches, Its Battles, Its Achievements* (New York: Neale Publishing, 1910), 134. The quotation "be depended upon" is from U.S. War Department, *War of the Rebellion*, vol. 19, ser. 1, pt. 1:66.

Stop 14   The quotation beginning "I wish you" is from Harsh, *Taken at the Flood*, 442.

Optional Excursion 1

The quotation "a galling" is from Carman, "Maryland Campaign," chap. 18, 13. The quotations "intensely American" and "bring them colors" are from Carman, "Maryland Campaign," chap. 18, 27, 33–34. The quotation "the impetuosity" is from U.S. War Department, *War of the Rebellion*, vol. 19, ser. 1, pt. 2:294. The quotation "standing erect" is from Robert K. Krick, "It Appeared As Though Mutual Extermination Would Put a Stop to the Awful Carnage: Confederates in Sharpsburg's Bloody Lane," in *The Antietam Campaign*, ed. Gary W. Gallagher (Chapel Hill: University of North Carolina Press, 1999), 237–38.

Optional Excursion 2

The quotation beginning "Come on boys" is from Stephen W. Sears, *Landscape Turned Red: The Battle of Antietam* (New York: Ticknor and Fields, 1982), 266. The quotation in the vignette is from Carman, "Maryland Campaign," chap. 21, 45.

Optional Excursion 3

The quotations in the first vignette are from John G. Walker, "Sharpsburg," in *Battles and Leaders of the Civil War*, ed. Robert U. Johnson and Clarence C. Buel (New York: Century, 1885–87), 2:682; and James V. Murfin, *The Gleam of Bayonets: The Battle of Antietam and the Maryland Campaign of 1862* (New York: Thomas Yoseloff, 1965), 304. The quoted exchange beginning "All?" and the quotation in the second vignette are from Mark A. Snell, "Baptism of Fire: The 118th Pennsylvania ('Corn Exchange') Infantry at the Battle of Shepherdstown," *Civil War Regiments: A Journal of the American Civil War* 5 (1997): 126, 131, 133.

SOUTH MOUNTAIN

Overview of the Battle of South Mountain

The quotation "Now I know what to do!" is from Harsh, *Taken at the Flood*, 242.

Stop 1

The quotation beginning "My God!" is from Jacob Cox, "Forcing Fox's Gap and Turner's Gap," in *Battles and Leaders of the Civil War*, ed. Robert U. Johnson and Clarence C. Buel (New York: Century, 1885–87), 2:586. The quotation in the first vignette is from T. Harry Williams, *Hayes of the 23rd: The Civil War Volunteer Officer* (New York: Knopf, 1965), 137. The quotations in the second vignette are from John Michael Priest, ed., *From New Bern to Fredericksburg: Captain James Wren's Diary, B Company 48th Pennsylvania Volunteers, February 20, 1862–December 17, 1862* (Shippensburg PA: White Mane Publishing, 1990), 65; and Strother, "Personal Recollections of the War," 278.

Stop 2

The quotations "as far as" and "as blank cartridge" are from Daniel H. Hill, "The Battle of South Mountain, or Boonsboro: Fighting for Time at Turner's and Fox's Gaps," in *Battles and Leaders of the Civil War*, ed. Robert U. Johnson and Clarence C. Buel (New York: Century, 1885–87), 2:564, 574. The quotation in the first vignette is from Edward Porter Alexander, *Fighting for the Confederacy: The Personal Recollections of General Edward Porter Alexander*, ed. Gary W. Gallagher (Chapel Hill: University of North Carolina Press, 1989), 143. The quotations in the second vignette are from John Bryson, Memoir, New York State Archives, Albany NY.

Stop 3   The quotation in the vignette is from Dawes, *Full Blown Yankee*, 81–83.

Stop 4   The quotation in the vignette is from Timothy J. Reese, *Sealed with Their Lives: The Battle for Crampton's Gap* (Baltimore: Butternut and Blue, 1998), 143–44.

Stop 5   The quotation in the first vignette is from Reese, *Sealed with Their Lives*, 155–56. The quotation from the second vignette is from W. W. Blackford, *War Years with Jeb Stuart* (New York: Charles Scribner's, 1945), 145.

HARPERS FERRY

Stop 1   The quotation "one of the most" is from Thomas Jefferson, *Notes on the State of Virginia* (1782; repr., New York: Library of America, 1984), 142–43.

Stop 2   The quotations beginning "You *can*" and "God Almighty!" are from Dennis Frye, "Drama Between the Rivers," in *Antietam: Essays on the 1862 Maryland Campaign*, ed. Gary W. Gallagher (Kent OH: Kent State University Press, 1989), 24, 27–28. The quotations "but if he was," "conducted the defense," and "an officer" are from U.S. War Department, *War of the Rebellion*, vol. 19, ser. 1, pt. 1:751, 720, 803, 799. The quotation in the first vignette is from an interpretive marker in Harpers Ferry National Historical Park. The quotation in the second vignette is from Henry Kyd Douglas, "Stonewall Jackson in Maryland," in *Battles and Leaders of the Civil War*, ed. Robert U. Johnson and Clarence C. Buel (New York: Century, 1885–87), 2:627. The quotation beginning "Had Halleck" is from Carman, "Maryland Campaign," chap. 6, 372.

After Antietam   The quotation "overcautiousness" is from U.S. War Department, *War of the Rebellion*, vol. 19, ser. 1, pt. 1:14.

Beating the long roll. BLCW 4:179

For Further Reading

This bibliography lists the works of most use in preparing this guide as well as suggestions for further reading.

Carman, Ezra Ayers. "The Maryland Campaign of 1862." Typescript with annotations by Thomas G. Clemens. Antietam National Battlefield Library. A massive study of the campaign and battle, by the leading member of the Antietam Battlefield Board. Although Carman's interpretations are open to debate, his narrative of events is authoritative, and no serious study of the campaign can be done without consulting it.

Carmichael, Peter S. "'We Don't Know What To Do With Him': William Nelson Pendleton and the Affair at Shepherdstown." In *The Antietam Campaign*, edited by Gary W. Gallagher, 259–88. Chapel Hill: University of North Carolina Press, 1999.

Clemens, Tom. "'Black Hats' off to the Original 'Iron Brigade.'" *Columbiad* 1 (Spring 1997): 47–58.

Cox, Jacob. "Forcing Fox's Gap and Turner's Gap." In *Battles and Leaders of the Civil War*, edited by Robert U. Johnson and Clarence C. Buel, 2:583–90. New York: Century, 1885–87.

Franklin, William B. "Notes on Crampton's Gap and Antietam." In *Battles and Leaders of the Civil War*, edited by Robert U. Johnson and Clarence C. Buel, 2:591–97. New York: Century, 1885–87.

Frassanito, William A. *Antietam: The Photographic Legacy of America's Bloodiest Day*. New York: Scribner's, 1978. A fascinating compilation of postbattle and contemporary photographs of sites, with insightful commentary, associated with the fighting at Antietam.

Frye, Dennis. "Drama Between the Rivers." In *Antietam: Essays on the 1862 Maryland Campaign*, edited by Gary W. Gallagher, 14–34. Kent OH: Kent State University Press, 1989.

Gallagher, Gary W., ed. *The Antietam Campaign*. Chapel Hill: University of North Carolina Press, 1999. A collection of superlative essays that cover a broader range of topics than Gallagher's earlier compilation.

——, ed. *Antietam: Essays on the 1862 Maryland Campaign*. Kent OH: Kent State University Press, 1989. A slim volume containing informative and well-written essays that focus on operations and command-level leadership during the campaign.

——. "'The Net Result of the Campaign Was in Our Favor': Confederate Reaction to the Maryland Campaign." In *The*

Antietam Campaign, edited by Gary W. Gallagher, 3-43. Chapel Hill: University of North Carolina Press, 1999.

Grimsley, Mark. "In Not so Dubious Battle: The Motivations of American Civil War Soldiers." *The Journal of Military History* 62 (January 1998): 175–88.

Harsh, Joseph L. *Sounding the Shallows: A Confederate Companion for the Maryland Campaign of 1862.* Kent OH: Kent State University Press, 2000. An invaluable compendium of information, ranging from weather reports to scrutiny of key sources and controversies, related to the campaign.

——. *Taken at the Flood: Robert E. Lee and Confederate Strategy in the Maryland Campaign of 1862.* Kent OH: Kent State University Press, 1999. Although its focus is on the Confederate side, this exhaustively researched, wonderfully insightful, and authoritative work is the best published study of the Maryland campaign.

Hartwig, D. Scott. "It Looked Like a Task to Storm." *North & South*, October 2002.

Hill, Daniel H. "The Battle of South Mountain, or Boonsboro: Fighting for Time at Turner's and Fox's Gaps." In *Battles and Leaders of the Civil War*, edited by Robert U. Johnson and Clarence C. Buel, 2:559–81. New York: Century, 1885–87.

Jamieson, Perry D. *Death in September: The Antietam Campaign.* Abilene TX: McWhiney Foundation Press, 1995. An excellent brief account of the campaign and battle.

Johnson, Robert U. and Clarence C. Buel, eds. *Battles and Leaders of the Civil War.* 4 vols. New York: Century, 1885–87. A compilation of postwar writings by participants in the Civil War. Volume 2 has over a half-dozen first-person accounts of the Maryland campaign, including contributions by George McClellan, James Longstreet, Jacob Cox, and others.

Krick, Robert K. "'It Appeared As Though Mutual Extermination Would Put a Stop to the Awful Carnage': Confederates in Sharpsburg's Bloody Lane." In *The Antietam Campaign*, edited by Gary W. Gallagher, 223–58. Chapel Hill: University of North Carolina Press, 1999.

Murfin, James V. *The Gleam of Bayonets: The Battle of Antietam and the Maryland Campaign of 1862.* New York: Thomas Yoseloff, 1965.

Priest, John Michael. *Antietam: A Soldier's Battle.* New York: Oxford University Press, 1989. Both of Priest's books are exhaustive in detail, with useful hand-drawn maps, and not recommended for the novice.

——. *Before Antietam: The Battle of South Mountain.* Shippensburg PA: White Mane Publishing, 1992.

Rafuse, Ethan S. *McClellan's War: The Failure of Moderation in the Struggle for the Union*. Bloomington: Indiana University Press, 2005.

Reese, Timothy J. *Sealed with Their Lives: The Battle for Crampton's Gap*. Baltimore: Butternut and Blue, 1998. A very useful and thorough account of this engagement by the leading authority.

Sears, Stephen W. *Landscape Turned Red: The Battle of Antietam*. New York: Ticknor and Fields, 1982. A well-researched, comprehensive, and entertaining study of the entire campaign that stood for many years as the standard work on the campaign.

Snell, Mark A. "Baptism of Fire: The 118th Pennsylvania ('Corn Exchange') Infantry at the Battle of Shepherdstown." *Civil War Regiments: A Journal of the American Civil War* 5 (1997): 119–42.

——, ed. Special issue, *Civil War Regiments: A Journal of the American Civil War* 6 (1998). A special issue of this journal dedicated to the Maryland campaign, which offers useful studies of particular topics.

U.S. War Department. *The War of the Rebellion: A Compilation of the Official Records of the Union and Confederate Armies*. 70 vols. Washington DC: Government Printing Office, 1880–1901. All references to this work are from series 1. Volume 19 contains official reports and correspondence that are essential for understanding the course and conduct of the Maryland campaign.

In This Hallowed Ground: Guides to the Civil War Battlefields series

Antietam, South Mountain, and Harpers Ferry:
A Battlefield Guide
Ethan S. Rafuse

Chickamauga: A Battlefield Guide
with a Section on Chattanooga
Steven E. Woodworth

Gettysburg: A Battlefield Guide
Mark Grimsley and Brooks D. Simpson

The Peninsula and Seven Days:
A Battlefield Guide
Brian K. Burton

Shiloh: A Battlefield Guide
Mark Grimsley and Steven E. Woodworth

Wilson's Creek, Pea Ridge, and Prairie Grove:
A Battlefield Guide with a Section on the Wire Road
Earl J. Hess, Richard W. Hatcher III,
William Garrett Piston, and William L. Shea